STAR WARS

THE ASHES OF JEDHA

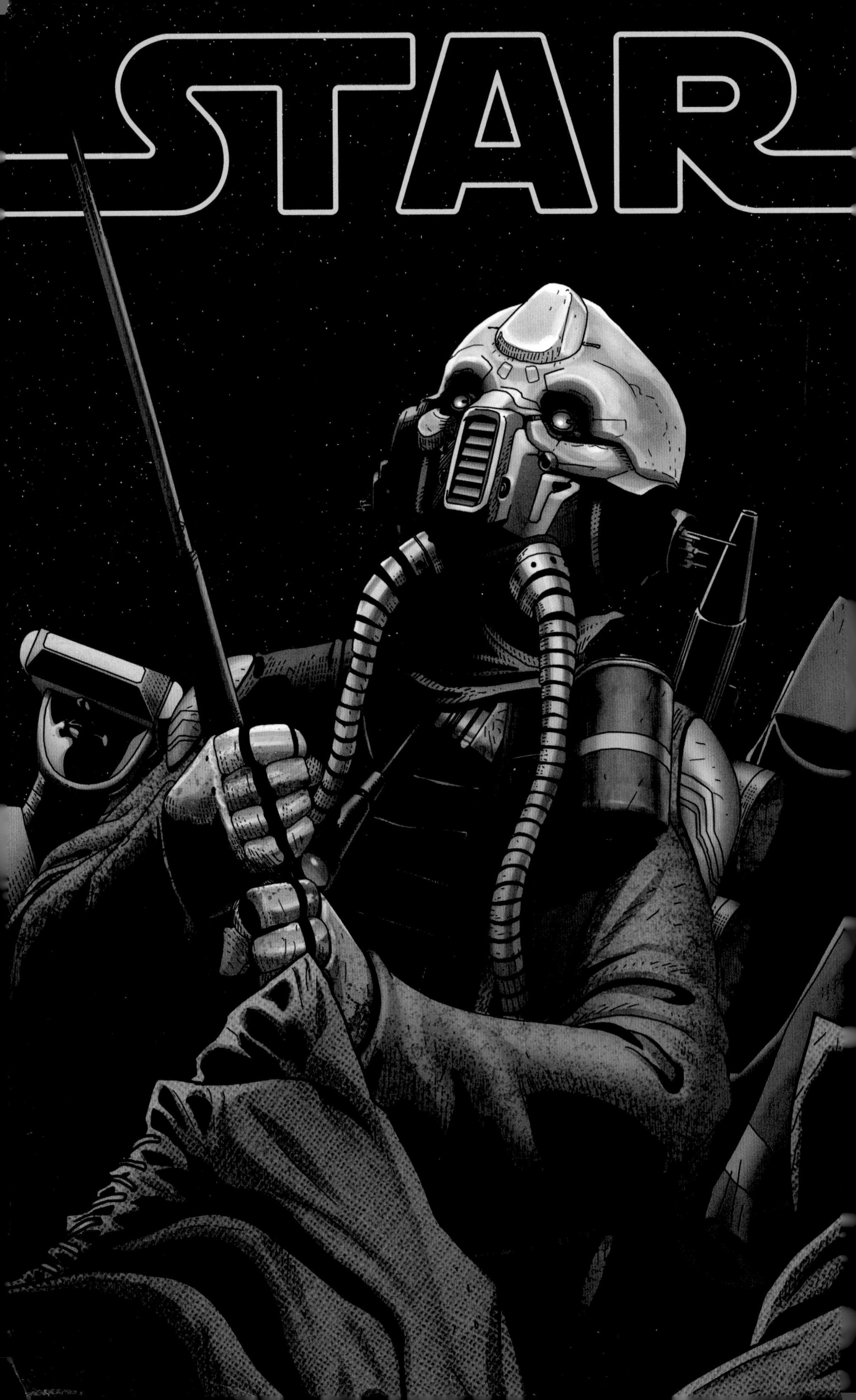

THE ASHES OF JEDHA

Writer	**KIERON GILLEN**
Artist	**SALVADOR LARROCA**
Color Artist	**GURU-eFX**
Letterer	**VC's JOE CARAMAGNA**
Cover Art	**DAVID MARQUEZ & MATTHEW WILSON**
Assistant Editor	**HEATHER ANTOS**
Editor	**JORDAN D. WHITE**
Editor in Chief	**C.B. CEBULSKI**
Chief Creative Officer	**JOE QUESADA**
President	**DAN BUCKLEY**

For Lucasfilm:

Assistant Editor	**NICK MARTINO**
Senior Editor	**JEN HEDDLE**
Creative Director	**MICHAEL SIGLAIN**
Lucasfilm Story Group	**JAMES WAUGH, LELAND CHEE, MATT MARTIN**

Collection Editor	**JENNIFER GRÜNWALD**	VP Production & Special Projects **JEFF YOUNGQUIST**
Assistant Editor	**CAITLIN O'CONNELL**	SVP Print, Sales & Marketing **DAVID GABRIEL**
Associate Managing Editor	**KATERI WOODY**	Book Designer **ADAM DEL RE**
Editor, Special Projects	**MARK D. BEAZLEY**	

 ·

STAR WARS VOL. 7: THE ASHES OF JEDHA. Contains material originally published in magazine form as STAR WARS #38-43. First printing 2018. ISBN 978-1-302-91052-5. Published by MARVEL WORLDWIDE, INC., a subsidiary of MARVEL ENTERTAINMENT, LLC. OFFICE OF PUBLICATION: 135 West 50th Street, New York, NY 10020. STAR WARS and related text and illustrations are trademarks and/or copyrights in the United States and other countries, of Lucasfilm Ltd. and/or its affiliates. © & TM Lucasfilm Ltd. No similarity between any of the names, characters, persons, and/or institutions in this magazine with those of any living or dead person or institution is intended, and any such similarity which may exist is purely coincidental. Marvel and its logos are TM Marvel Characters, Inc. Printed in the U.S.A. DAN BUCKLEY, President, Marvel Entertainment; JOE QUESADA, Chief Creative Officer; TOM BREVOORT, SVP of Publishing; DAVID BOGART, SVP of Business Affairs & Operations, Publishing & Partnership; DAVID GABRIEL, SVP of Sales & Marketing, Publishing; JEFF YOUNGQUIST, VP of Production & Special Projects; DAN CARR, Executive Director of Publishing Technology; ALEX MORALES, Director of Publishing Operations; SUSAN CRESPI, Production Manager; STAN LEE, Chairman Emeritus. For information regarding advertising in Marvel Comics or on Marvel.com, please contact Vit DeBellis, Custom Solutions & Integrated Advertising Manager, at vdebellis@marvel.com. For Marvel subscription inquiries, please call 888-511-5480. Manufactured between 2/9/2018 and 3/13/2018 by LSC COMMUNICATIONS INC., KENDALLVILLE, IN, USA.

10 9 8 7 6 5 4 3 2 1

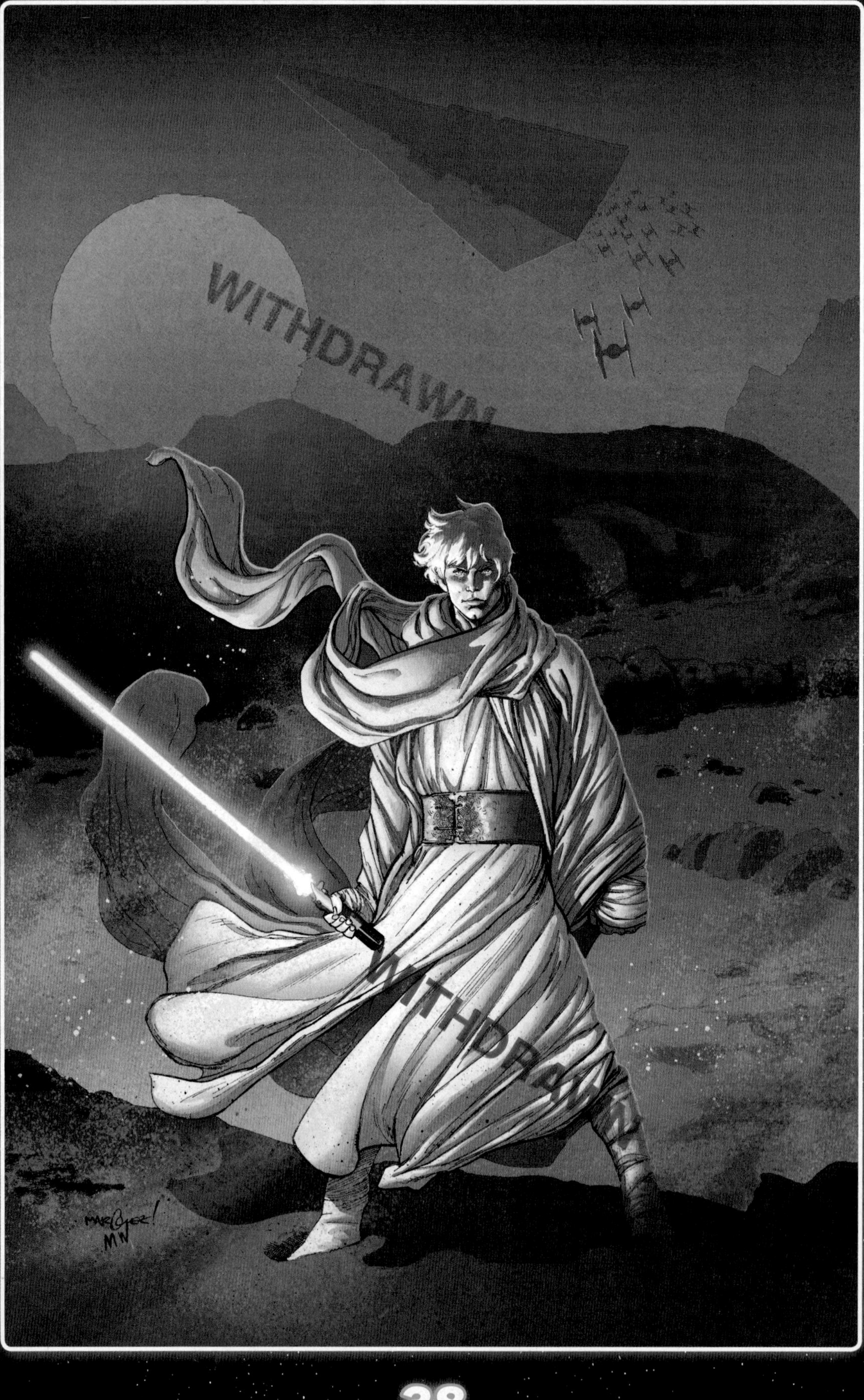

THE ASHES OF JEDHA

It is period of high tension in the galaxy.

Rebellion leaders Princess Leia and Luke Skywalker, joined by smugglers Han Solo and Sana Starros, are leading the mission to find a new base for their operation.

Meanwhile, the Galactic Empire has returned to Jedha in an attempt to collect the remaining kyber crystals that survived the Death Star's attack....

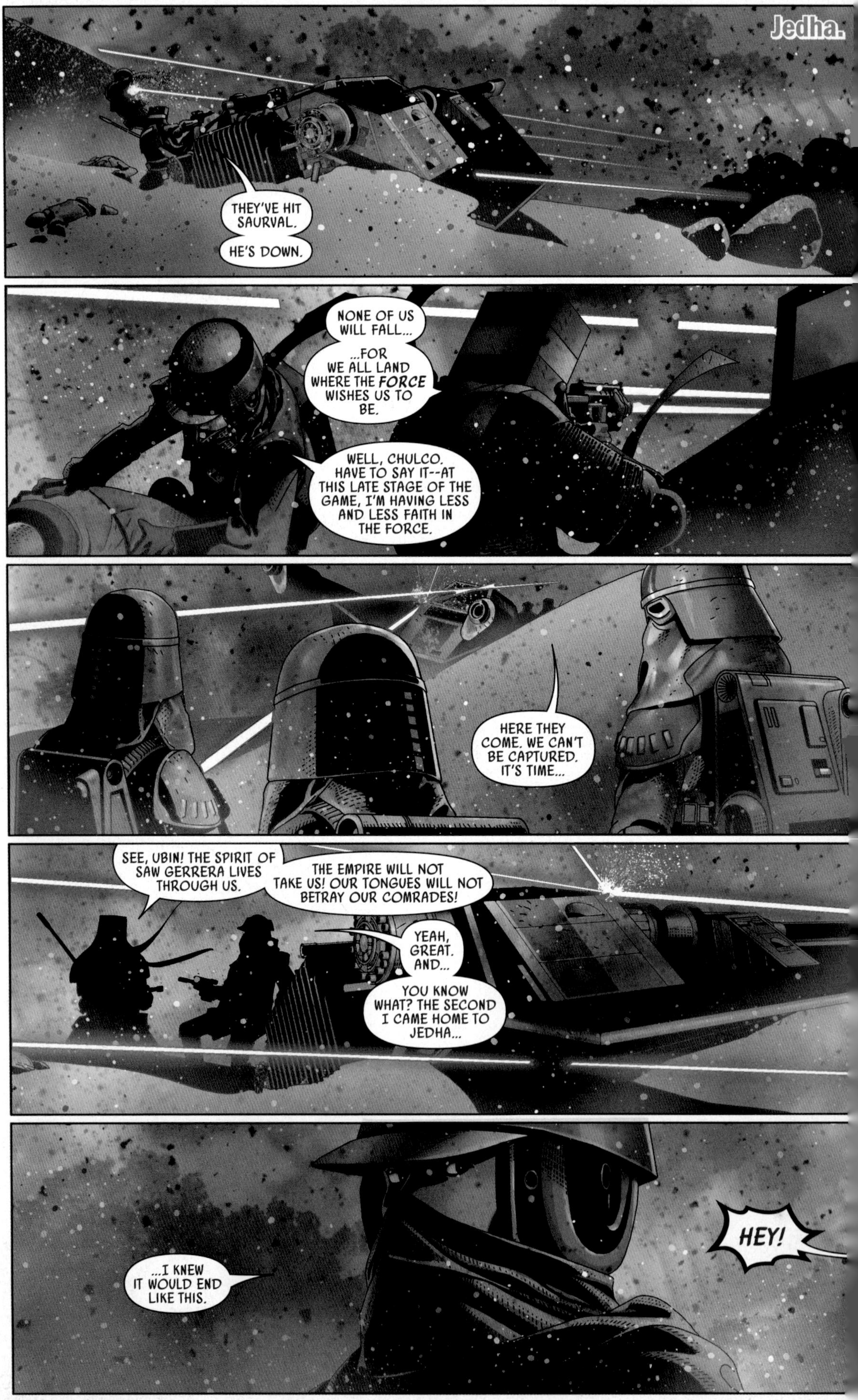
Jedha.
THEY'VE HIT SAURVAL.
HE'S DOWN.
NONE OF US WILL FALL...
...FOR WE ALL LAND WHERE THE FORCE WISHES US TO BE.
WELL, CHULCO. HAVE TO SAY IT--AT THIS LATE STAGE OF THE GAME, I'M HAVING LESS AND LESS FAITH IN THE FORCE.
HERE THEY COME. WE CAN'T BE CAPTURED. IT'S TIME...
SEE, UBIN! THE SPIRIT OF SAW GERRERA LIVES THROUGH US.
THE EMPIRE WILL NOT TAKE US! OUR TONGUES WILL NOT BETRAY OUR COMRADES!
YEAH, GREAT. AND...
YOU KNOW WHAT? THE SECOND I CAME HOME TO JEDHA...
HEY!
...I KNEW IT WOULD END LIKE THIS.

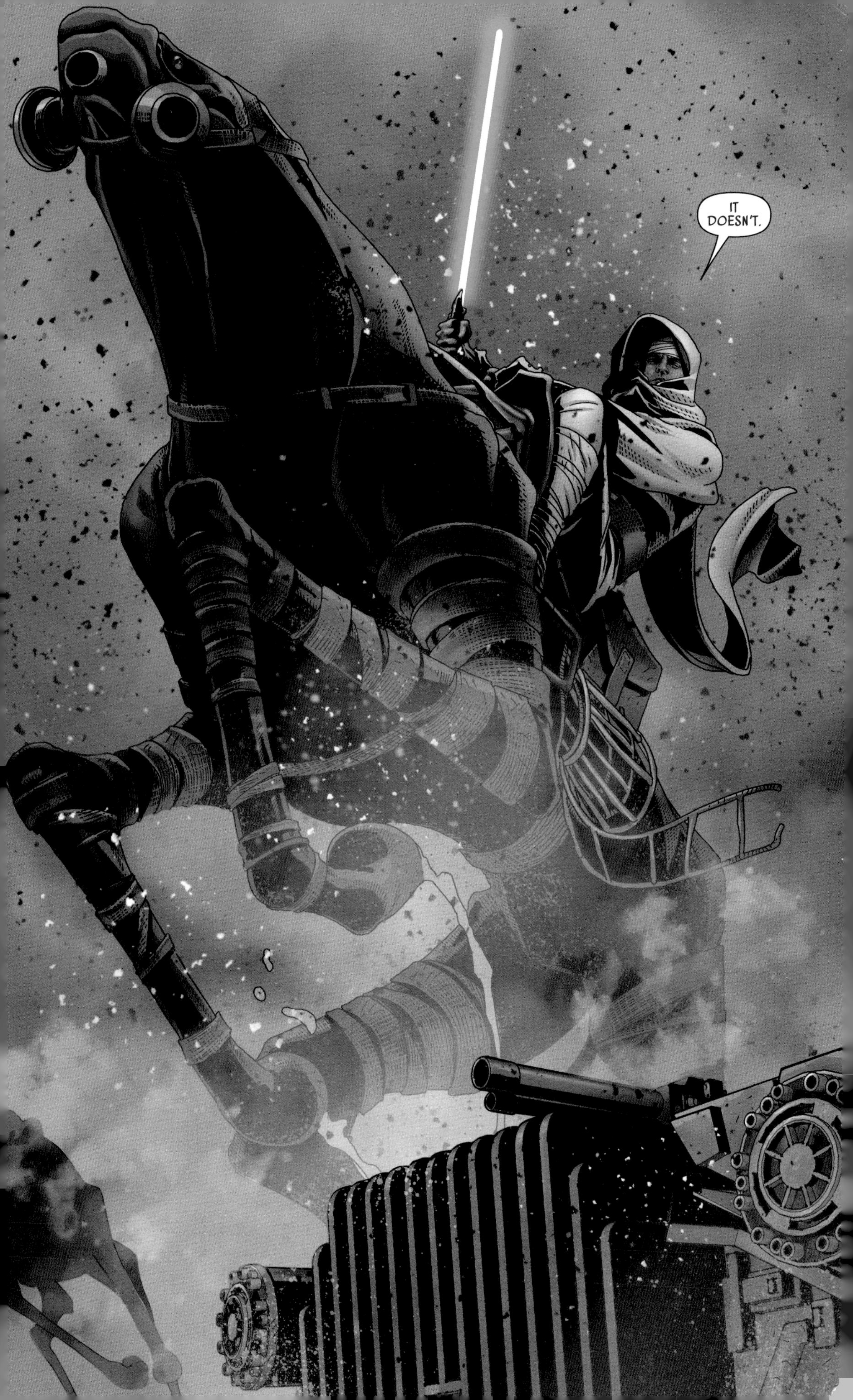
IT DOESN'T.

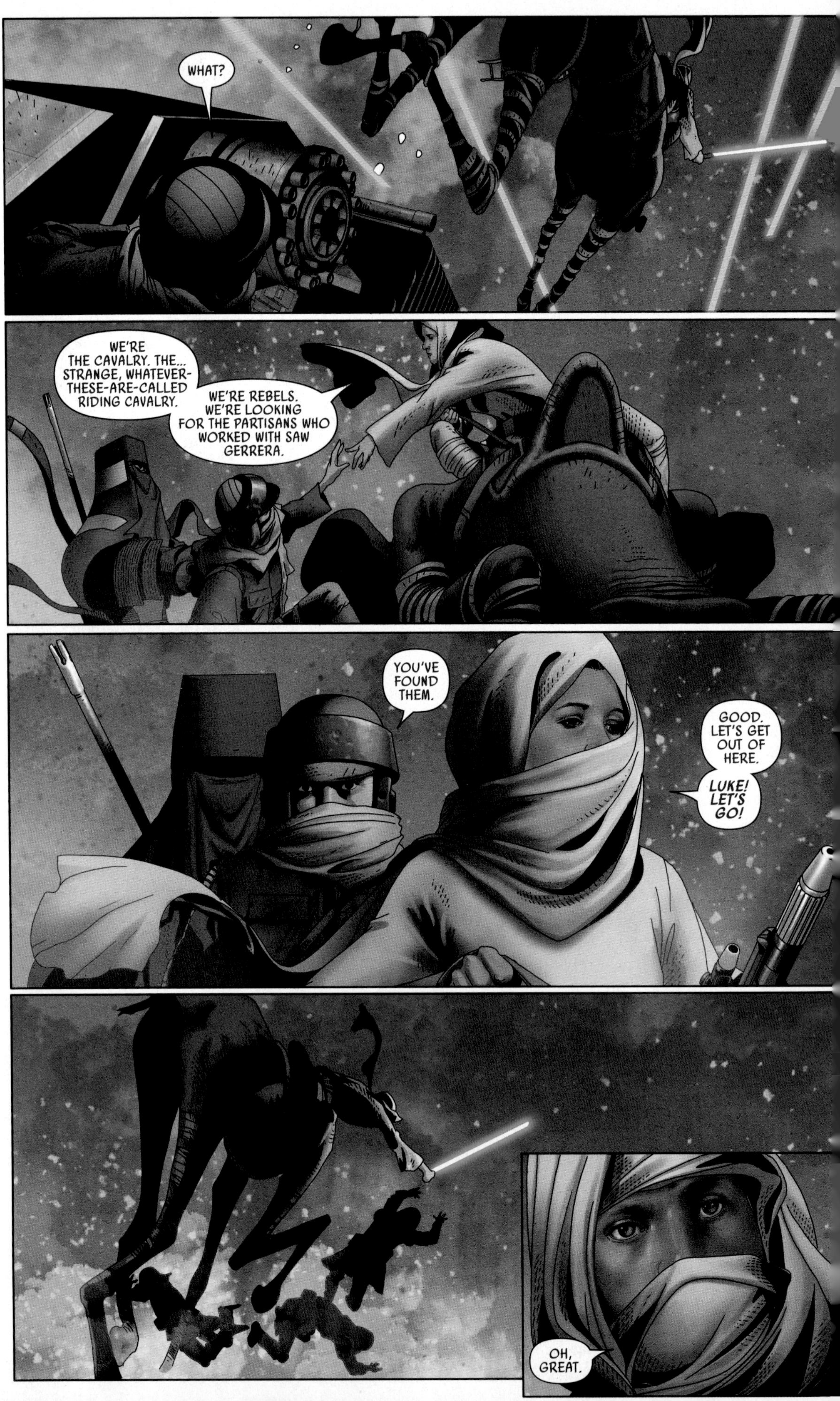
WHAT?
WE'RE THE CAVALRY. THE... STRANGE, WHATEVER-THESE-ARE-CALLED RIDING CAVALRY.
WE'RE REBELS. WE'RE LOOKING FOR THE PARTISANS WHO WORKED WITH SAW GERRERA.
YOU'VE FOUND THEM.
GOOD. LET'S GET OUT OF HERE.
LUKE! LET'S GO!
OH, GREAT.

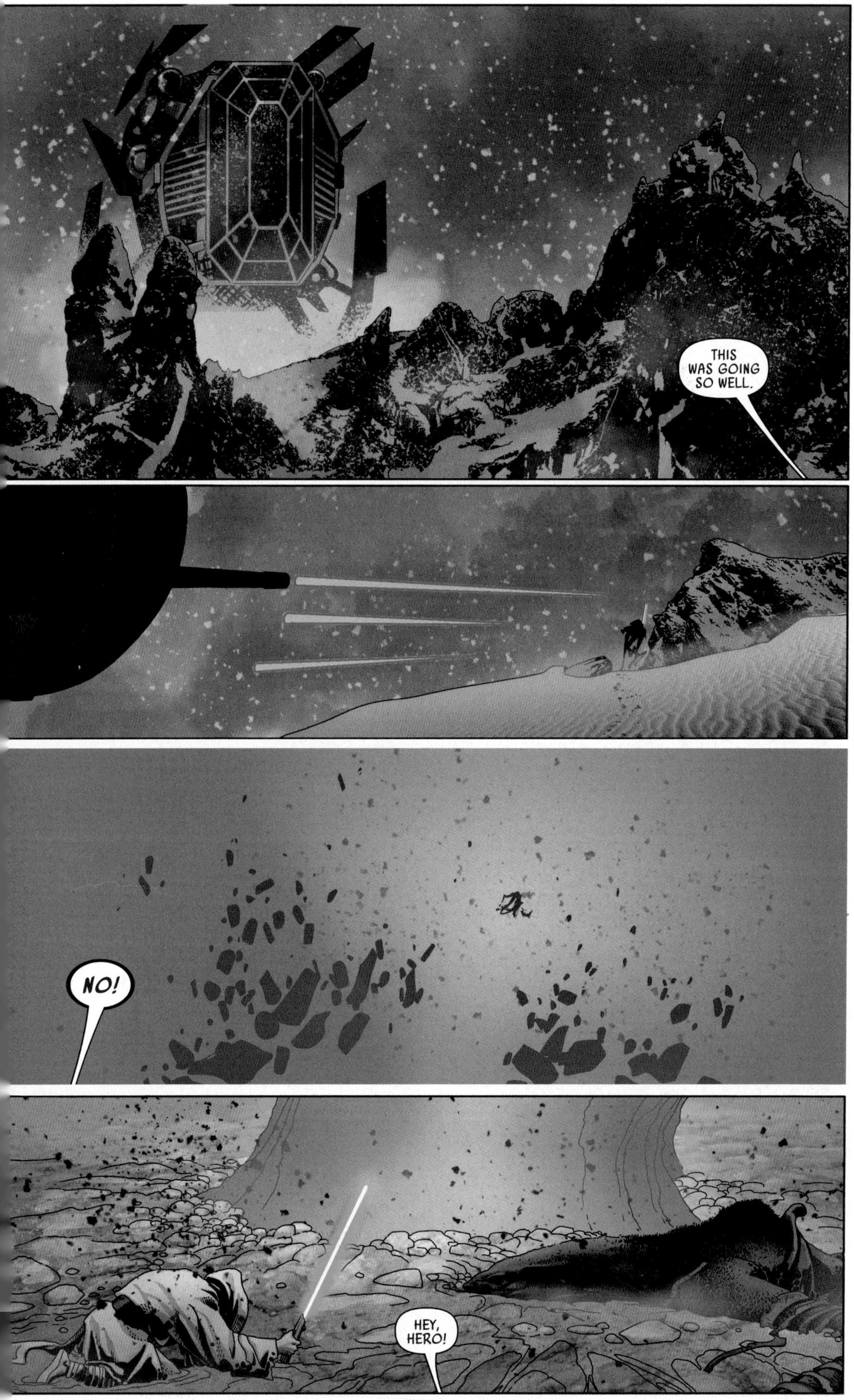
THIS WAS GOING SO WELL.
NO!
HEY, HERO!

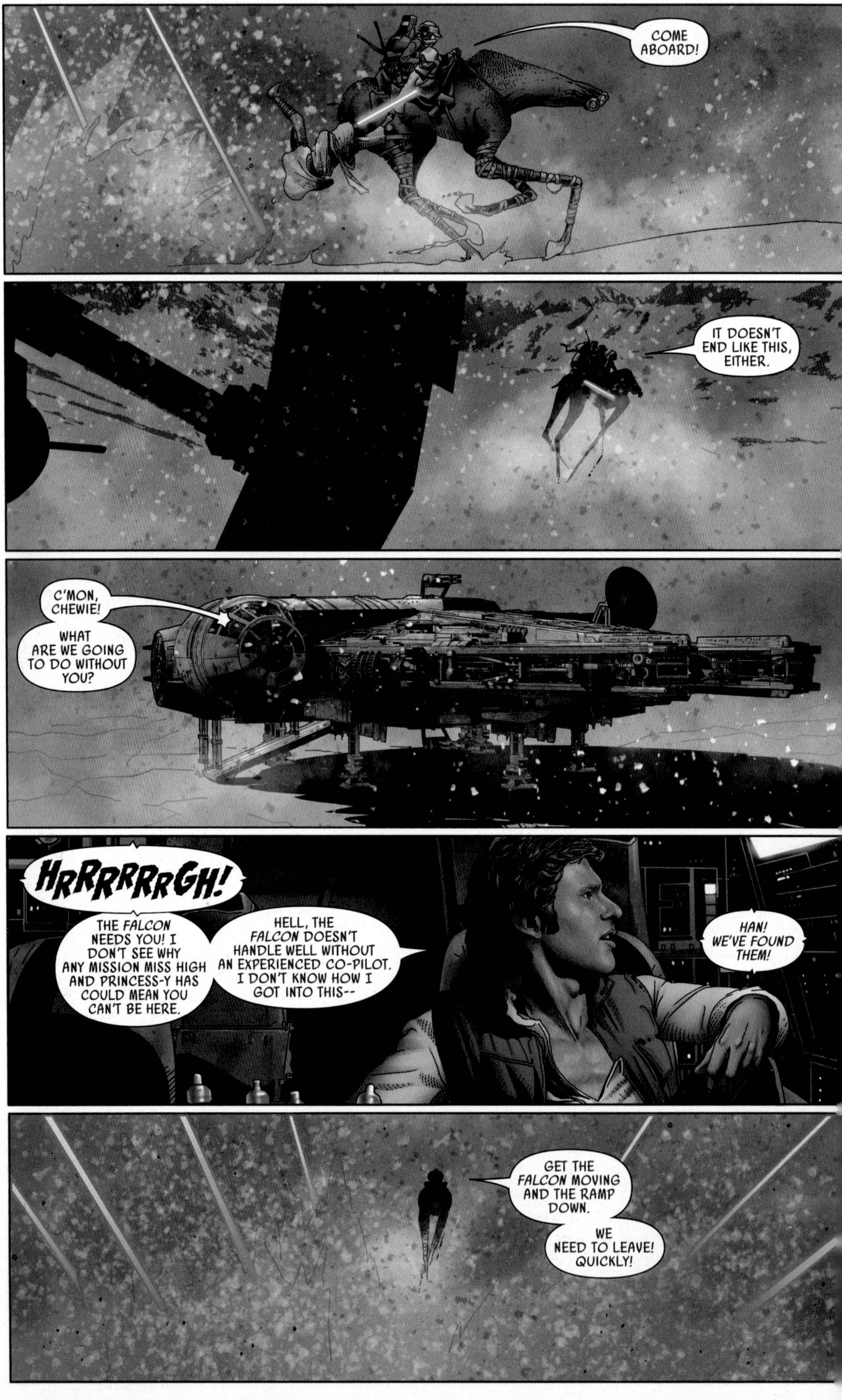
COME ABOARD!
IT DOESN'T END LIKE THIS, EITHER.
C'MON, CHEWIE!
WHAT ARE WE GOING TO DO WITHOUT YOU?
HRRRRRRGH!
THE *FALCON* NEEDS YOU! I DON'T SEE WHY ANY MISSION MISS HIGH AND PRINCESS-Y HAS COULD MEAN YOU CAN'T BE HERE.
HELL, THE *FALCON* DOESN'T HANDLE WELL WITHOUT AN EXPERIENCED CO-PILOT. I DON'T KNOW HOW I GOT INTO THIS--
HAN! WE'VE FOUND THEM!
GET THE *FALCON* MOVING AND THE RAMP DOWN.
WE NEED TO LEAVE! QUICKLY!

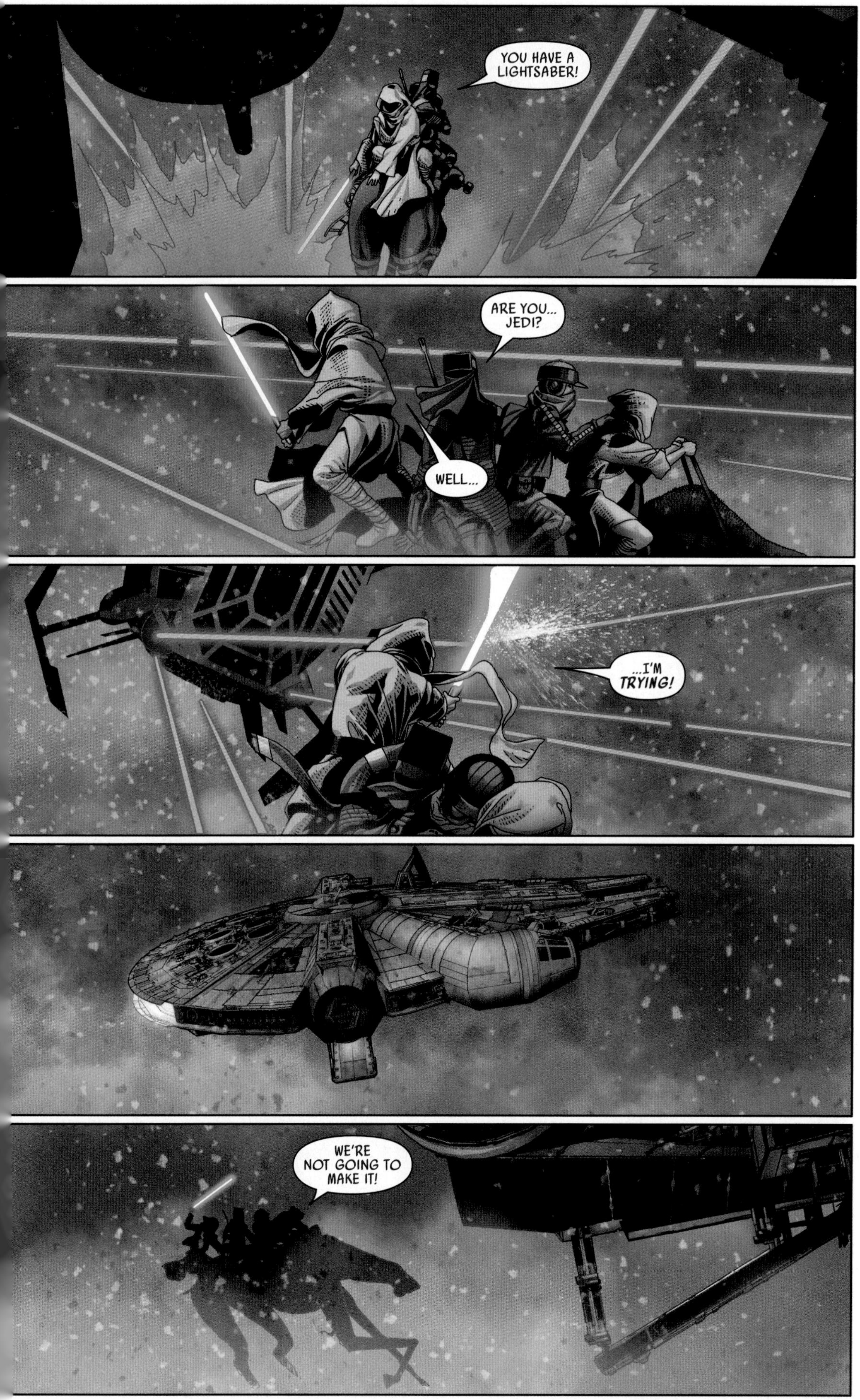
YOU HAVE A LIGHTSABER!
ARE YOU... JEDI?
WELL...
...I'M TRYING!
WE'RE NOT GOING TO MAKE IT!

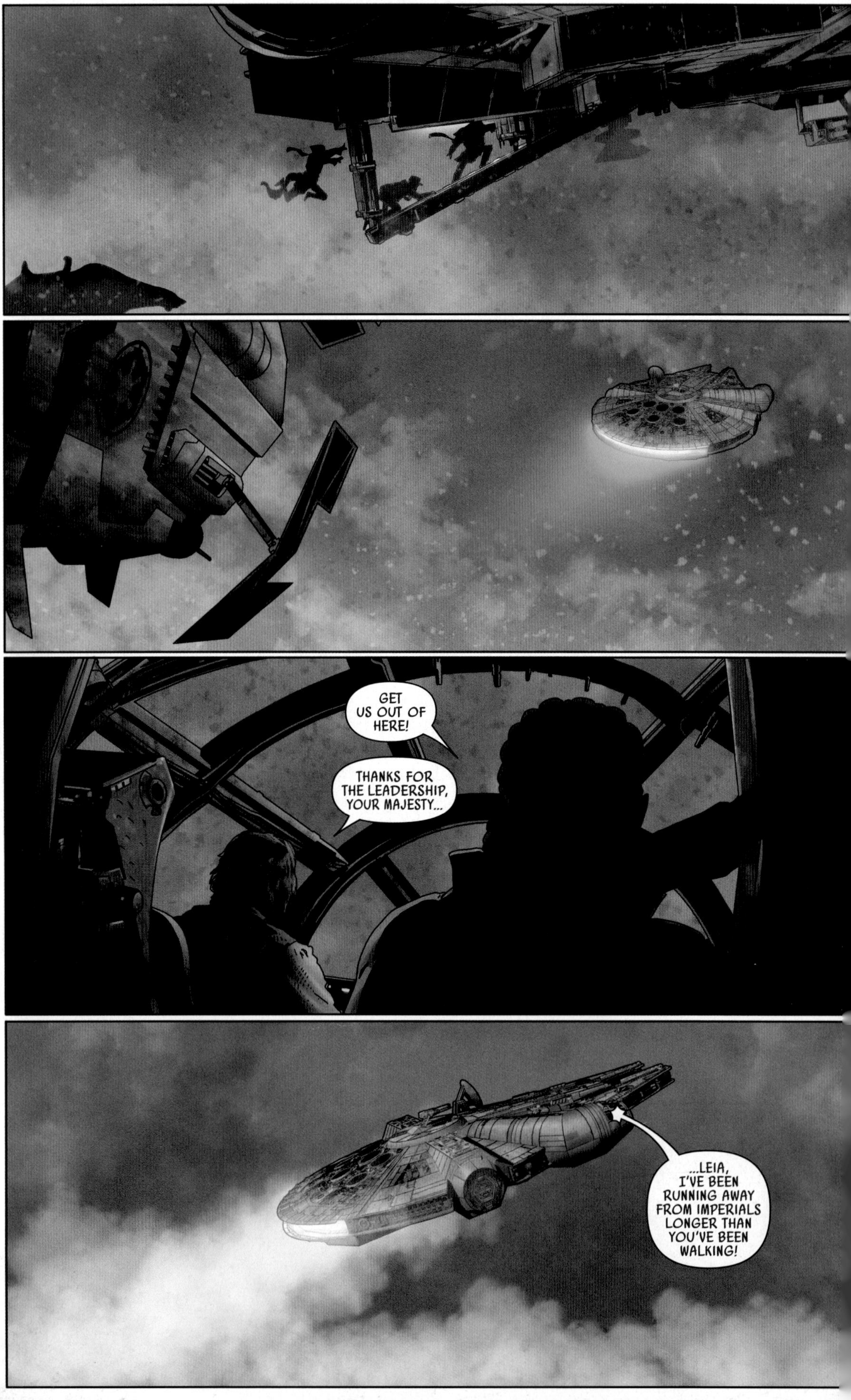
GET US OUT OF HERE!
THANKS FOR THE LEADERSHIP, YOUR MAJESTY...
...LEIA, I'VE BEEN RUNNING AWAY FROM IMPERIALS LONGER THAN YOU'VE BEEN WALKING!

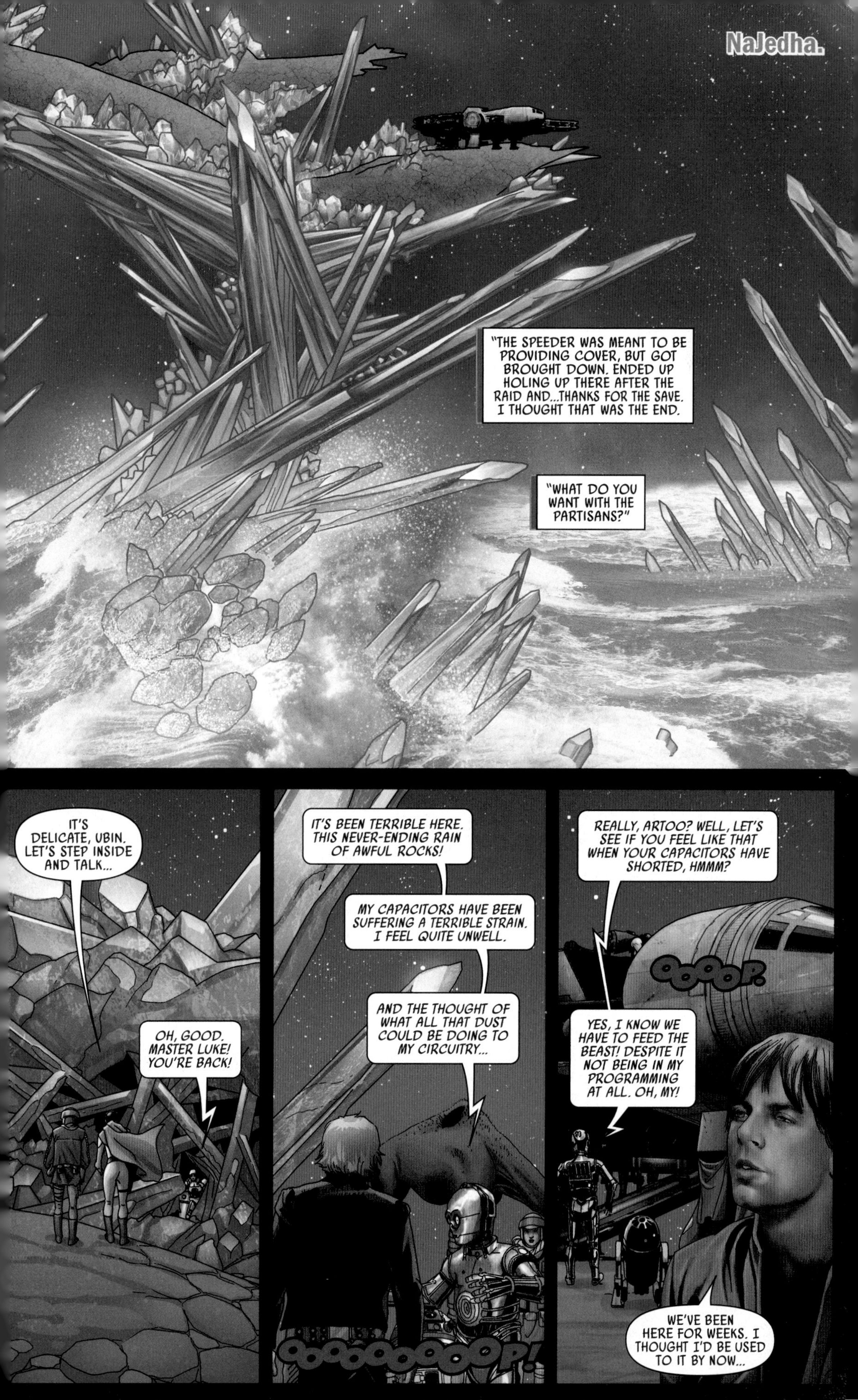
"THE SPEEDER WAS MEANT TO BE PROVIDING COVER, BUT GOT BROUGHT DOWN. ENDED UP HOLING UP THERE AFTER THE RAID AND...THANKS FOR THE SAVE. I THOUGHT THAT WAS THE END.
"WHAT DO YOU WANT WITH THE PARTISANS?"
IT'S DELICATE, UBIN. LET'S STEP INSIDE AND TALK...
OH, GOOD. MASTER LUKE! YOU'RE BACK!
IT'S BEEN TERRIBLE HERE. THIS NEVER-ENDING RAIN OF AWFUL ROCKS!
MY CAPACITORS HAVE BEEN SUFFERING A TERRIBLE STRAIN. I FEEL QUITE UNWELL.
AND THE THOUGHT OF WHAT ALL THAT DUST COULD BE DOING TO MY CIRCUITRY...
OOOOOOOOOOP!
REALLY, ARTOO? WELL, LET'S SEE IF YOU FEEL LIKE THAT WHEN YOUR CAPACITORS HAVE SHORTED, HMMM?
OOOOP.
YES, I KNOW WE HAVE TO FEED THE BEAST! DESPITE IT NOT BEING IN MY PROGRAMMING AT ALL. OH, MY!
WE'VE BEEN HERE FOR WEEKS. I THOUGHT I'D BE USED TO IT BY NOW...

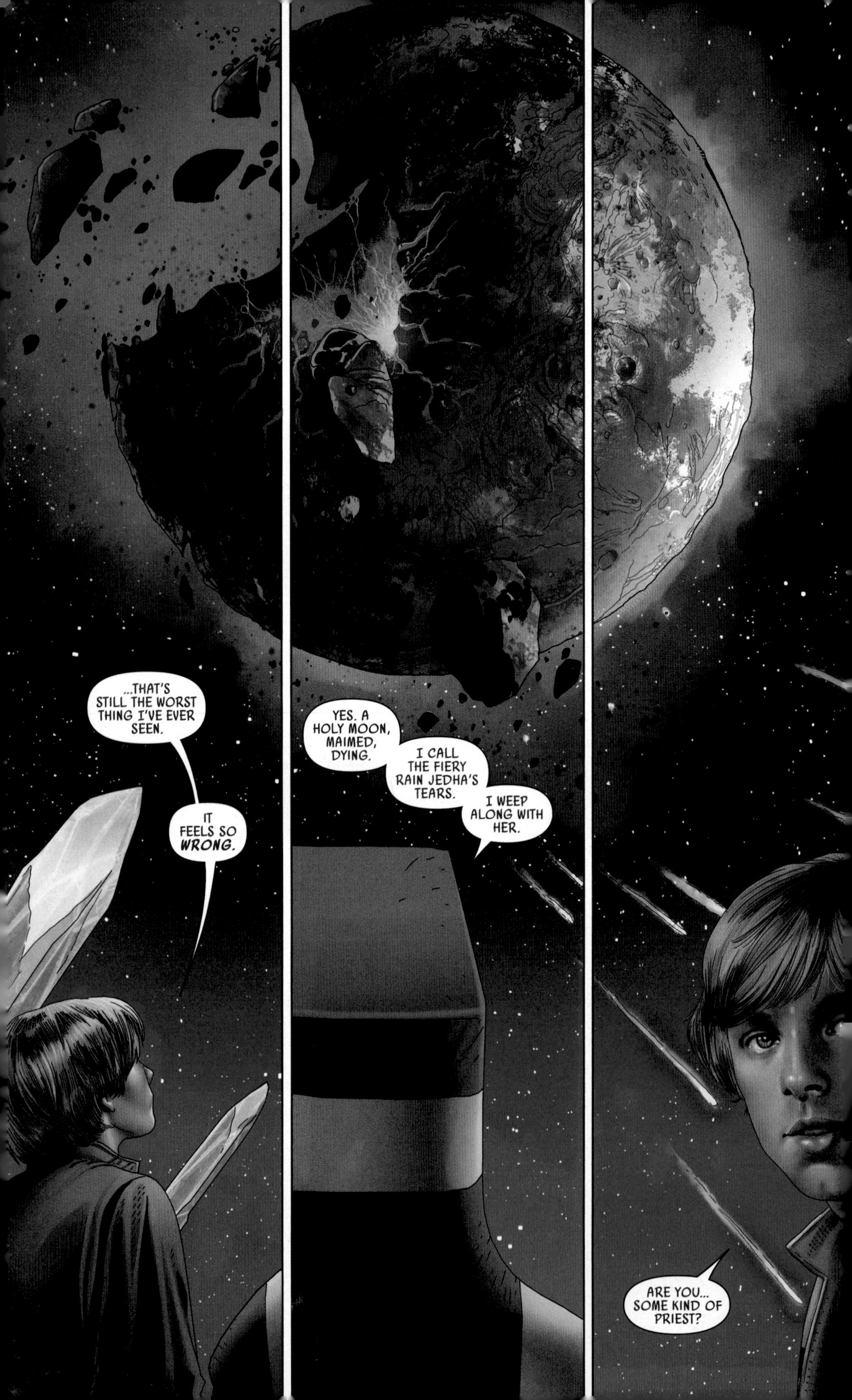
...THAT'S STILL THE WORST THING I'VE EVER SEEN.
IT FEELS SO *WRONG*.
YES. A HOLY MOON, MAIMED, DYING.
I CALL THE FIERY RAIN JEDHA'S TEARS.
I WEEP ALONG WITH HER.
ARE YOU... SOME KIND OF PRIEST?

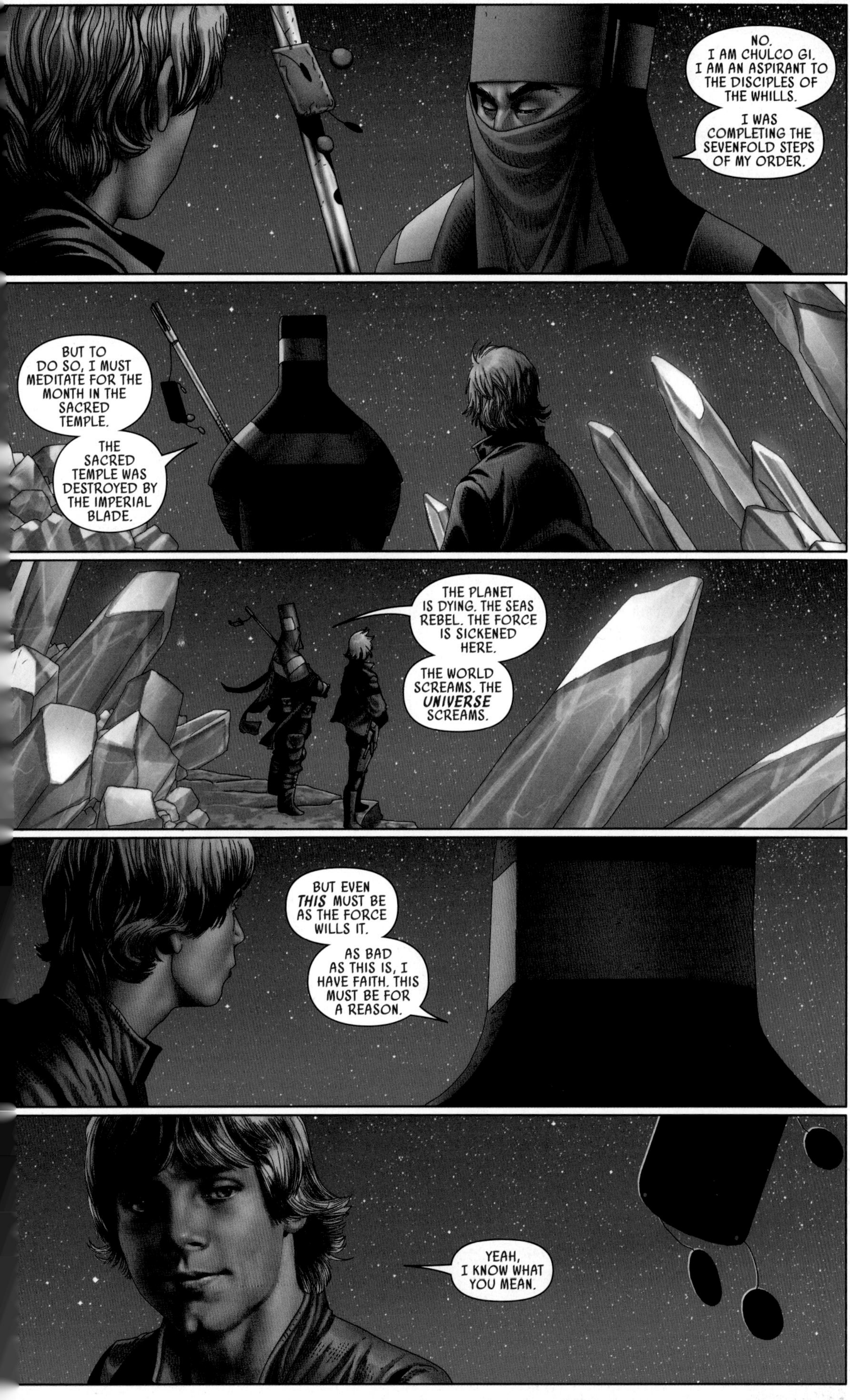
NO. I AM CHULCO GI. I AM AN ASPIRANT TO THE DISCIPLES OF THE WHILLS.
I WAS COMPLETING THE SEVENFOLD STEPS OF MY ORDER.
BUT TO DO SO, I MUST MEDITATE FOR THE MONTH IN THE SACRED TEMPLE.
THE SACRED TEMPLE WAS DESTROYED BY THE IMPERIAL BLADE.
THE PLANET IS DYING. THE SEAS REBEL. THE FORCE IS SICKENED HERE.
THE WORLD SCREAMS. THE *UNIVERSE* SCREAMS.
BUT EVEN *THIS* MUST BE AS THE FORCE WILLS IT.
AS BAD AS THIS IS, I HAVE FAITH. THIS MUST BE FOR A REASON.
YEAH, I KNOW WHAT YOU MEAN.

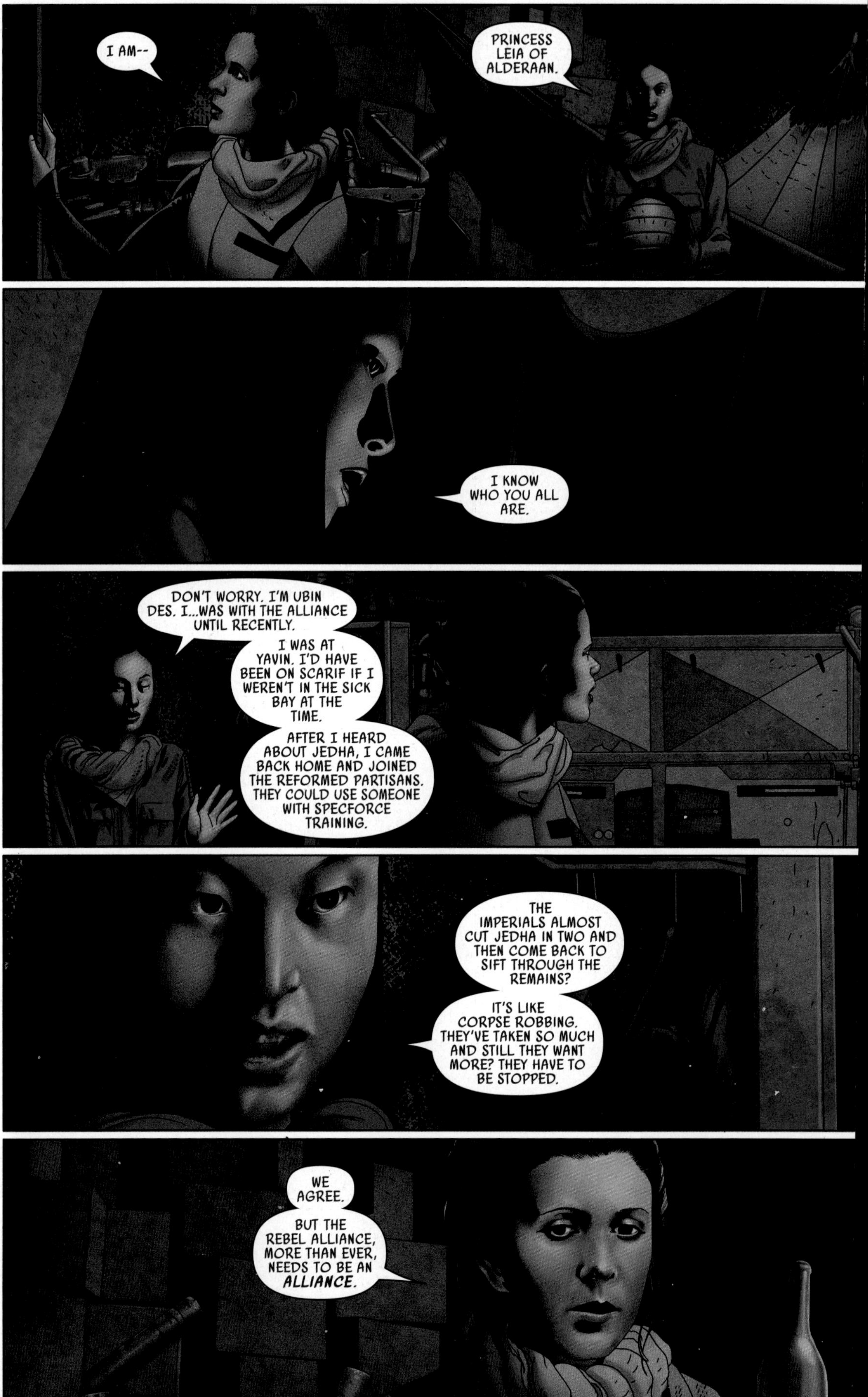
I AM--
PRINCESS LEIA OF ALDERAAN.
I KNOW WHO YOU ALL ARE.
DON'T WORRY. I'M UBIN DES. I...WAS WITH THE ALLIANCE UNTIL RECENTLY.
I WAS AT YAVIN. I'D HAVE BEEN ON SCARIF IF I WEREN'T IN THE SICK BAY AT THE TIME.
AFTER I HEARD ABOUT JEDHA, I CAME BACK HOME AND JOINED THE REFORMED PARTISANS. THEY COULD USE SOMEONE WITH SPECFORCE TRAINING.
THE IMPERIALS ALMOST CUT JEDHA IN TWO AND THEN COME BACK TO SIFT THROUGH THE REMAINS?
IT'S LIKE CORPSE ROBBING. THEY'VE TAKEN SO MUCH AND STILL THEY WANT MORE? THEY HAVE TO BE STOPPED.
WE AGREE.
BUT THE REBEL ALLIANCE, MORE THAN EVER, NEEDS TO BE AN *ALLIANCE*.

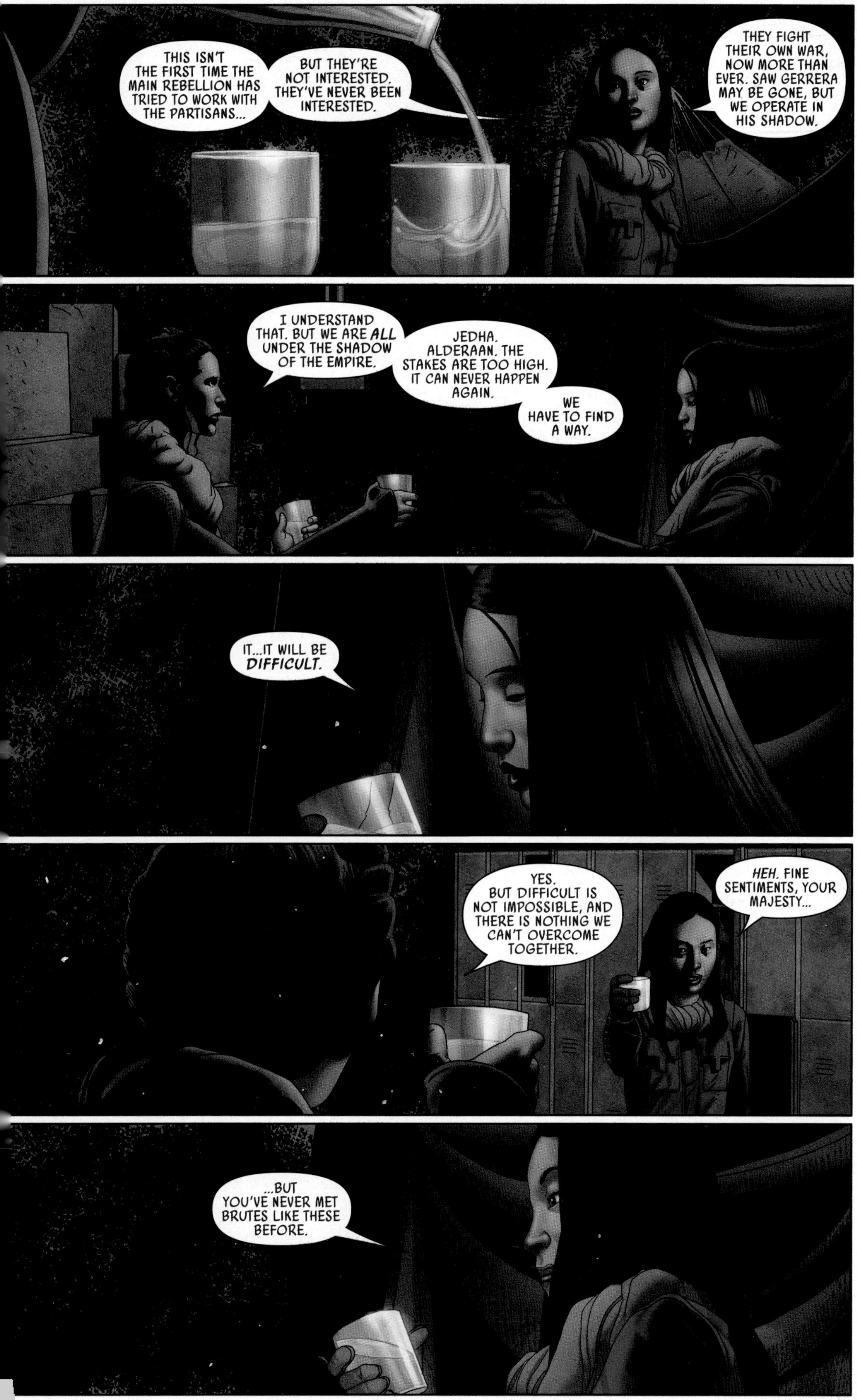
THIS ISN'T THE FIRST TIME THE MAIN REBELLION HAS TRIED TO WORK WITH THE PARTISANS...
BUT THEY'RE NOT INTERESTED. THEY'VE NEVER BEEN INTERESTED.
THEY FIGHT THEIR OWN WAR, NOW MORE THAN EVER. SAW GERRERA MAY BE GONE, BUT WE OPERATE IN HIS SHADOW.
I UNDERSTAND THAT. BUT WE ARE ALL UNDER THE SHADOW OF THE EMPIRE.
JEDHA. ALDERAAN. THE STAKES ARE TOO HIGH. IT CAN NEVER HAPPEN AGAIN.
WE HAVE TO FIND A WAY.
IT...IT WILL BE DIFFICULT.
YES. BUT DIFFICULT IS NOT IMPOSSIBLE, AND THERE IS NOTHING WE CAN'T OVERCOME TOGETHER.
HEH. FINE SENTIMENTS, YOUR MAJESTY...
...BUT YOU'VE NEVER MET BRUTES LIKE THESE BEFORE.

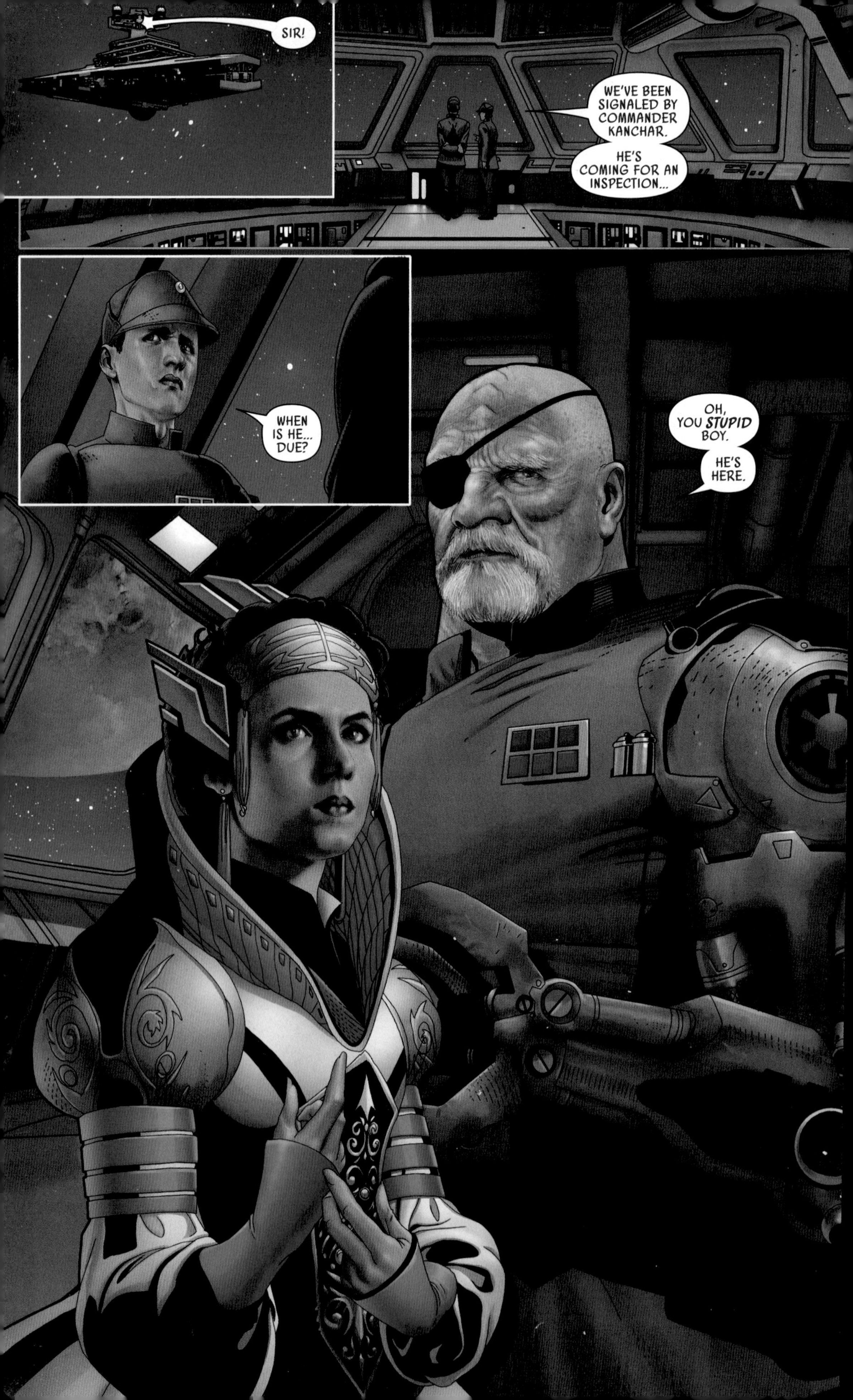
SIR!
WE'VE BEEN SIGNALED BY COMMANDER KANCHAR.
HE'S COMING FOR AN INSPECTION...
WHEN IS HE... DUE?
OH, YOU **STUPID** BOY.
HE'S HERE.

SIR, THIS IS AN UNEXPECTED PLEASURE.

AND WHO IS THE BEAUTIFUL--

DON'T TRY TO SWEET-TALK ME, BEFA. IT'S NO "UNEXPECTED PLEASURE."

AND HANDS OFF THE ADVISER.

I'M QUEEN TRIOS OF SHU-TORUN.

I AM, AS THE GOOD COMMANDER PUTS IT, MERELY A CIVILIAN WITH EXPERIENCE IN MINERAL EXTRACTION.

I ONLY WISH TO ASSIST THE EMPIRE.

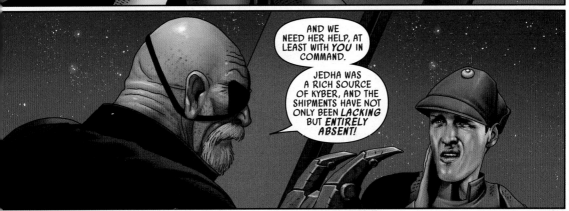

AND WE NEED HER HELP, AT LEAST WITH YOU IN COMMAND.

JEDHA WAS A RICH SOURCE OF KYBER, AND THE SHIPMENTS HAVE NOT ONLY BEEN LACKING BUT ENTIRELY ABSENT!

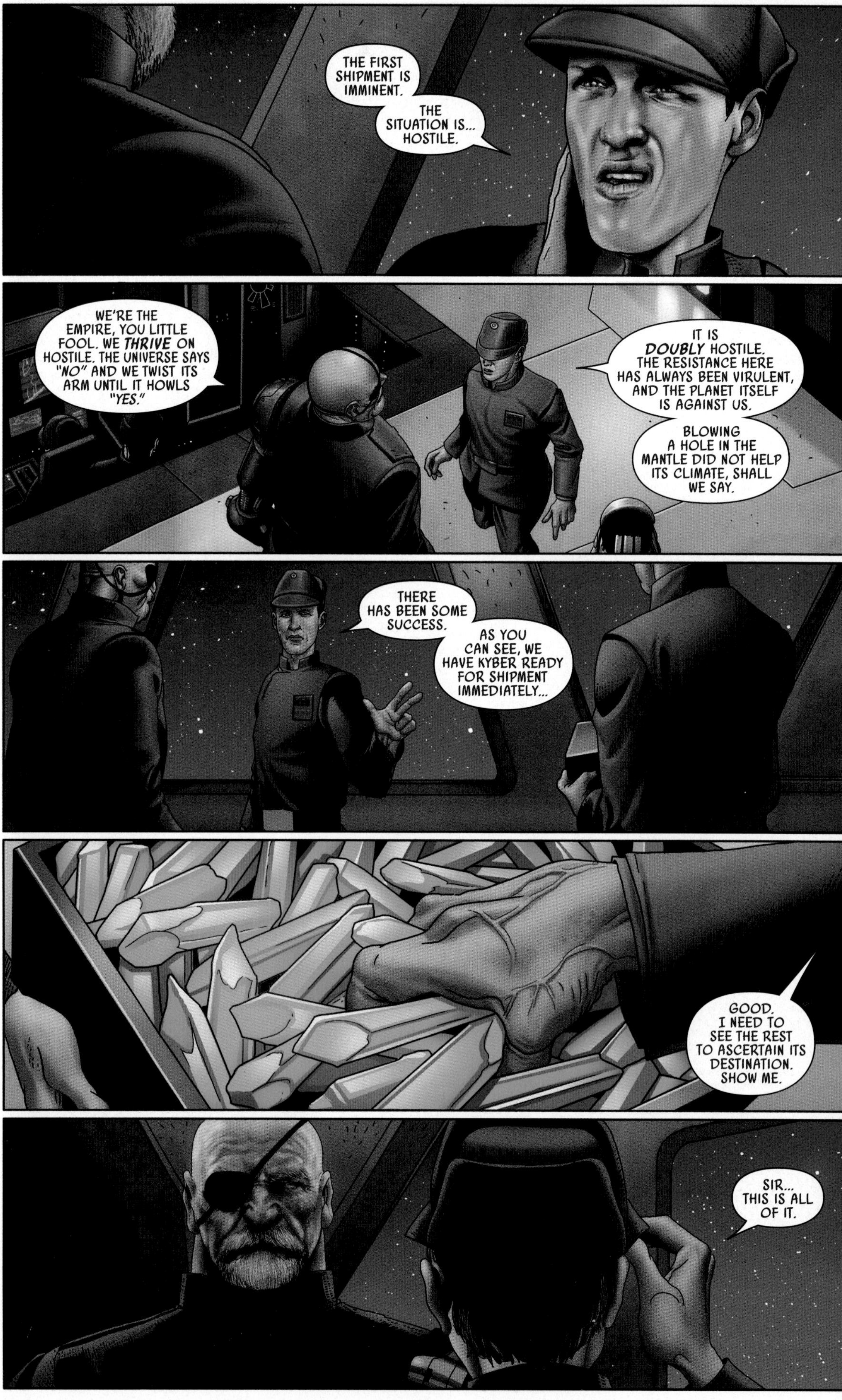
THE FIRST SHIPMENT IS IMMINENT.
THE SITUATION IS... HOSTILE.
WE'RE THE EMPIRE, YOU LITTLE FOOL. WE THRIVE ON HOSTILE. THE UNIVERSE SAYS "NO" AND WE TWIST ITS ARM UNTIL IT HOWLS "YES."
IT IS DOUBLY HOSTILE. THE RESISTANCE HERE HAS ALWAYS BEEN VIRULENT, AND THE PLANET ITSELF IS AGAINST US.
BLOWING A HOLE IN THE MANTLE DID NOT HELP ITS CLIMATE, SHALL WE SAY.
THERE HAS BEEN SOME SUCCESS.
AS YOU CAN SEE, WE HAVE KYBER READY FOR SHIPMENT IMMEDIATELY...
GOOD. I NEED TO SEE THE REST TO ASCERTAIN ITS DESTINATION. SHOW ME.
SIR... THIS IS ALL OF IT.

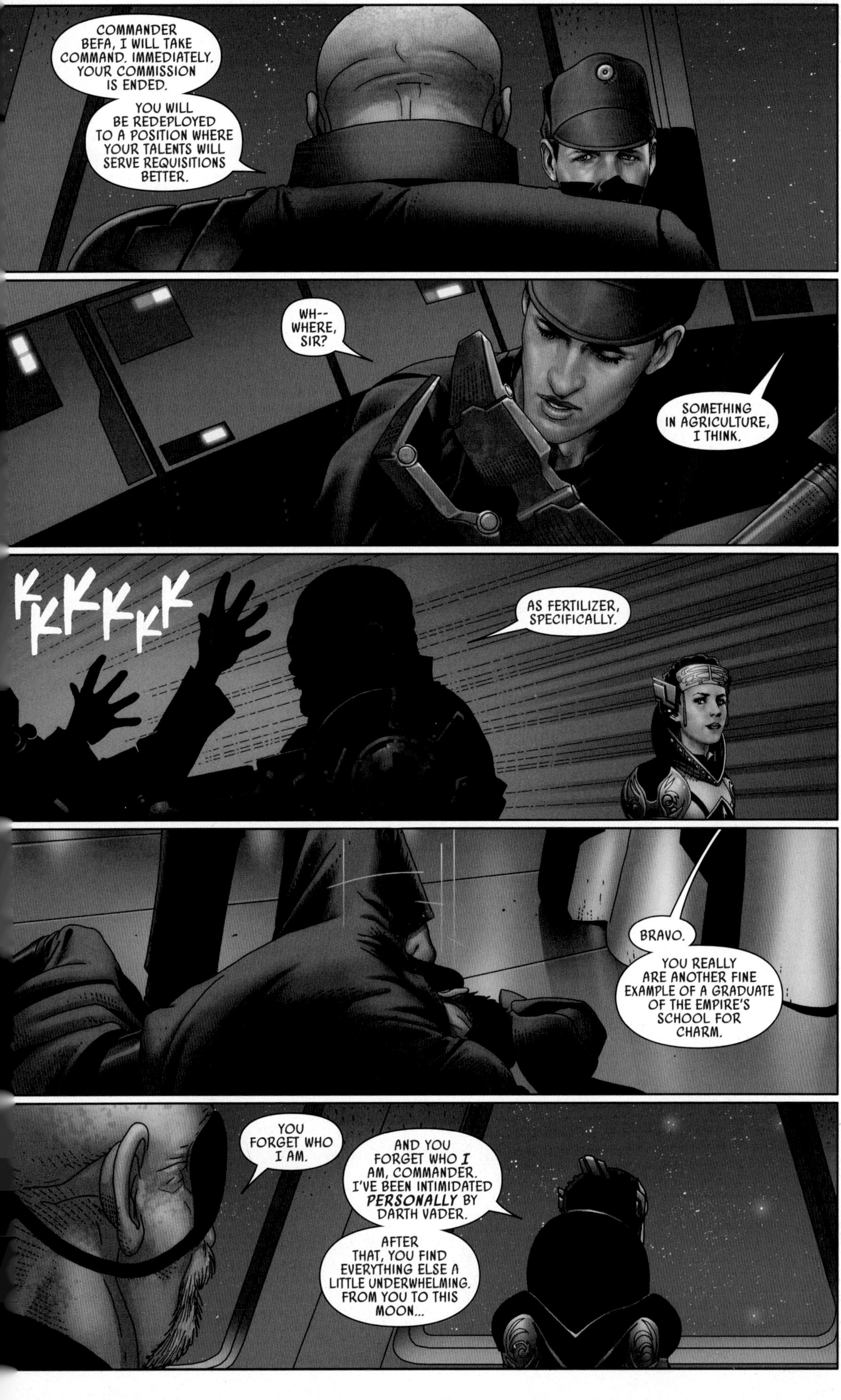
COMMANDER BEFA, I WILL TAKE COMMAND. IMMEDIATELY. YOUR COMMISSION IS ENDED.
YOU WILL BE REDEPLOYED TO A POSITION WHERE YOUR TALENTS WILL SERVE REQUISITIONS BETTER.
WH-- WHERE, SIR?
SOMETHING IN AGRICULTURE, I THINK.
KKKKKK
AS FERTILIZER, SPECIFICALLY.
BRAVO.
YOU REALLY ARE ANOTHER FINE EXAMPLE OF A GRADUATE OF THE EMPIRE'S SCHOOL FOR CHARM.
YOU FORGET WHO I AM.
AND YOU FORGET WHO *I* AM, COMMANDER. I'VE BEEN INTIMIDATED ***PERSONALLY*** BY DARTH VADER.
AFTER THAT, YOU FIND EVERYTHING ELSE A LITTLE UNDERWHELMING. FROM YOU TO THIS MOON...

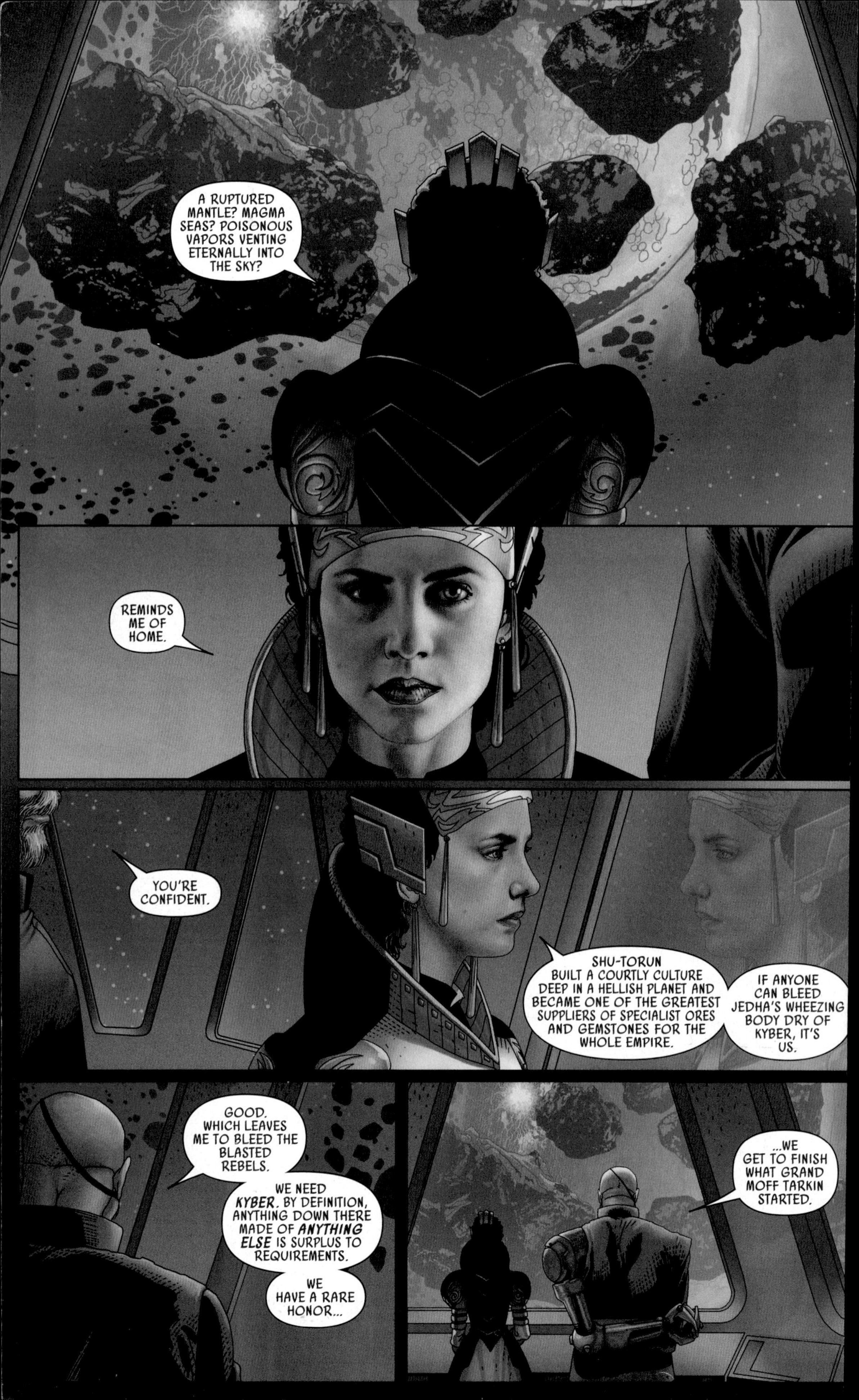
A RUPTURED MANTLE? MAGMA SEAS? POISONOUS VAPORS VENTING ETERNALLY INTO THE SKY?
REMINDS ME OF HOME.
YOU'RE CONFIDENT.
SHU-TORUN BUILT A COURTLY CULTURE DEEP IN A HELLISH PLANET AND BECAME ONE OF THE GREATEST SUPPLIERS OF SPECIALIST ORES AND GEMSTONES FOR THE WHOLE EMPIRE.
IF ANYONE CAN BLEED JEDHA'S WHEEZING BODY DRY OF KYBER, IT'S US.
GOOD. WHICH LEAVES ME TO BLEED THE BLASTED REBELS.
WE NEED ***KYBER***. BY DEFINITION, ANYTHING DOWN THERE MADE OF ***ANYTHING ELSE*** IS SURPLUS TO REQUIREMENTS.
WE HAVE A RARE HONOR...
...WE GET TO FINISH WHAT GRAND MOFF TARKIN STARTED.

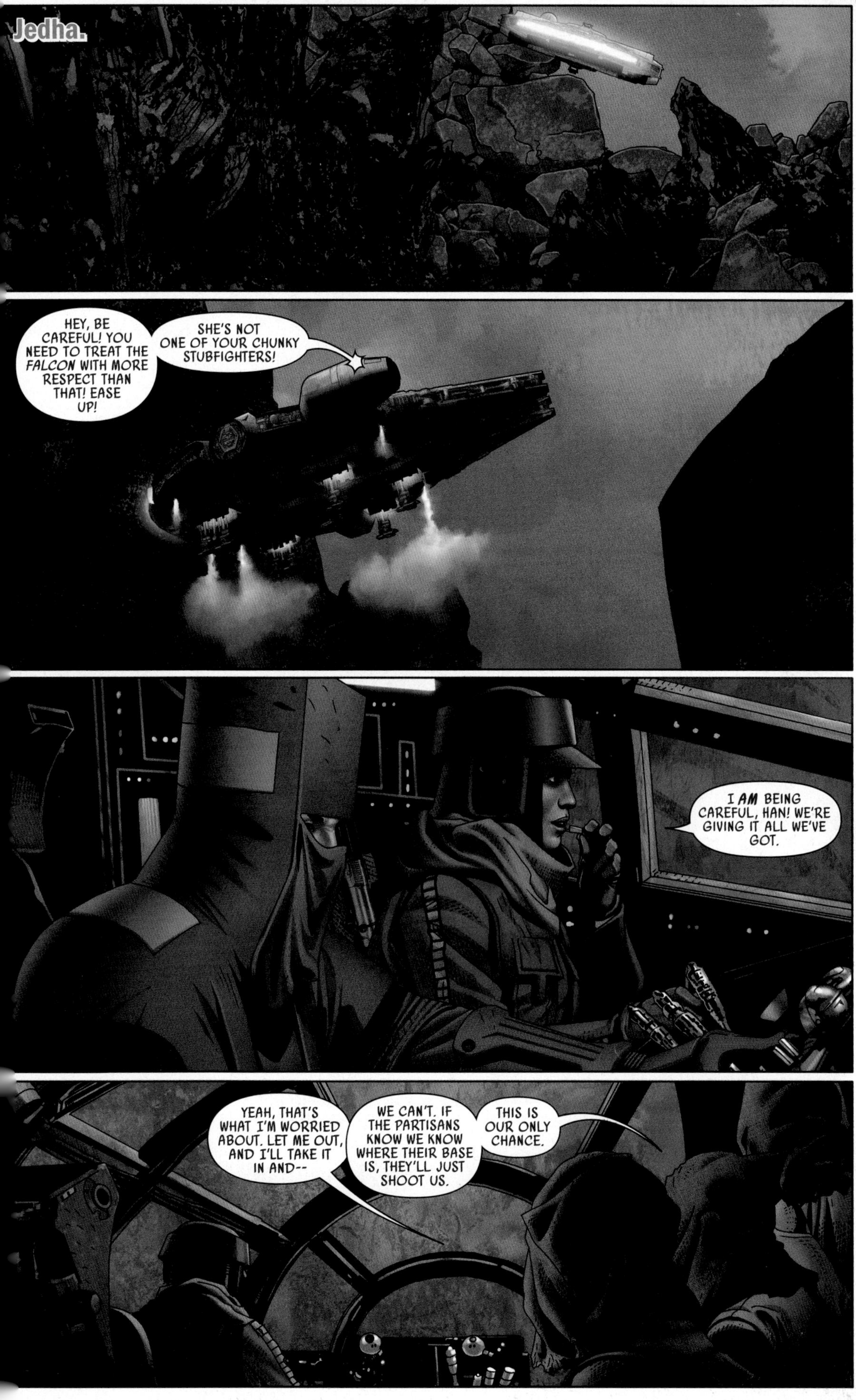
Jedha.
HEY, BE CAREFUL! YOU NEED TO TREAT THE *FALCON* WITH MORE RESPECT THAN THAT! EASE UP!
SHE'S NOT ONE OF YOUR CHUNKY STUBFIGHTERS!
I **AM** BEING CAREFUL, HAN! WE'RE GIVING IT ALL WE'VE GOT.
YEAH, THAT'S WHAT I'M WORRIED ABOUT. LET ME OUT, AND I'LL TAKE IT IN AND--
WE CAN'T. IF THE PARTISANS KNOW WE KNOW WHERE THEIR BASE IS, THEY'LL JUST SHOOT US.
THIS IS OUR ONLY CHANCE.

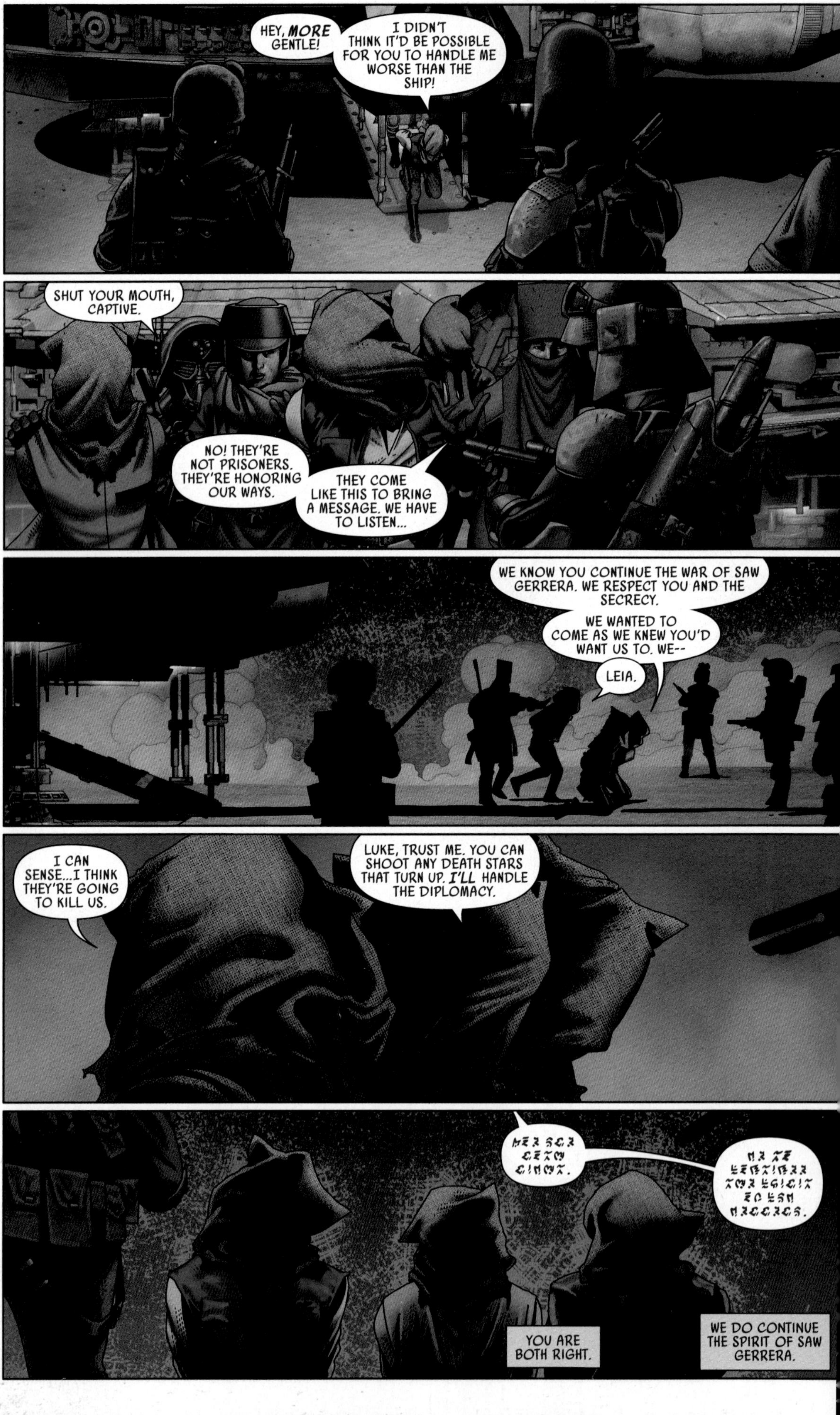
HEY, MORE GENTLE!
I DIDN'T THINK IT'D BE POSSIBLE FOR YOU TO HANDLE ME WORSE THAN THE SHIP!
SHUT YOUR MOUTH, CAPTIVE.
NO! THEY'RE NOT PRISONERS. THEY'RE HONORING OUR WAYS.
THEY COME LIKE THIS TO BRING A MESSAGE. WE HAVE TO LISTEN...
WE KNOW YOU CONTINUE THE WAR OF SAW GERRERA. WE RESPECT YOU AND THE SECRECY.
WE WANTED TO COME AS WE KNEW YOU'D WANT US TO. WE--
LEIA.
I CAN SENSE...I THINK THEY'RE GOING TO KILL US.
LUKE, TRUST ME. YOU CAN SHOOT ANY DEATH STARS THAT TURN UP. I'LL HANDLE THE DIPLOMACY.
YOU ARE BOTH RIGHT.
WE DO CONTINUE THE SPIRIT OF SAW GERRERA.

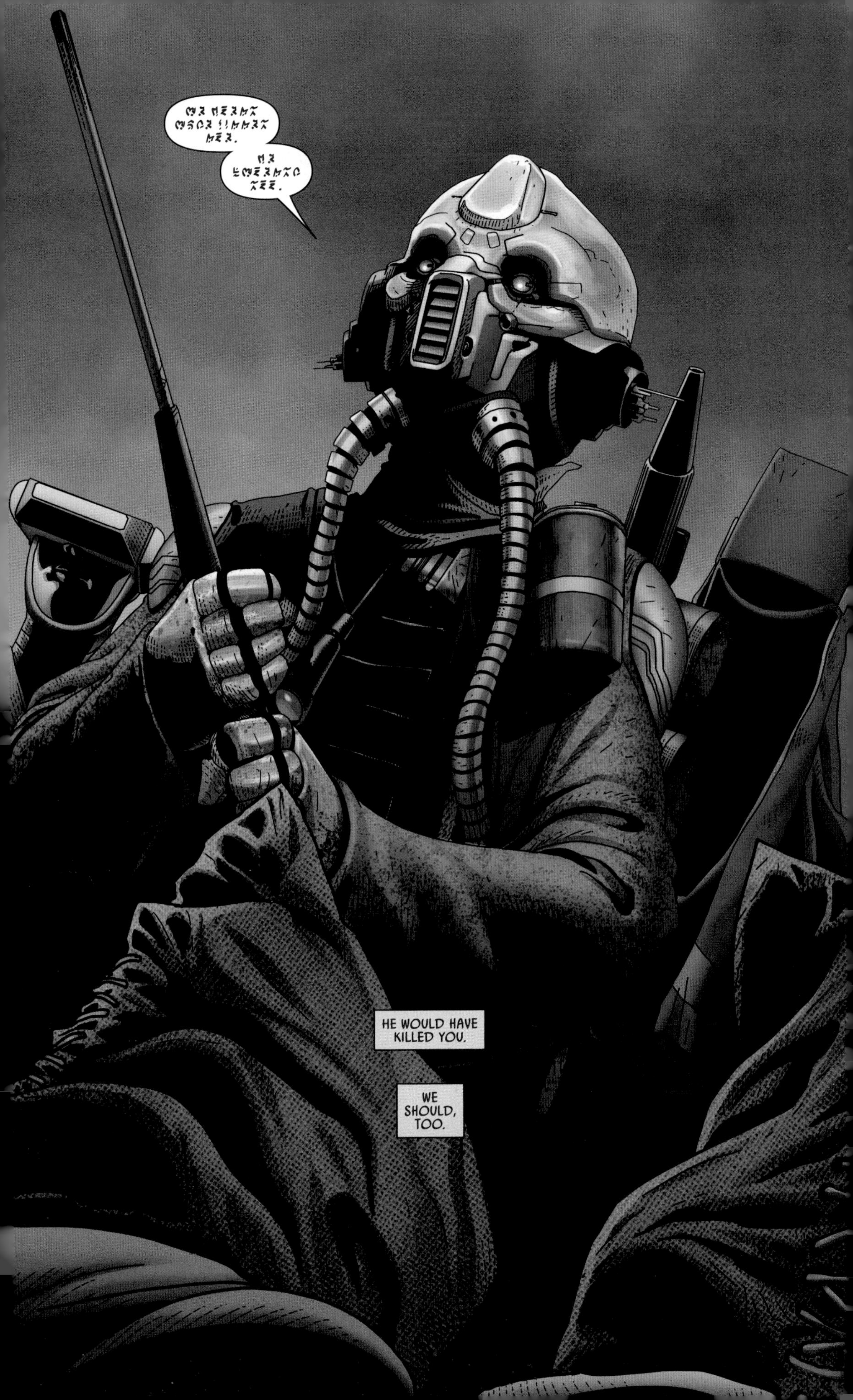
HE WOULD HAVE KILLED YOU.
WE SHOULD, TOO.

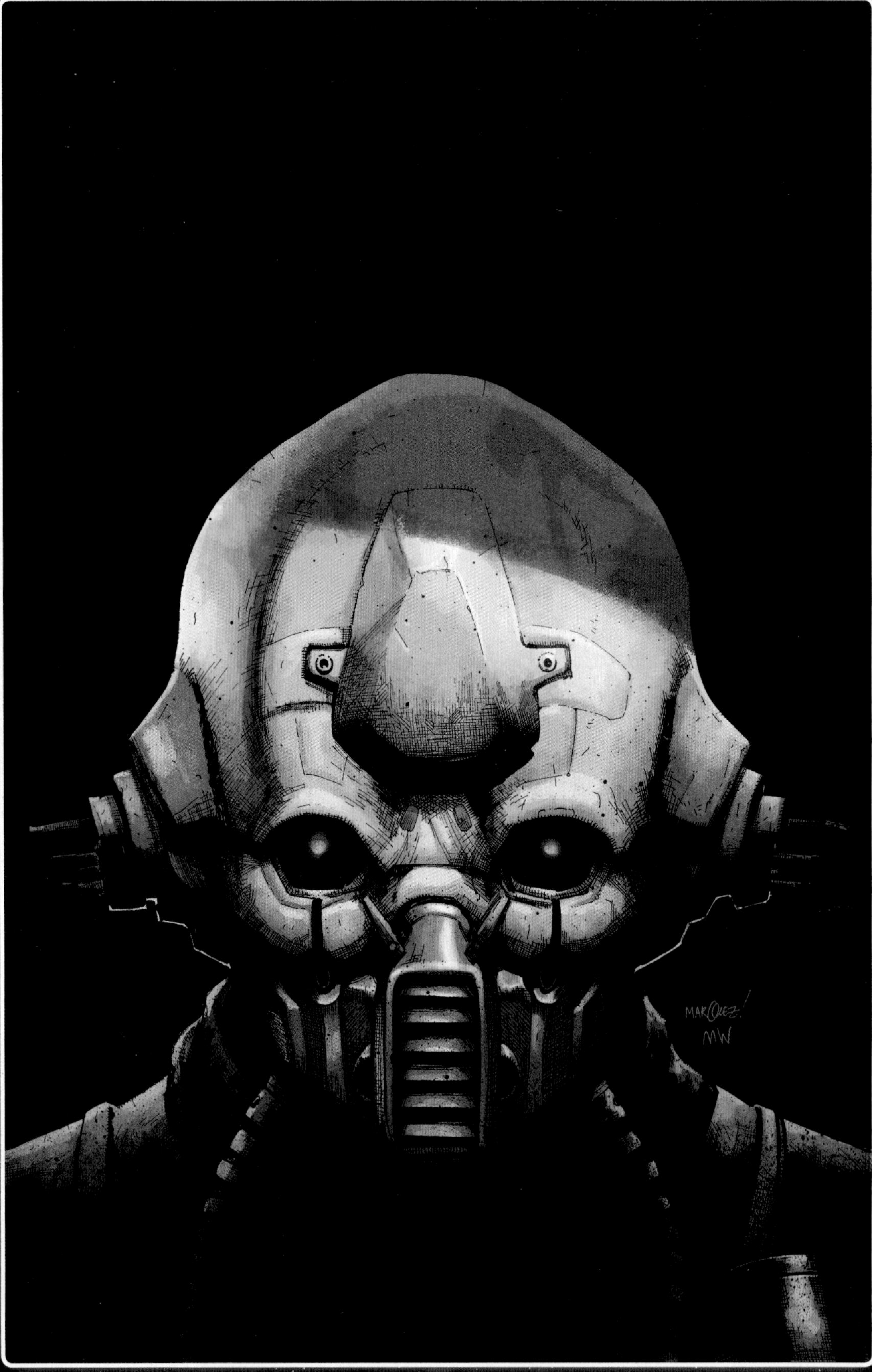
MARQUEZ!
MW

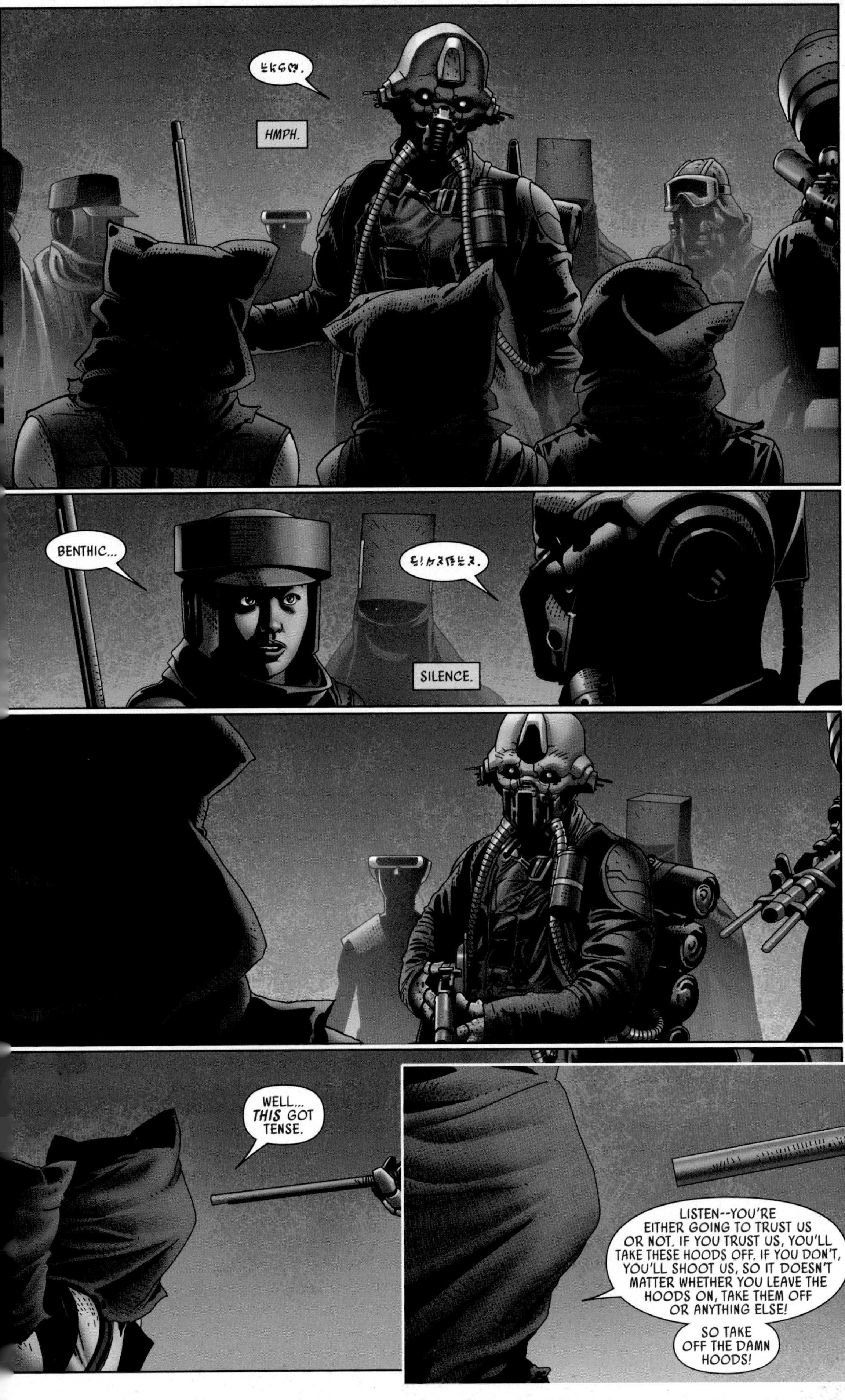
HMPH.
BENTHIC...
SILENCE.
WELL... *THIS* GOT TENSE.
LISTEN--YOU'RE EITHER GOING TO TRUST US OR NOT. IF YOU TRUST US, YOU'LL TAKE THESE HOODS OFF. IF YOU DON'T, YOU'LL SHOOT US, SO IT DOESN'T MATTER WHETHER YOU LEAVE THE HOODS ON, TAKE THEM OFF OR ANYTHING ELSE!
SO TAKE OFF THE DAMN HOODS!

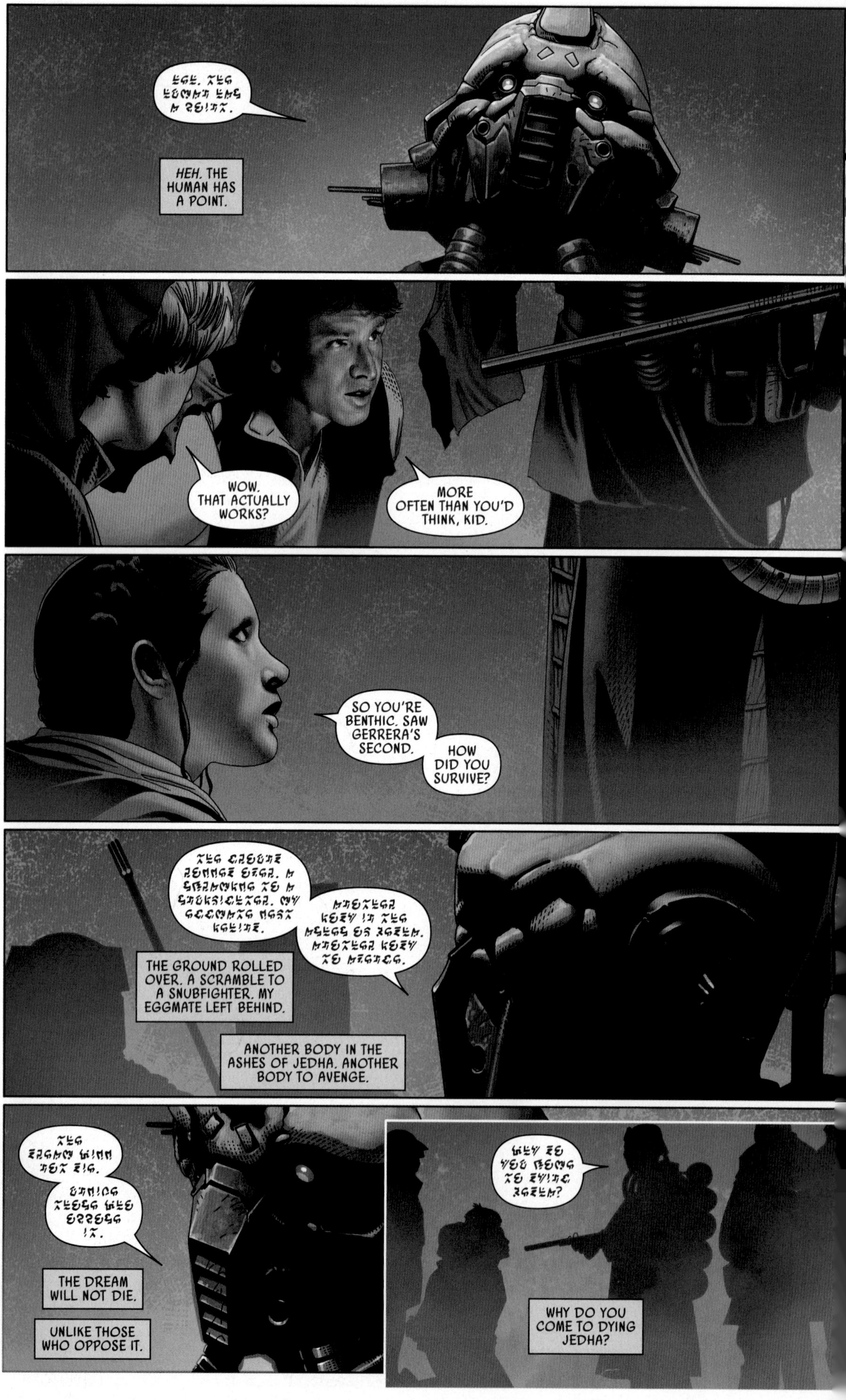
HEH. THE HUMAN HAS A POINT.
WOW. THAT ACTUALLY WORKS?
MORE OFTEN THAN YOU'D THINK, KID.
SO YOU'RE BENTHIC. SAW GERRERA'S SECOND.
HOW DID YOU SURVIVE?
THE GROUND ROLLED OVER. A SCRAMBLE TO A SNUBFIGHTER. MY EGGMATE LEFT BEHIND.
ANOTHER BODY IN THE ASHES OF JEDHA. ANOTHER BODY TO AVENGE.
THE DREAM WILL NOT DIE.
UNLIKE THOSE WHO OPPOSE IT.
WHY DO YOU COME TO DYING JEDHA?

THE DEATH STAR.

WE HAVE *NO IDEA* WHAT THE IMPERIALS COULD BUILD NEXT.

ONE THING WE DO KNOW--WHATEVER THEY TRY, WE HAVE TO STOP IT.

THEY'RE MINING KYBER CRYSTALS AGAIN? WE MAKE THAT AS HARD AS POSSIBLE. THE ALLIANCE WILL SUPPORT ANYONE WHO'S DOING THAT.

ᗷᗴ ᗯᎥᏞᏞ ᑎᗴᐯᗴᖇ ᔑᗝᒪᒪᗝᗯ Ƴᗝᑌᖇ ᗝᖇᗞᗴᖇᔑ.

WE WILL NEVER FOLLOW YOUR ORDERS.

WE KNOW. WE DON'T WANT YOU TO.

THE PARTISANS ON JEDHA DID MAGNIFICENTLY BY THEMSELVES...

...THEY'D DO BETTER IF THEY WERE BETTER SUPPLIED.

YOU'LL FIND THE FIRST SHIPMENT ABOARD OUR SHIP. I'M HERE TO SECURE WHATEVER FUTURE ARRANGEMENT THAT WILL WORK FOR YOU.

WHILE WE'RE WITH YOU, YOU'LL HAVE FULL USE OF OUR SKILLS AND TALENTS.

ᔑᏆᎿᗴ. ᗰᑌᗰᗷᒪᎥᑎᏩ ᔑᏆᖇᗩᑎᏩᗴᖇ.

PTTH. ALLIANCE "TALENTS."

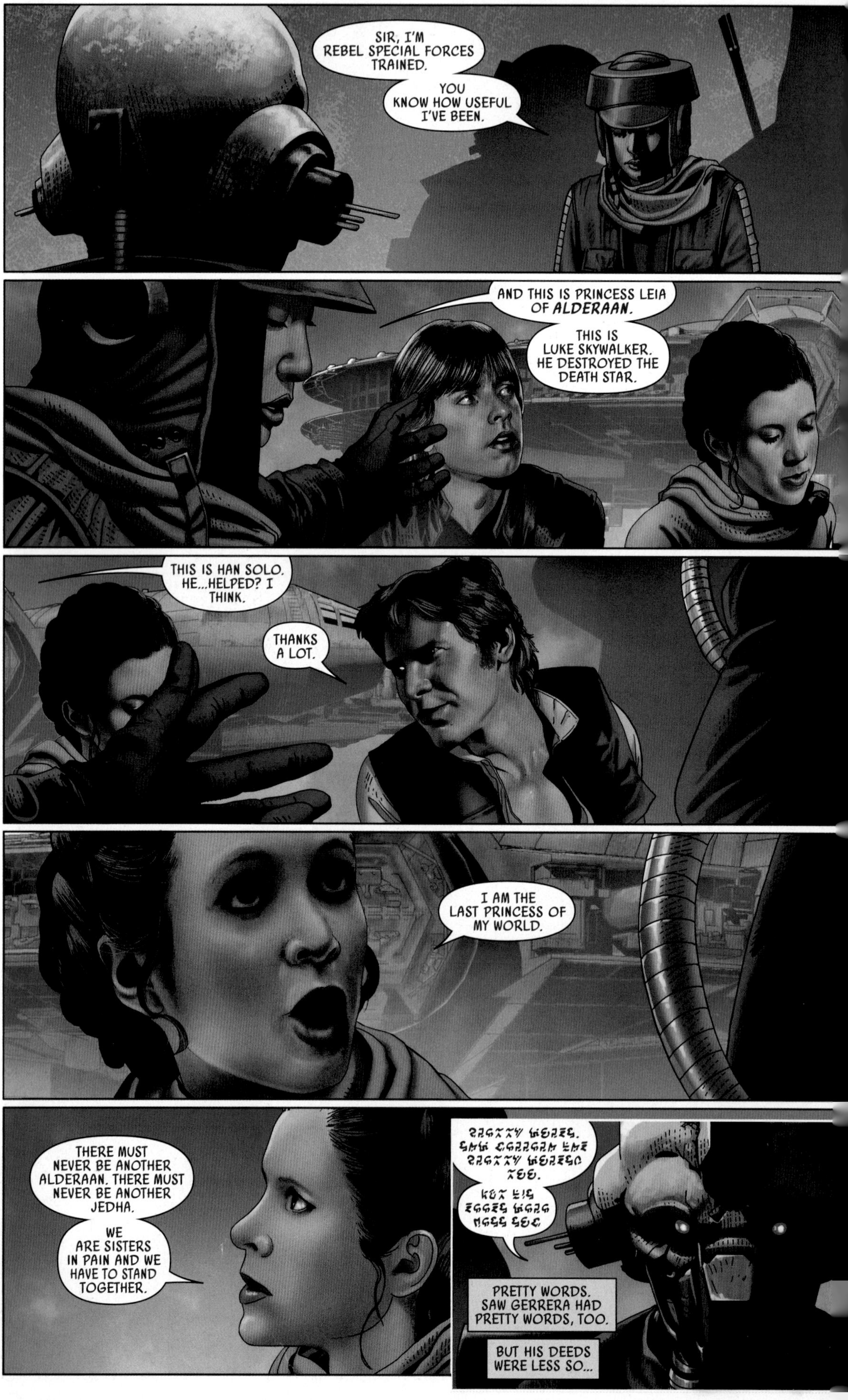
SIR, I'M REBEL SPECIAL FORCES TRAINED.
YOU KNOW HOW USEFUL I'VE BEEN.
AND THIS IS PRINCESS LEIA OF ALDERAAN.
THIS IS LUKE SKYWALKER. HE DESTROYED THE DEATH STAR.
THIS IS HAN SOLO. HE...HELPED? I THINK.
THANKS A LOT.
I AM THE LAST PRINCESS OF MY WORLD.
THERE MUST NEVER BE ANOTHER ALDERAAN. THERE MUST NEVER BE ANOTHER JEDHA.
WE ARE SISTERS IN PAIN AND WE HAVE TO STAND TOGETHER.
PRETTY WORDS. SAW GERRERA HAD PRETTY WORDS, TOO.
BUT HIS DEEDS WERE LESS SO...

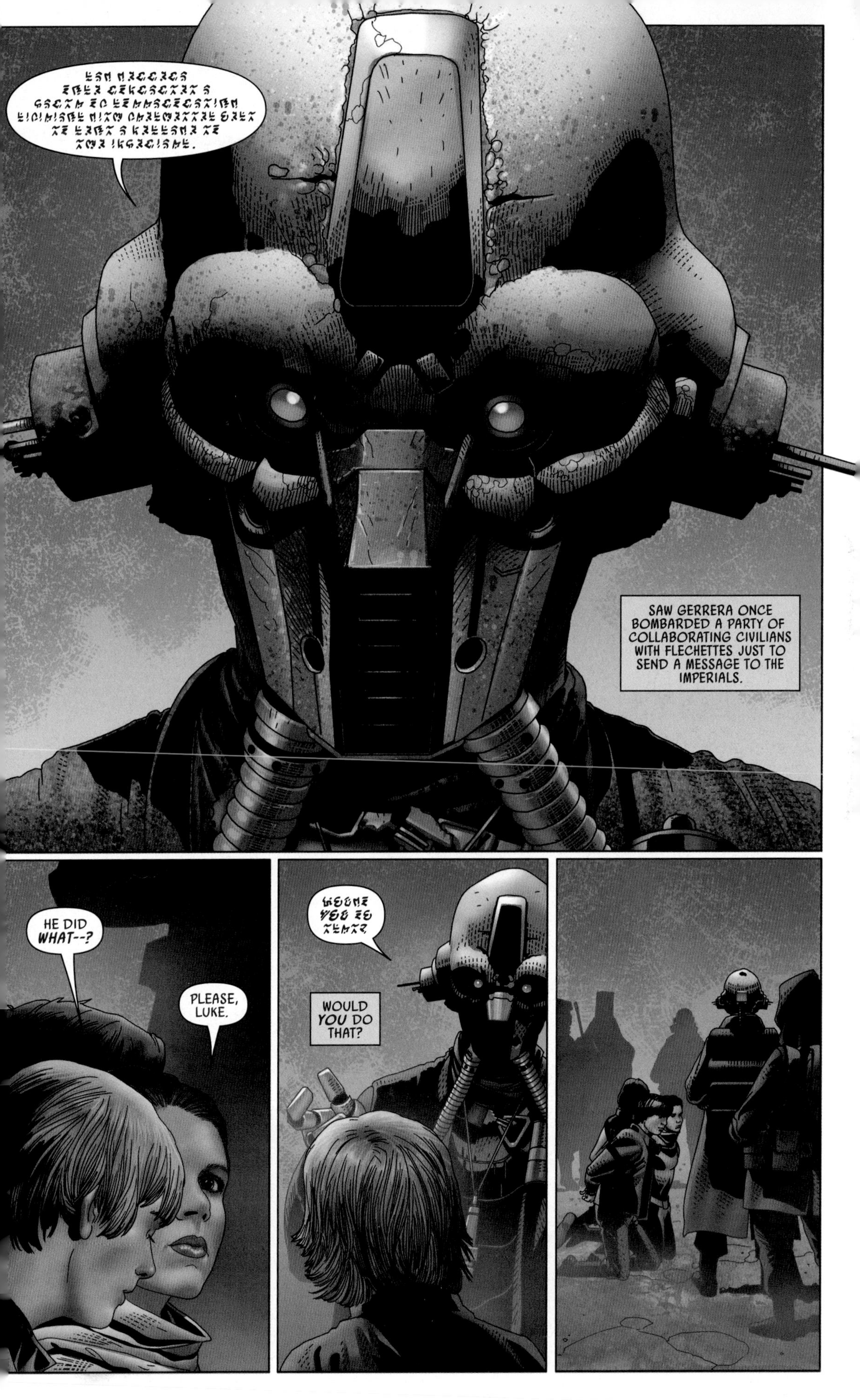
SAW GERRERA ONCE BOMBARDED A PARTY OF COLLABORATING CIVILIANS WITH FLECHETTES JUST TO SEND A MESSAGE TO THE IMPERIALS.
HE DID *WHAT--?*
PLEASE, LUKE.
WOULD *YOU* DO THAT?

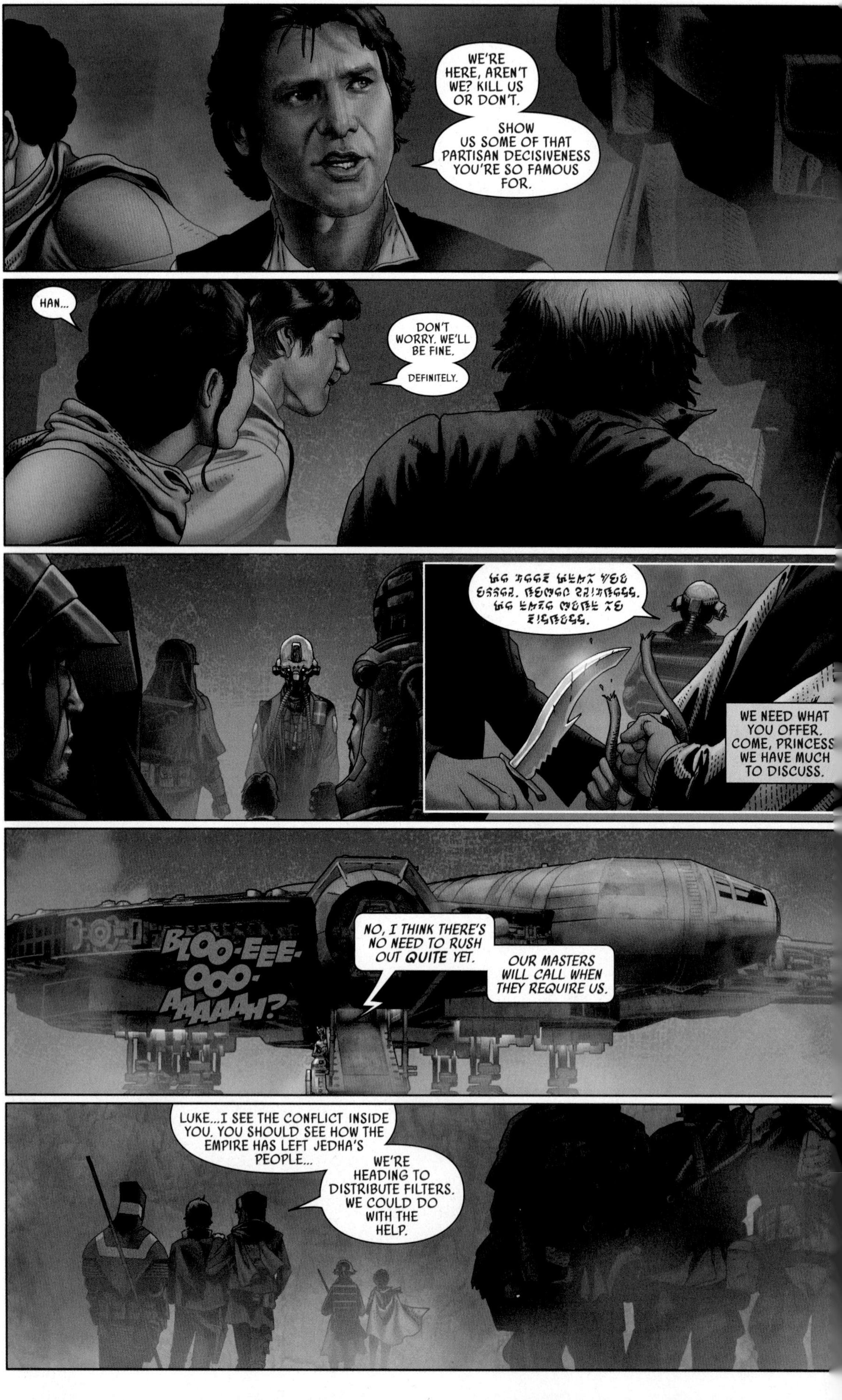
WE'RE HERE, AREN'T WE? KILL US OR DON'T.
SHOW US SOME OF THAT PARTISAN DECISIVENESS YOU'RE SO FAMOUS FOR.
HAN...
DON'T WORRY. WE'LL BE FINE.
DEFINITELY.
WE NEED WHAT YOU OFFER. COME, PRINCESS. WE HAVE MUCH TO DISCUSS.
BLOO-EEE-OOO-AAAAAH?
NO, I THINK THERE'S NO NEED TO RUSH OUT QUITE YET.
OUR MASTERS WILL CALL WHEN THEY REQUIRE US.
LUKE...I SEE THE CONFLICT INSIDE YOU. YOU SHOULD SEE HOW THE EMPIRE HAS LEFT JEDHA'S PEOPLE...
WE'RE HEADING TO DISTRIBUTE FILTERS. WE COULD DO WITH THE HELP.

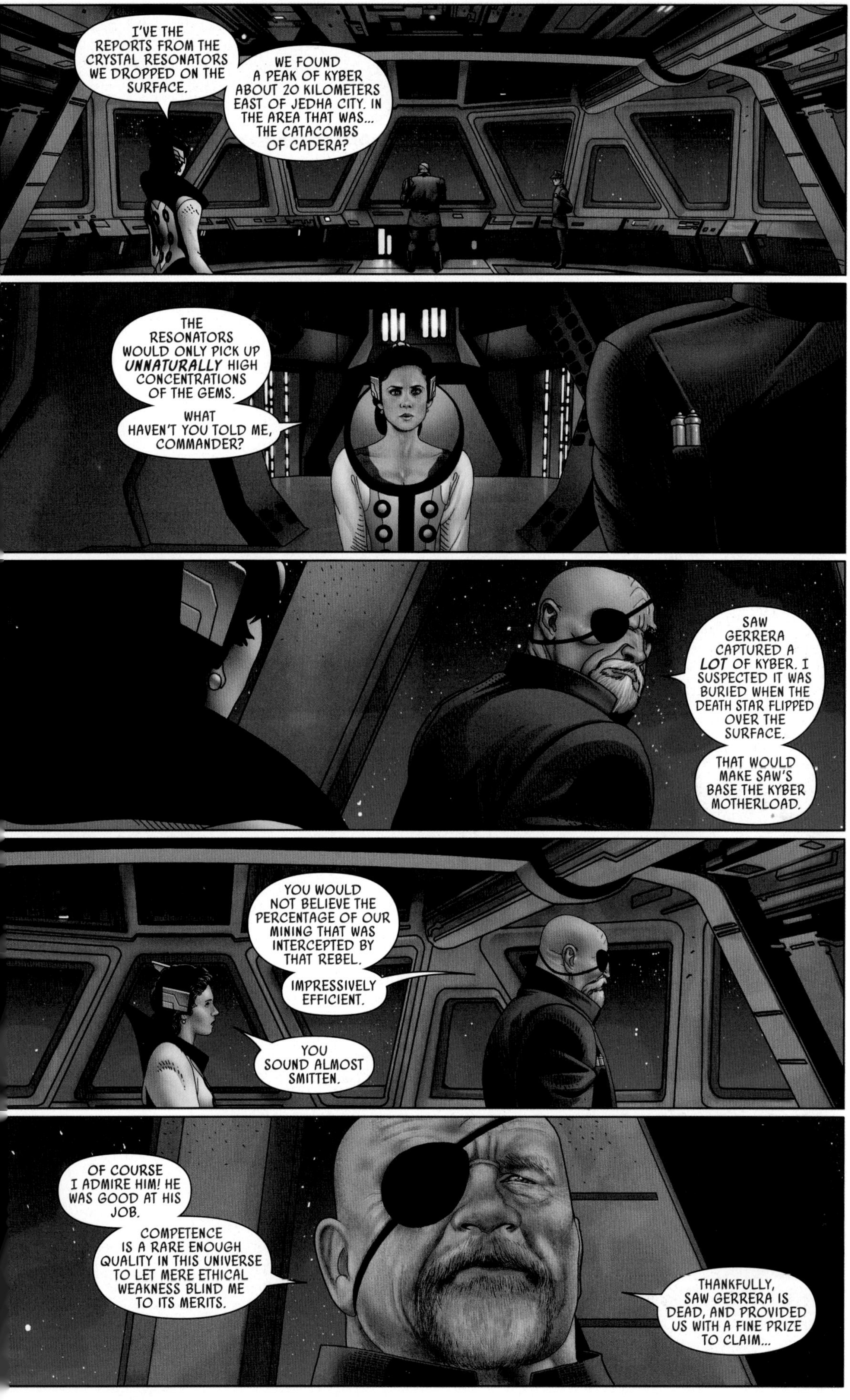
I'VE THE REPORTS FROM THE CRYSTAL RESONATORS WE DROPPED ON THE SURFACE.
WE FOUND A PEAK OF KYBER ABOUT 20 KILOMETERS EAST OF JEDHA CITY. IN THE AREA THAT WAS... THE CATACOMBS OF CADERA?
THE RESONATORS WOULD ONLY PICK UP UNNATURALLY HIGH CONCENTRATIONS OF THE GEMS.
WHAT HAVEN'T YOU TOLD ME, COMMANDER?
SAW GERRERA CAPTURED A LOT OF KYBER. I SUSPECTED IT WAS BURIED WHEN THE DEATH STAR FLIPPED OVER THE SURFACE.
THAT WOULD MAKE SAW'S BASE THE KYBER MOTHERLOAD.
YOU WOULD NOT BELIEVE THE PERCENTAGE OF OUR MINING THAT WAS INTERCEPTED BY THAT REBEL.
IMPRESSIVELY EFFICIENT.
YOU SOUND ALMOST SMITTEN.
OF COURSE I ADMIRE HIM! HE WAS GOOD AT HIS JOB.
COMPETENCE IS A RARE ENOUGH QUALITY IN THIS UNIVERSE TO LET MERE ETHICAL WEAKNESS BLIND ME TO ITS MERITS.
THANKFULLY, SAW GERRERA IS DEAD, AND PROVIDED US WITH A FINE PRIZE TO CLAIM...

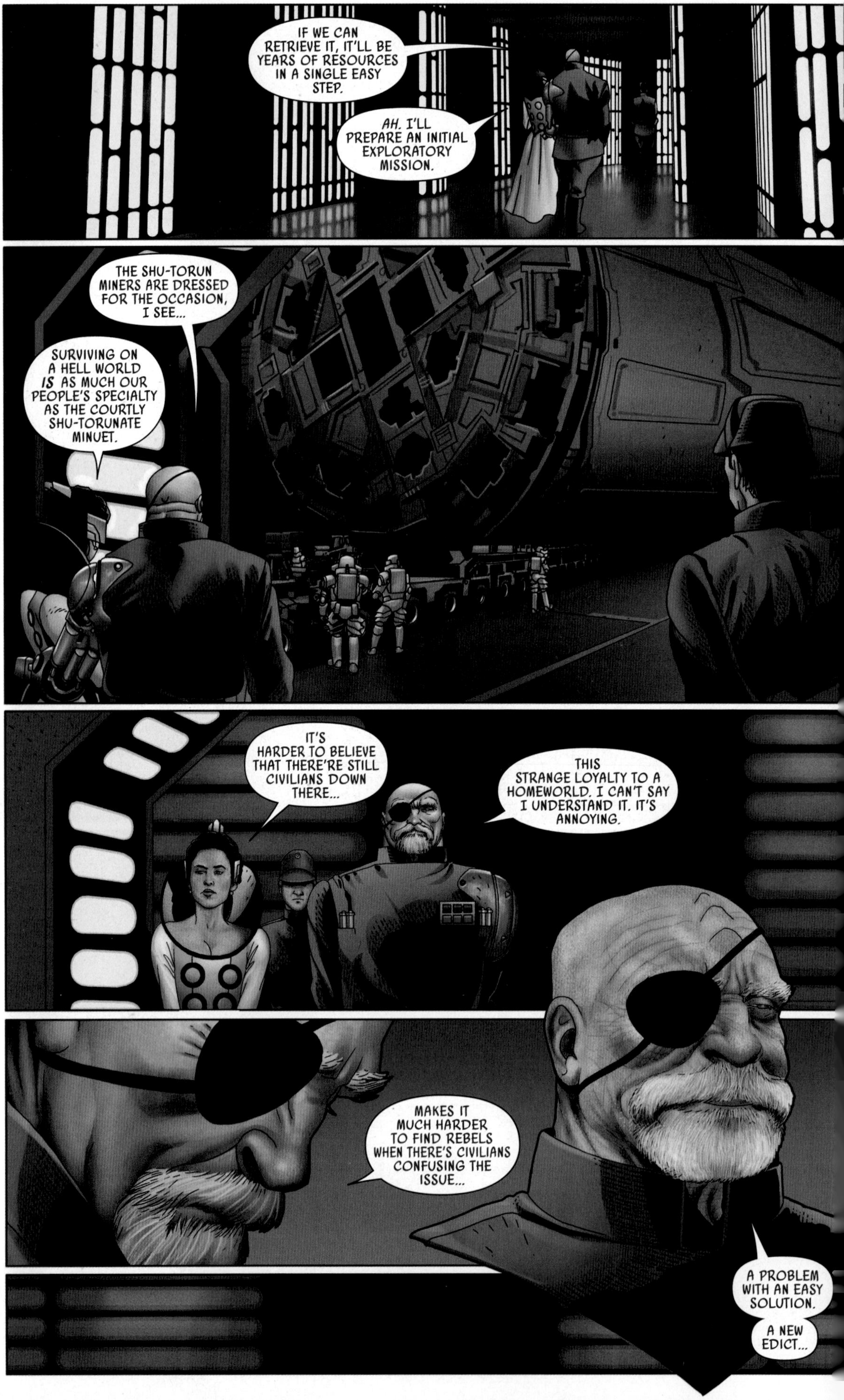
IF WE CAN RETRIEVE IT, IT'LL BE YEARS OF RESOURCES IN A SINGLE EASY STEP.
AH. I'LL PREPARE AN INITIAL EXPLORATORY MISSION.
THE SHU-TORUN MINERS ARE DRESSED FOR THE OCCASION, I SEE...
SURVIVING ON A HELL WORLD IS AS MUCH OUR PEOPLE'S SPECIALTY AS THE COURTLY SHU-TORUNATE MINUET.
IT'S HARDER TO BELIEVE THAT THERE'RE STILL CIVILIANS DOWN THERE...
THIS STRANGE LOYALTY TO A HOMEWORLD. I CAN'T SAY I UNDERSTAND IT. IT'S ANNOYING.
MAKES IT MUCH HARDER TO FIND REBELS WHEN THERE'S CIVILIANS CONFUSING THE ISSUE...
A PROBLEM WITH AN EASY SOLUTION.
A NEW EDICT...

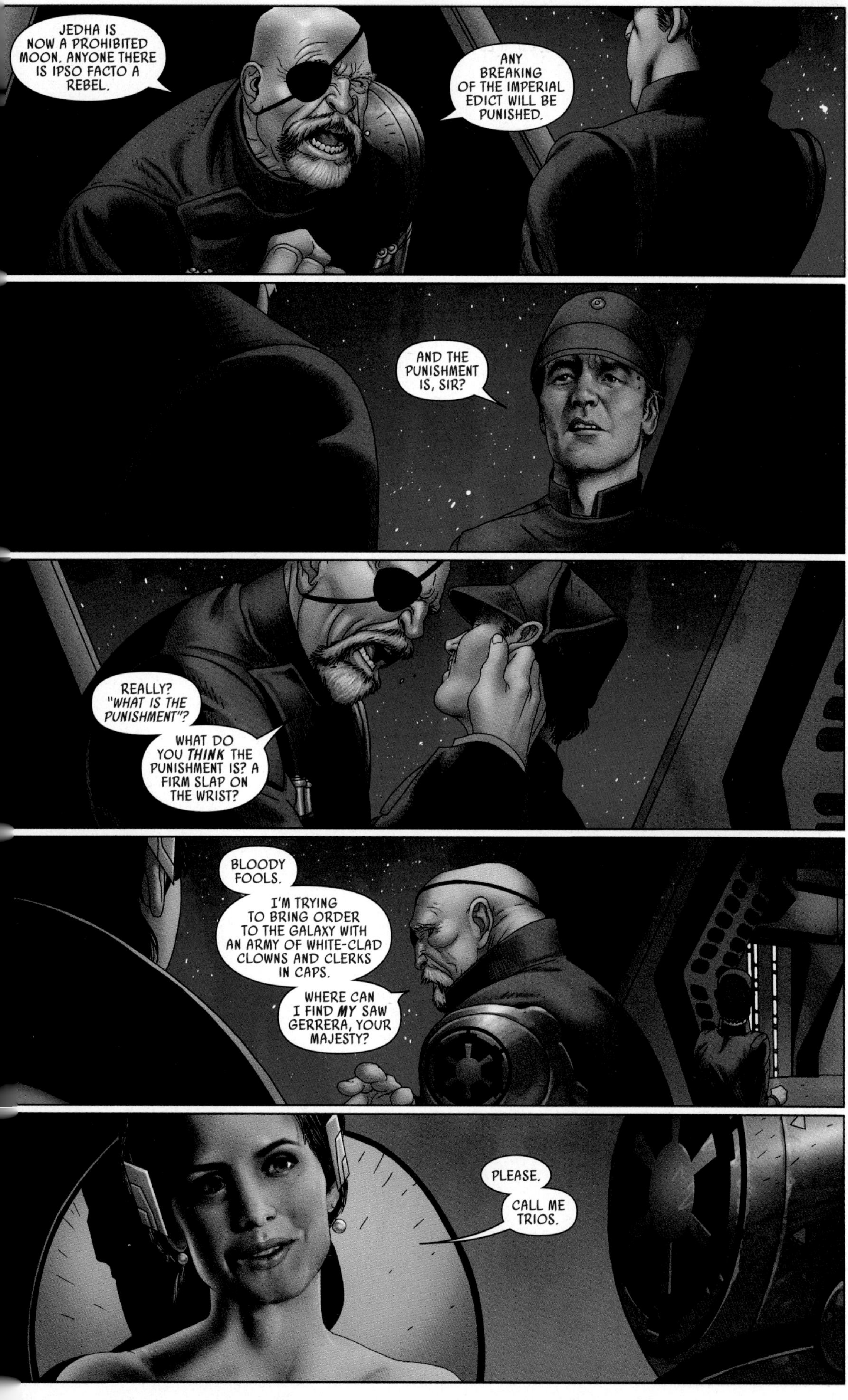
JEDHA IS NOW A PROHIBITED MOON. ANYONE THERE IS IPSO FACTO A REBEL.
ANY BREAKING OF THE IMPERIAL EDICT WILL BE PUNISHED.
AND THE PUNISHMENT IS, SIR?
REALLY? "WHAT IS THE PUNISHMENT"?
WHAT DO YOU THINK THE PUNISHMENT IS? A FIRM SLAP ON THE WRIST?
BLOODY FOOLS.
I'M TRYING TO BRING ORDER TO THE GALAXY WITH AN ARMY OF WHITE-CLAD CLOWNS AND CLERKS IN CAPS.
WHERE CAN I FIND MY SAW GERRERA, YOUR MAJESTY?
PLEASE.
CALL ME TRIOS.

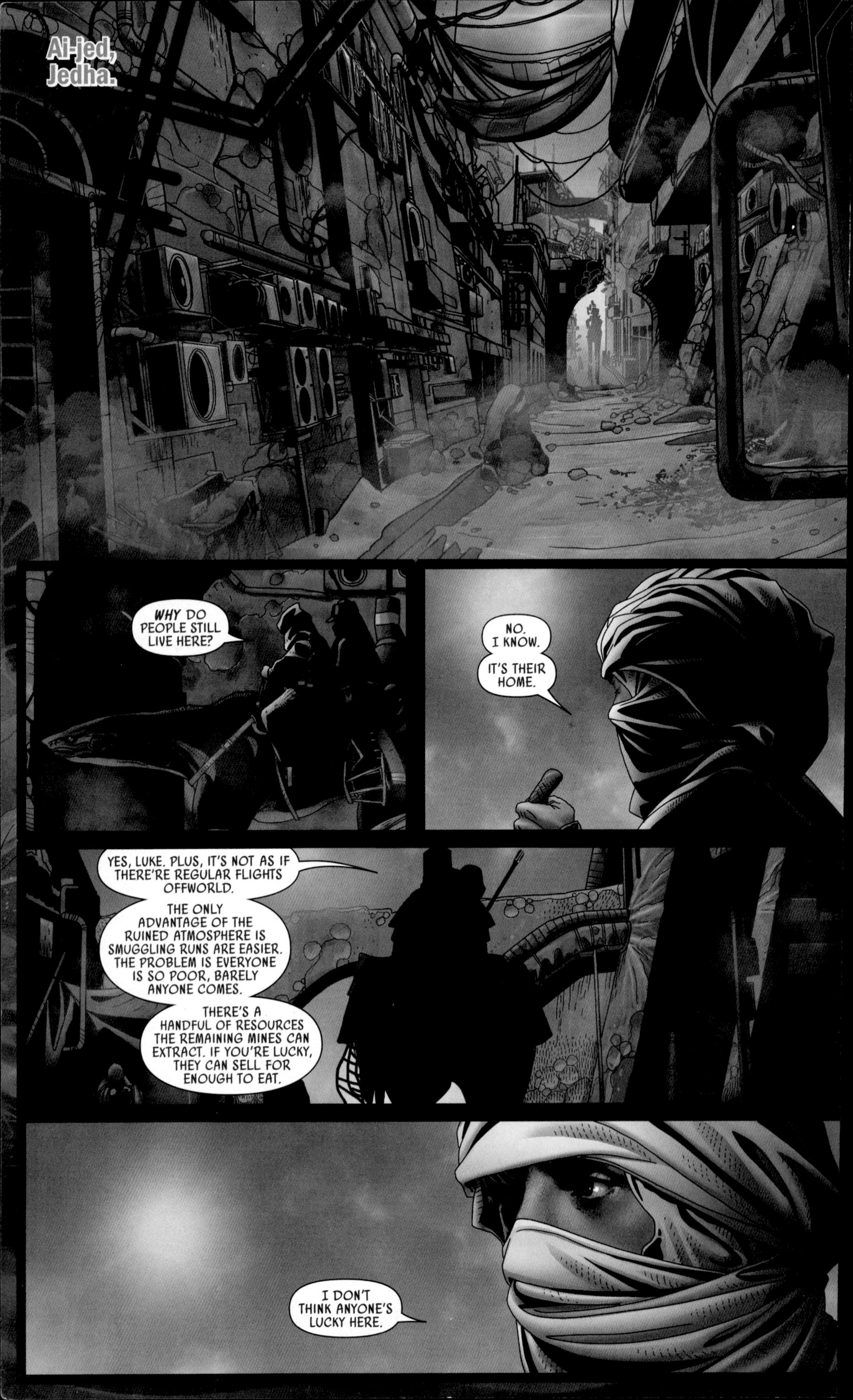
Ai-jed,
Jedha.
WHY DO PEOPLE STILL LIVE HERE?
NO. I KNOW.
IT'S THEIR HOME.
YES, LUKE. PLUS, IT'S NOT AS IF THERE'RE REGULAR FLIGHTS OFFWORLD.
THE ONLY ADVANTAGE OF THE RUINED ATMOSPHERE IS SMUGGLING RUNS ARE EASIER. THE PROBLEM IS EVERYONE IS SO POOR, BARELY ANYONE COMES.
THERE'S A HANDFUL OF RESOURCES THE REMAINING MINES CAN EXTRACT. IF YOU'RE LUCKY, THEY CAN SELL FOR ENOUGH TO EAT.
I DON'T THINK ANYONE'S LUCKY HERE.

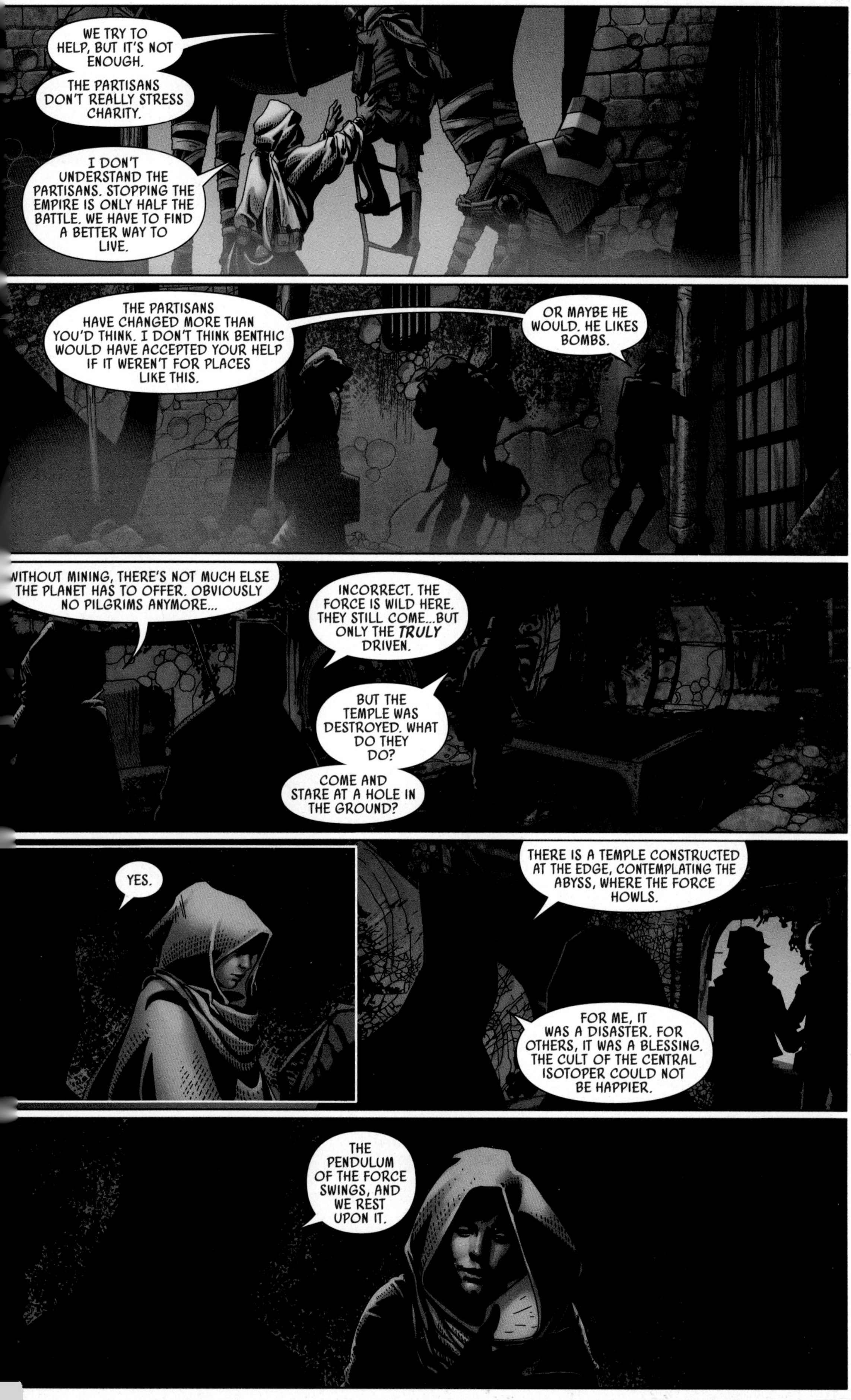
WE TRY TO HELP, BUT IT'S NOT ENOUGH.
THE PARTISANS DON'T REALLY STRESS CHARITY.
I DON'T UNDERSTAND THE PARTISANS. STOPPING THE EMPIRE IS ONLY HALF THE BATTLE. WE HAVE TO FIND A BETTER WAY TO LIVE.
THE PARTISANS HAVE CHANGED MORE THAN YOU'D THINK. I DON'T THINK BENTHIC WOULD HAVE ACCEPTED YOUR HELP IF IT WEREN'T FOR PLACES LIKE THIS.
OR MAYBE HE WOULD. HE LIKES BOMBS.
WITHOUT MINING, THERE'S NOT MUCH ELSE THE PLANET HAS TO OFFER. OBVIOUSLY NO PILGRIMS ANYMORE...
INCORRECT. THE FORCE IS WILD HERE. THEY STILL COME...BUT ONLY THE *TRULY* DRIVEN.
BUT THE TEMPLE WAS DESTROYED. WHAT DO THEY DO?
COME AND STARE AT A HOLE IN THE GROUND?
YES.
THERE IS A TEMPLE CONSTRUCTED AT THE EDGE, CONTEMPLATING THE ABYSS, WHERE THE FORCE HOWLS.
FOR ME, IT WAS A DISASTER. FOR OTHERS, IT WAS A BLESSING. THE CULT OF THE CENTRAL ISOTOPER COULD NOT BE HAPPIER.
THE PENDULUM OF THE FORCE SWINGS, AND WE REST UPON IT.

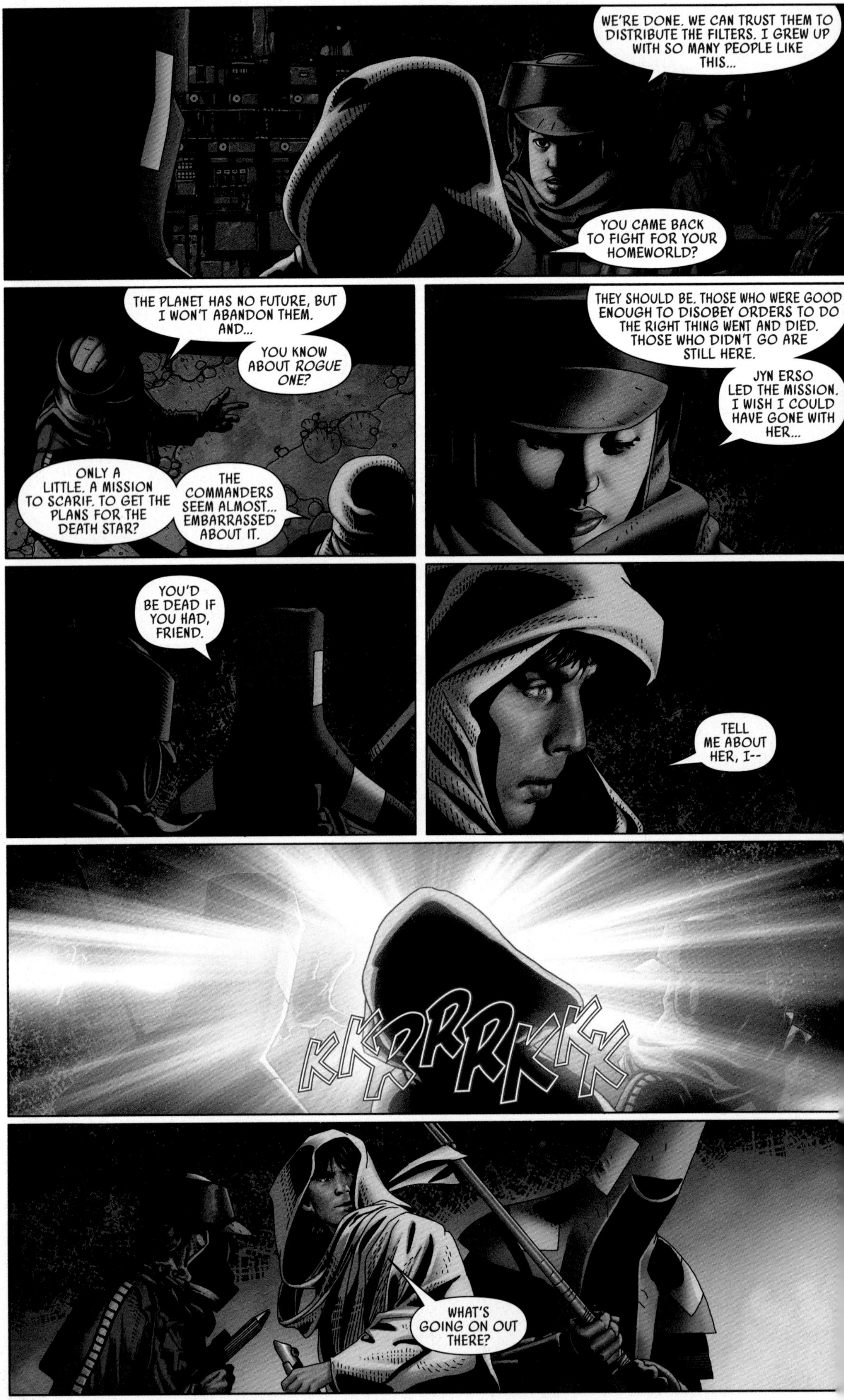

WE'RE DONE. WE CAN TRUST THEM TO DISTRIBUTE THE FILTERS. I GREW UP WITH SO MANY PEOPLE LIKE THIS...
YOU CAME BACK TO FIGHT FOR YOUR HOMEWORLD?
THE PLANET HAS NO FUTURE, BUT I WON'T ABANDON THEM. AND...
YOU KNOW ABOUT ROGUE ONE?
ONLY A LITTLE. A MISSION TO SCARIF. TO GET THE PLANS FOR THE DEATH STAR?
THE COMMANDERS SEEM ALMOST... EMBARRASSED ABOUT IT.
THEY SHOULD BE. THOSE WHO WERE GOOD ENOUGH TO DISOBEY ORDERS TO DO THE RIGHT THING WENT AND DIED. THOSE WHO DIDN'T GO ARE STILL HERE.
JYN ERSO LED THE MISSION. I WISH I COULD HAVE GONE WITH HER...
YOU'D BE DEAD IF YOU HAD, FRIEND.
TELL ME ABOUT HER, I--
KKRRRKK
WHAT'S GOING ON OUT THERE?

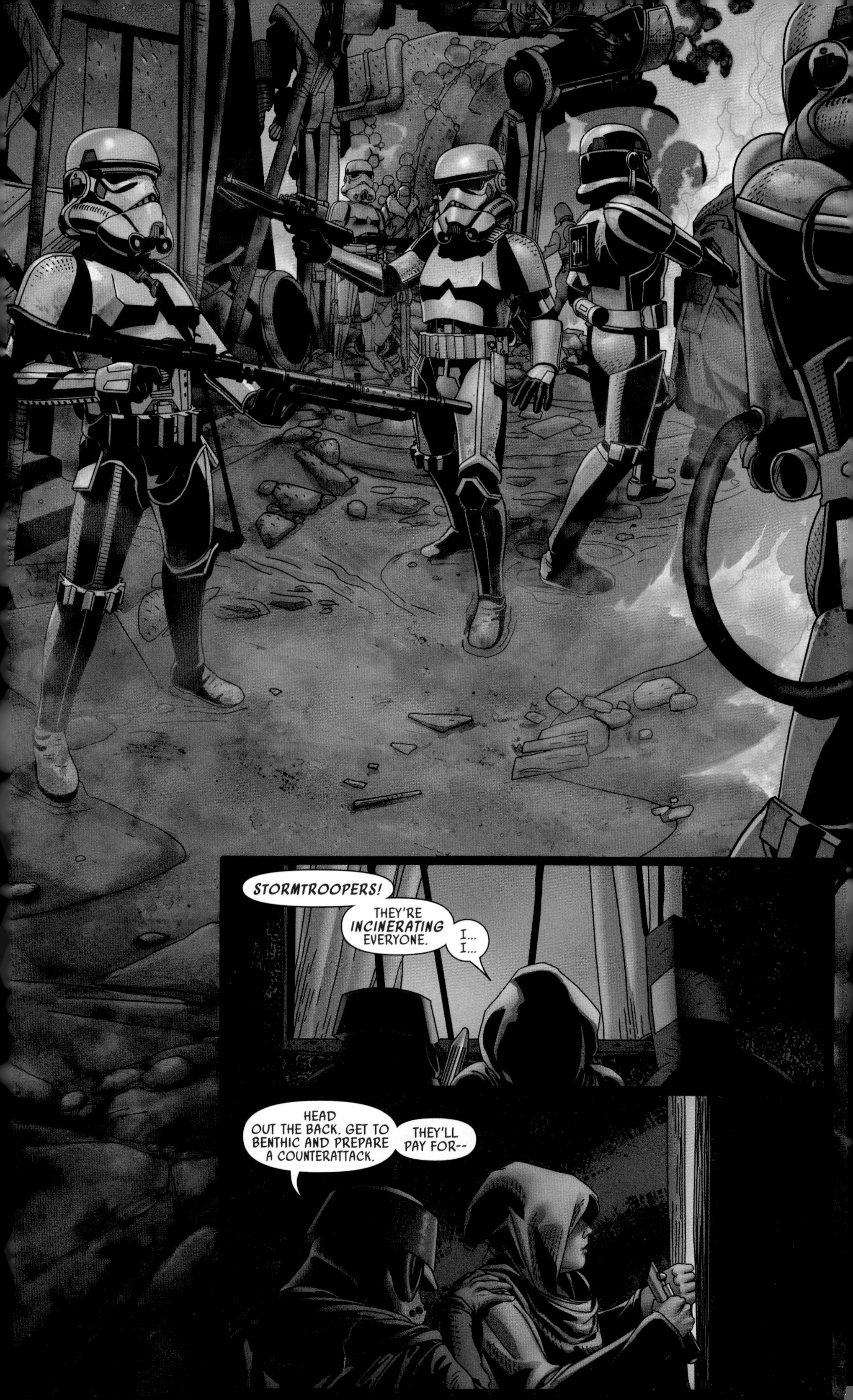
STORMTROOPERS!
THEY'RE INCINERATING EVERYONE.
I... I...
HEAD OUT THE BACK. GET TO BENTHIC AND PREPARE A COUNTERATTACK.
THEY'LL PAY FOR--

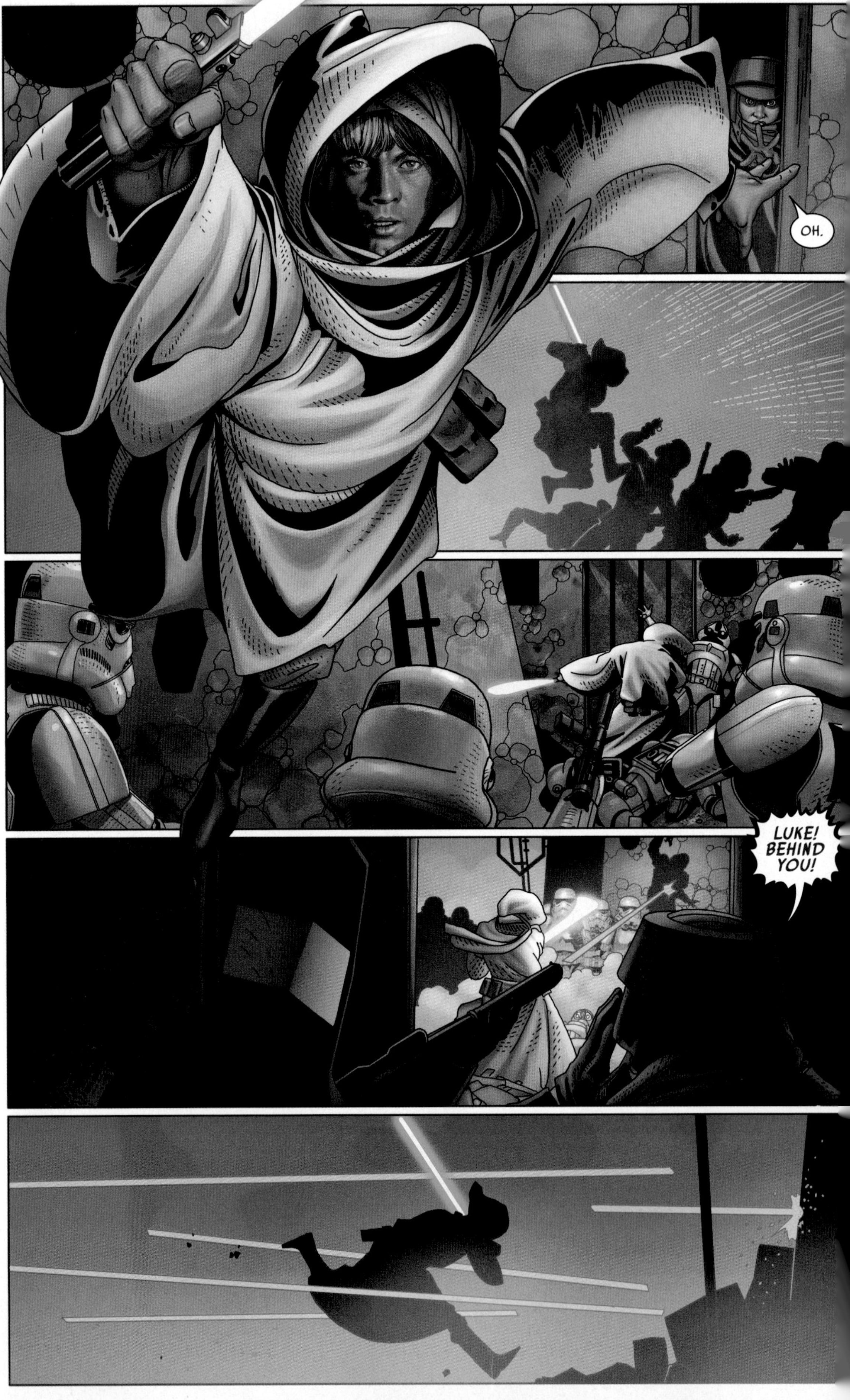
OH.
LUKE! BEHIND YOU!

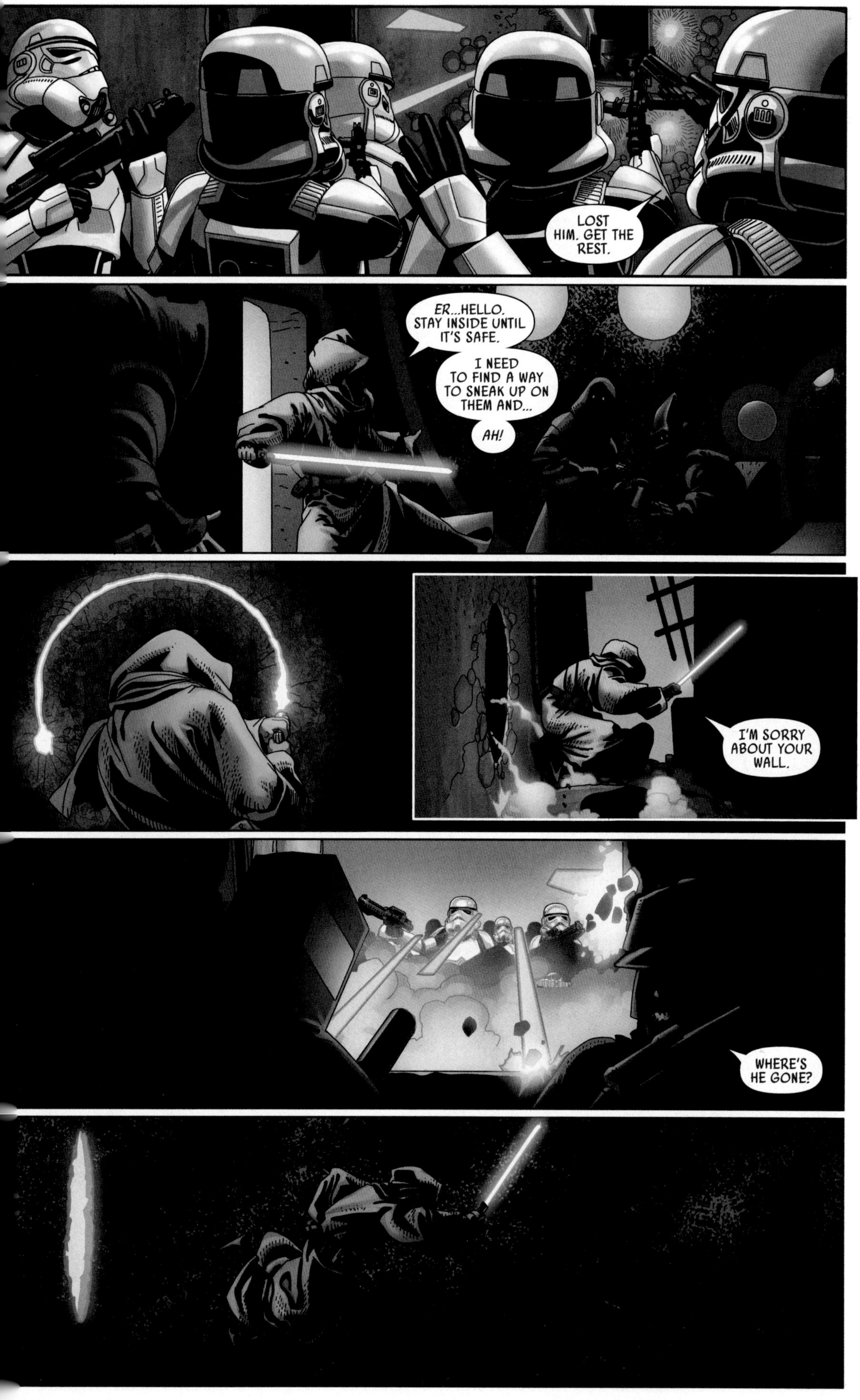
LOST HIM. GET THE REST.
ER...HELLO. STAY INSIDE UNTIL IT'S SAFE.
I NEED TO FIND A WAY TO SNEAK UP ON THEM AND...
AH!
I'M SORRY ABOUT YOUR WALL.
WHERE'S HE GONE?

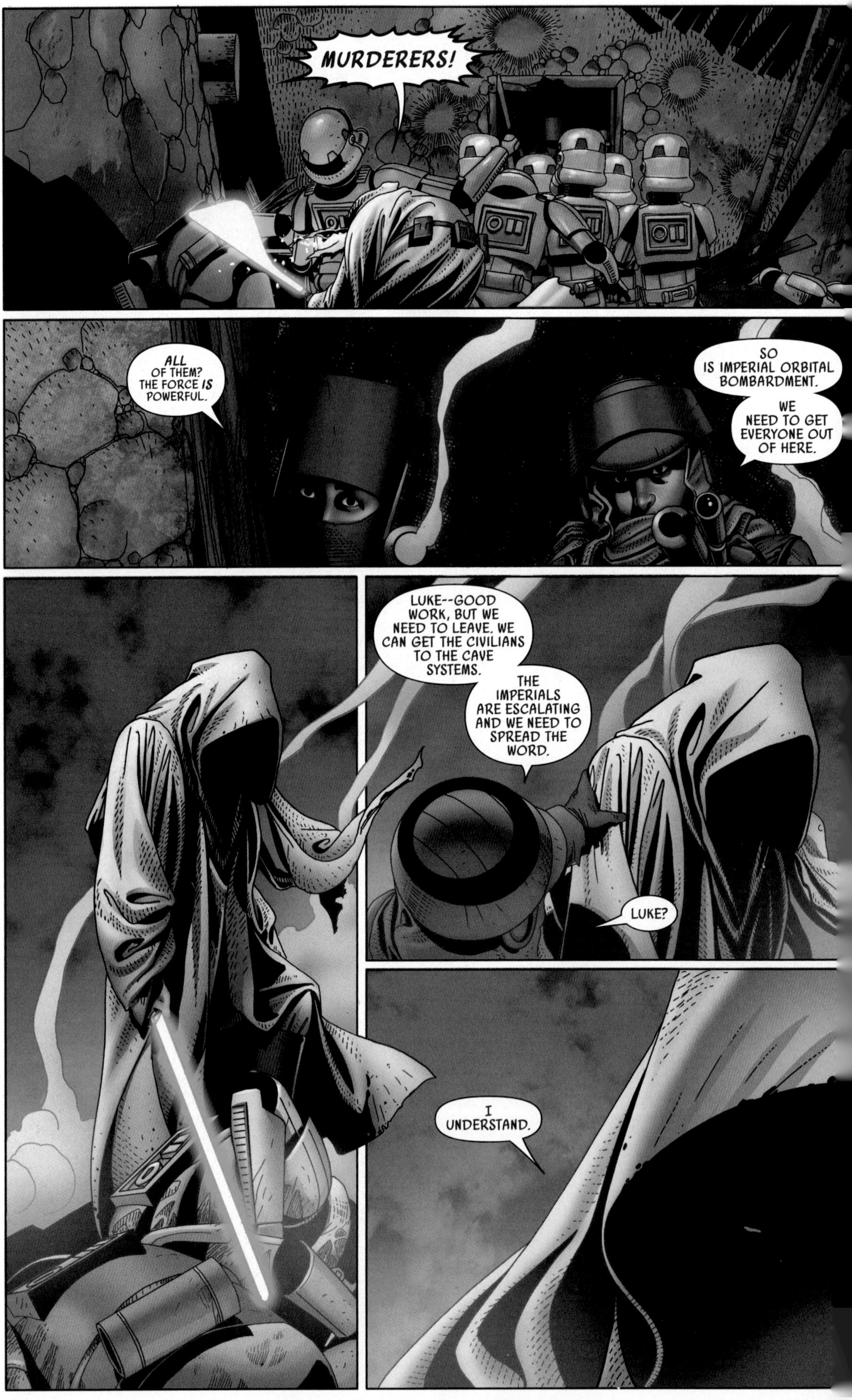
MURDERERS!
ALL OF THEM? THE FORCE IS POWERFUL.
SO IS IMPERIAL ORBITAL BOMBARDMENT.
WE NEED TO GET EVERYONE OUT OF HERE.
LUKE--GOOD WORK, BUT WE NEED TO LEAVE. WE CAN GET THE CIVILIANS TO THE CAVE SYSTEMS.
THE IMPERIALS ARE ESCALATING AND WE NEED TO SPREAD THE WORD.
LUKE?
I UNDERSTAND.

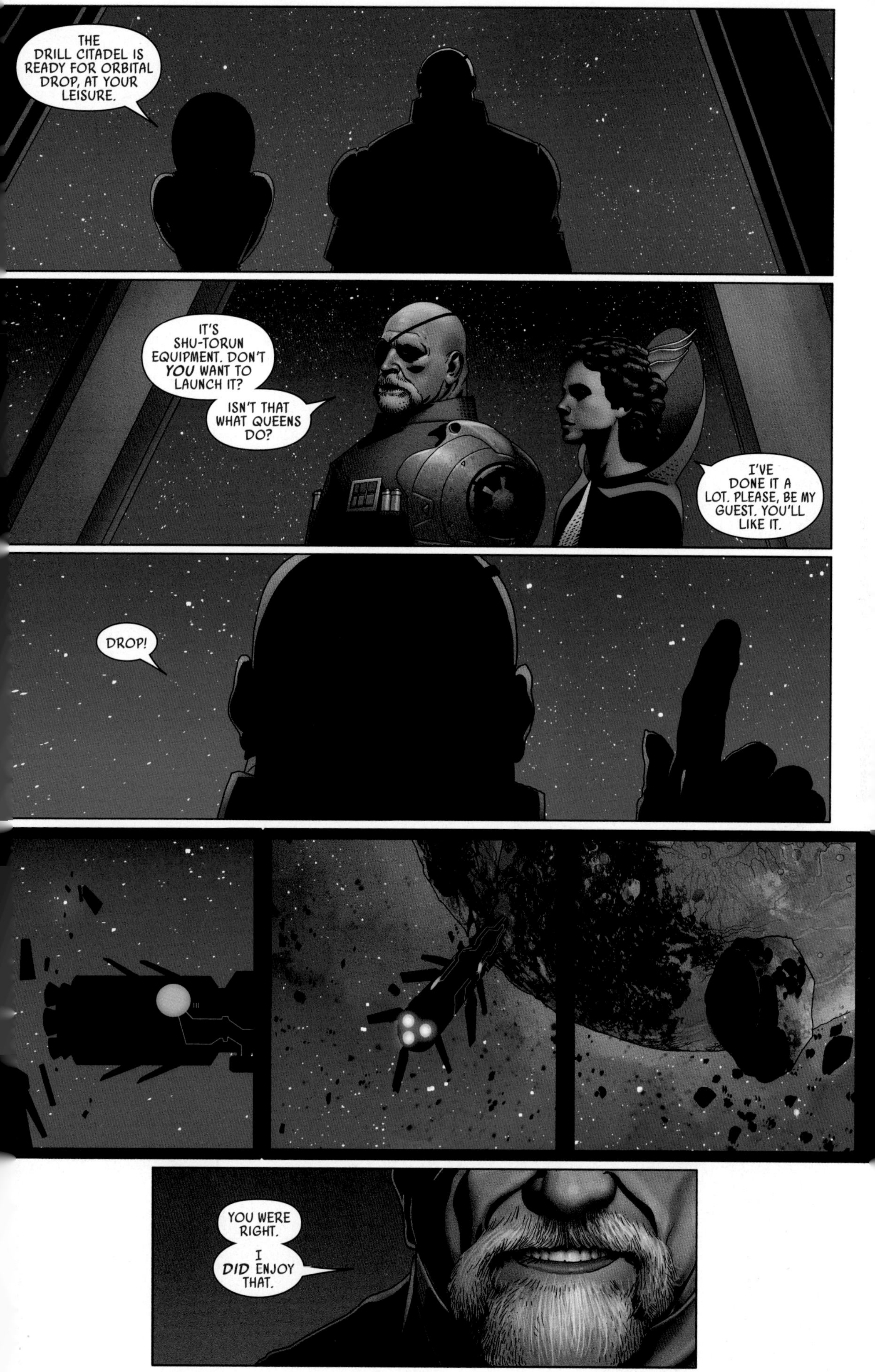
THE DRILL CITADEL IS READY FOR ORBITAL DROP, AT YOUR LEISURE.
IT'S SHU-TORUN EQUIPMENT. DON'T *YOU* WANT TO LAUNCH IT?
ISN'T THAT WHAT QUEENS DO?
I'VE DONE IT A LOT. PLEASE, BE MY GUEST. YOU'LL LIKE IT.
DROP!
YOU WERE RIGHT.
I *DID* ENJOY THAT.

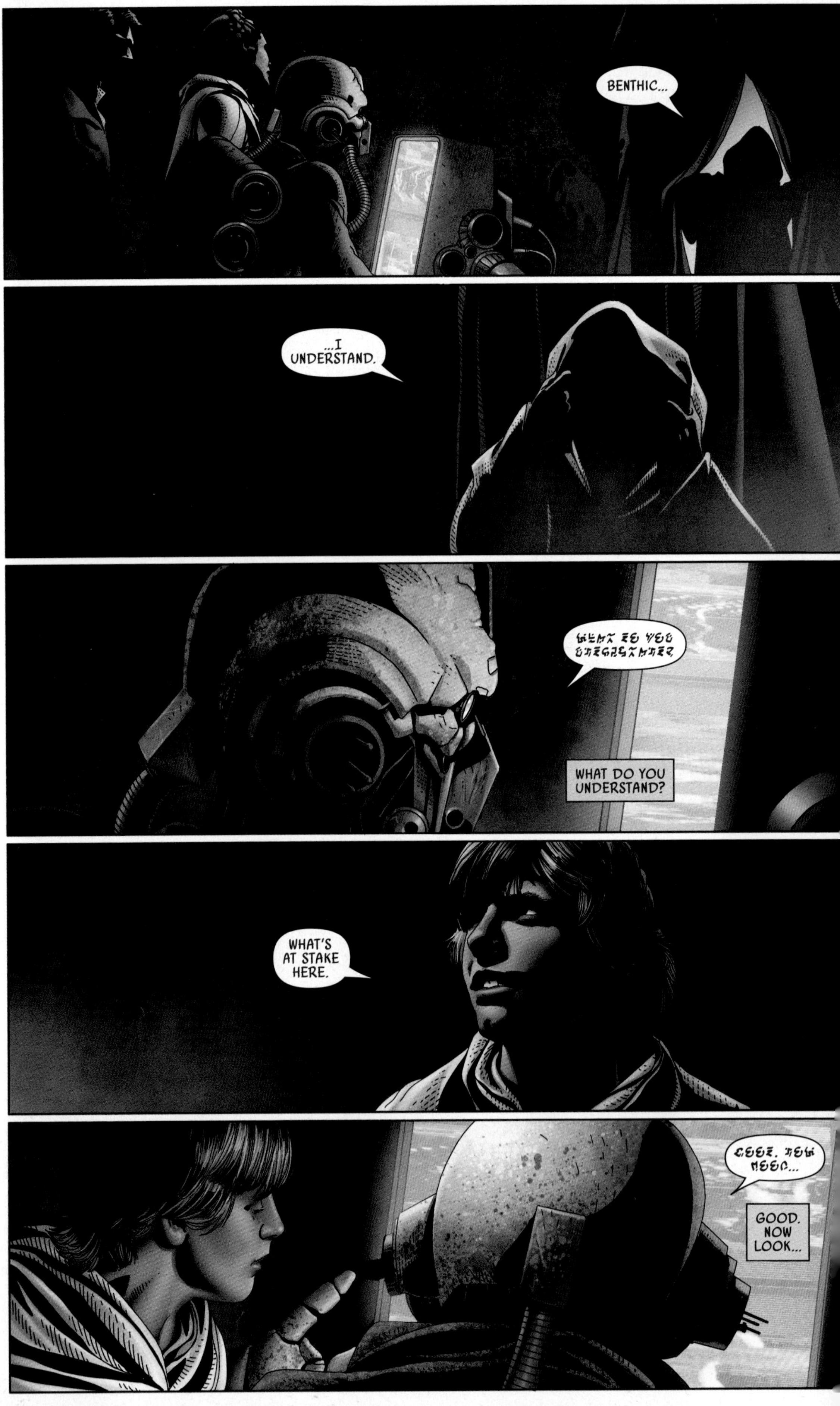
BENTHIC...
...I UNDERSTAND.
WHAT DO YOU UNDERSTAND?
WHAT'S AT STAKE HERE.
GOOD. NOW LOOK...

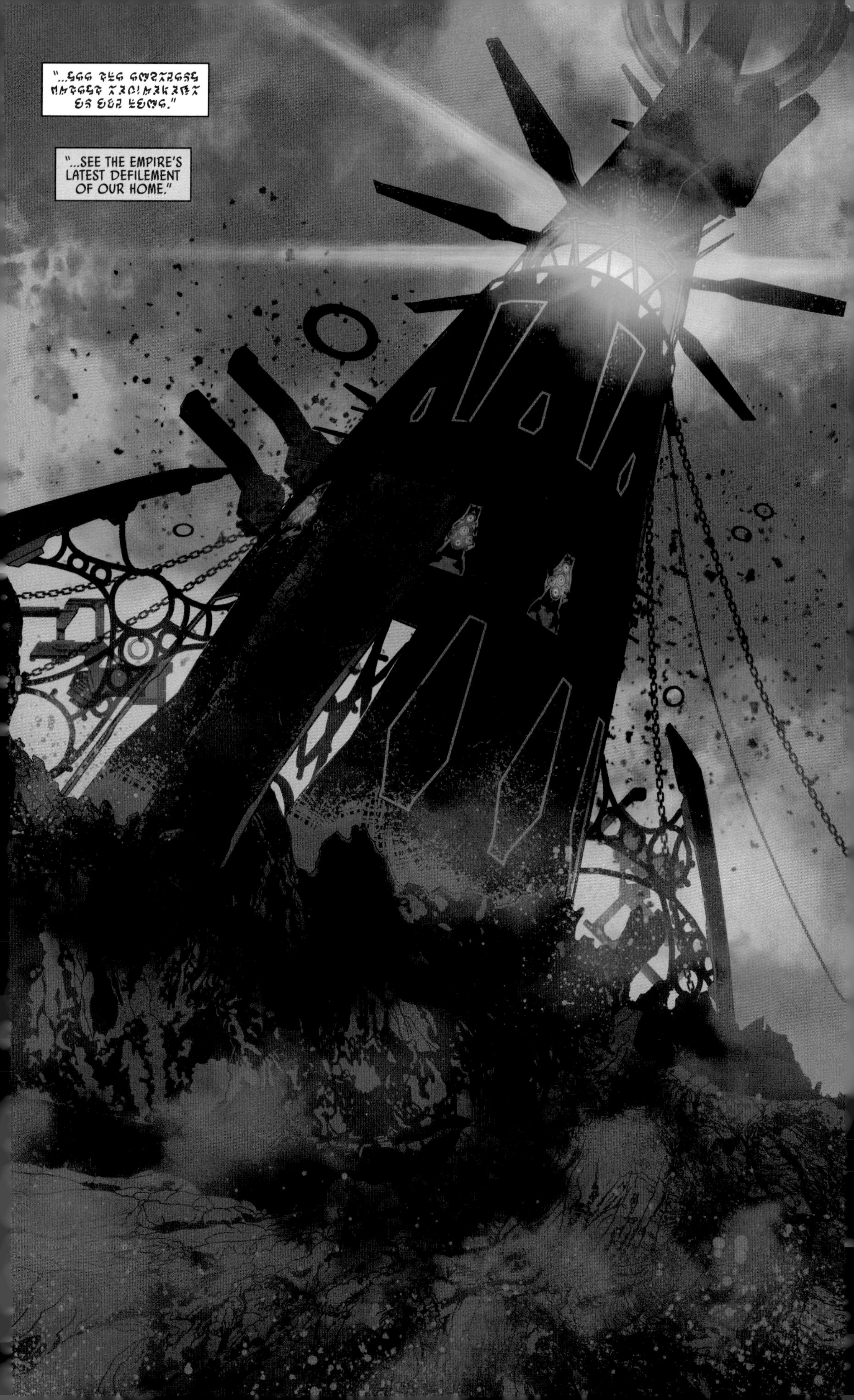
"...SEE THE EMPIRE'S LATEST DEFILEMENT OF OUR HOME."

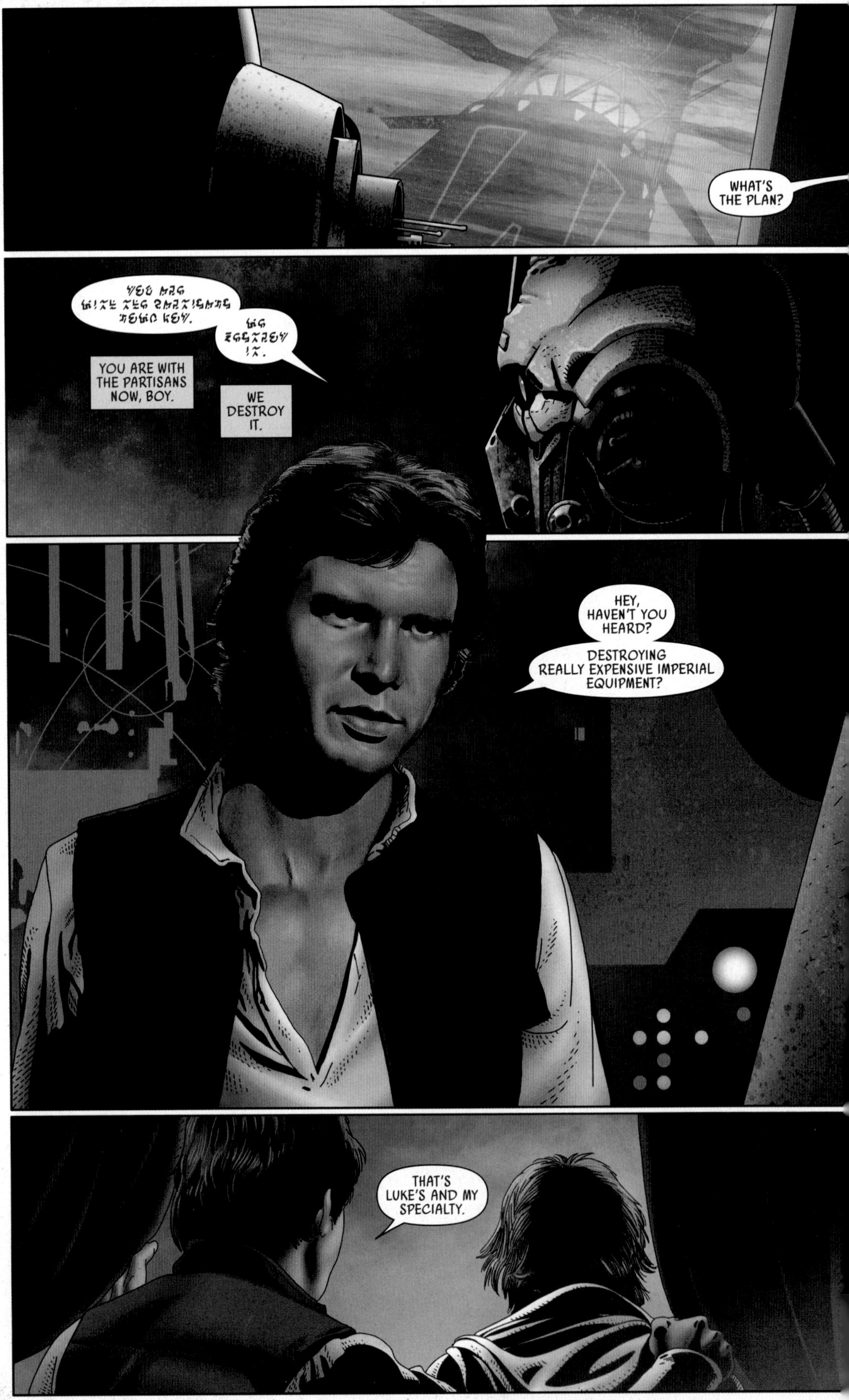
WHAT'S THE PLAN?
YOU ARE WITH THE PARTISANS NOW, BOY.
WE DESTROY IT.
HEY, HAVEN'T YOU HEARD?
DESTROYING REALLY EXPENSIVE IMPERIAL EQUIPMENT?
THAT'S LUKE'S AND MY SPECIALTY.

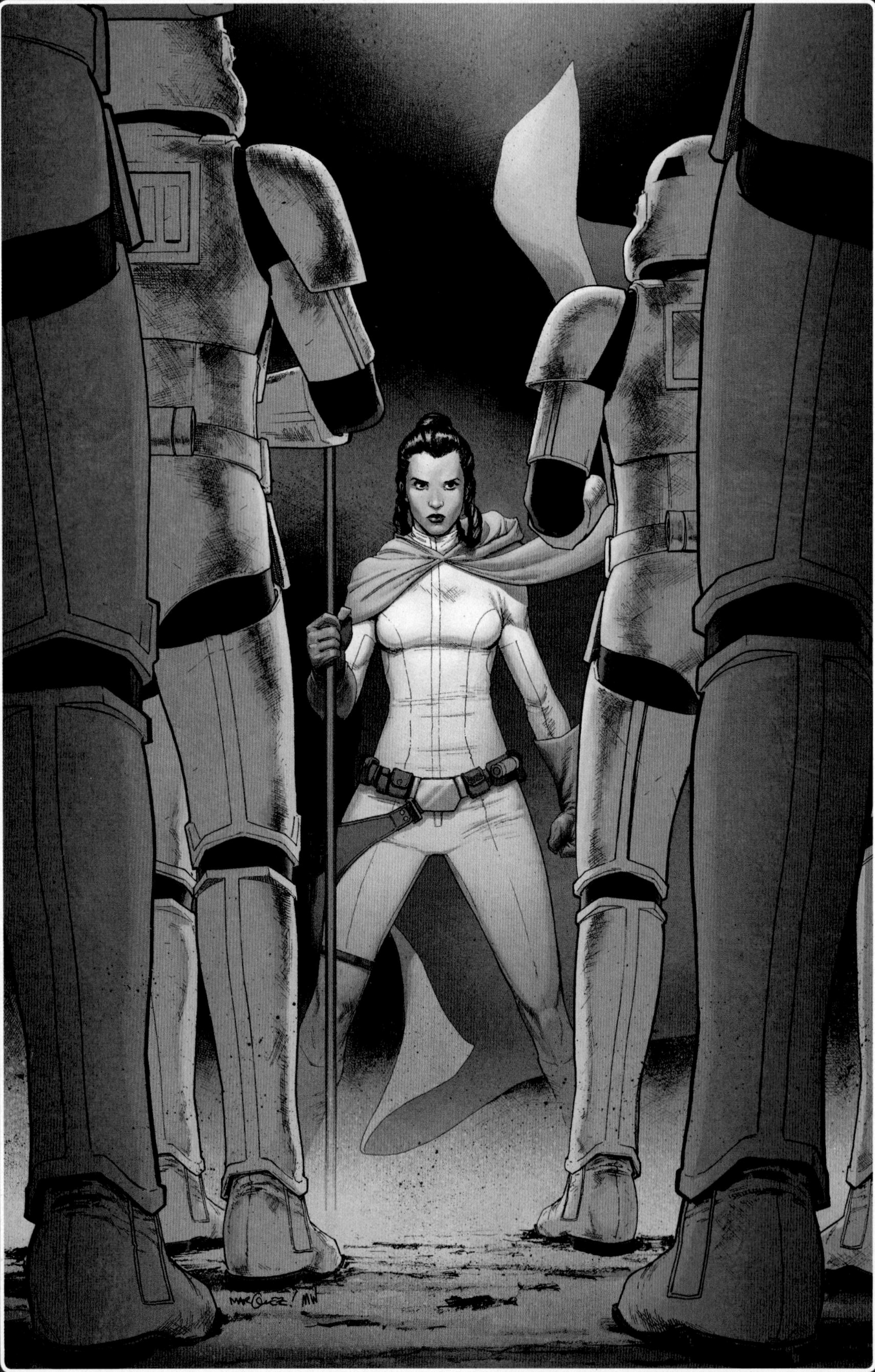

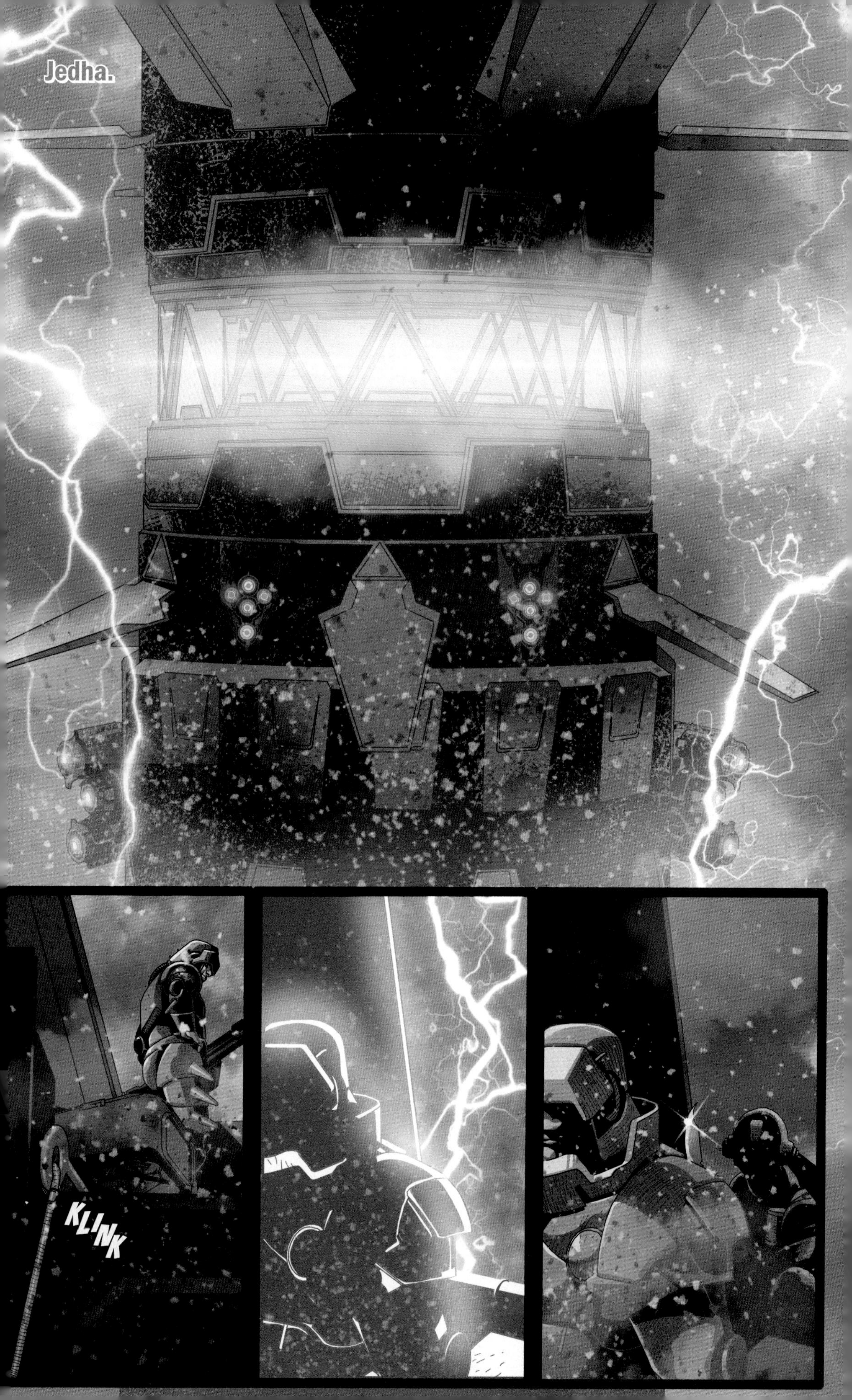
Jedha.
KLINK

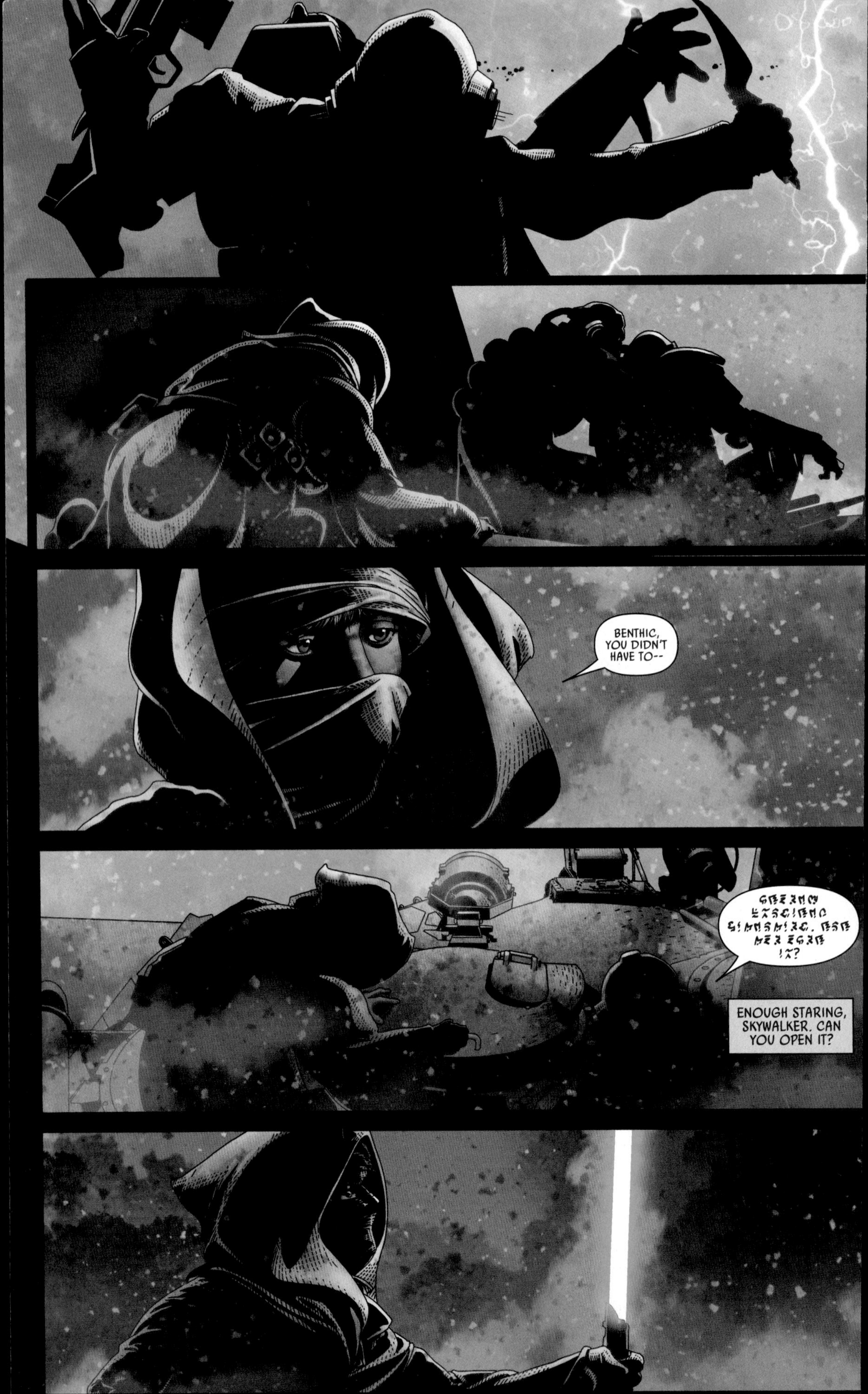
BENTHIC, YOU DIDN'T HAVE TO--
ENOUGH STARING, SKYWALKER. CAN YOU OPEN IT?

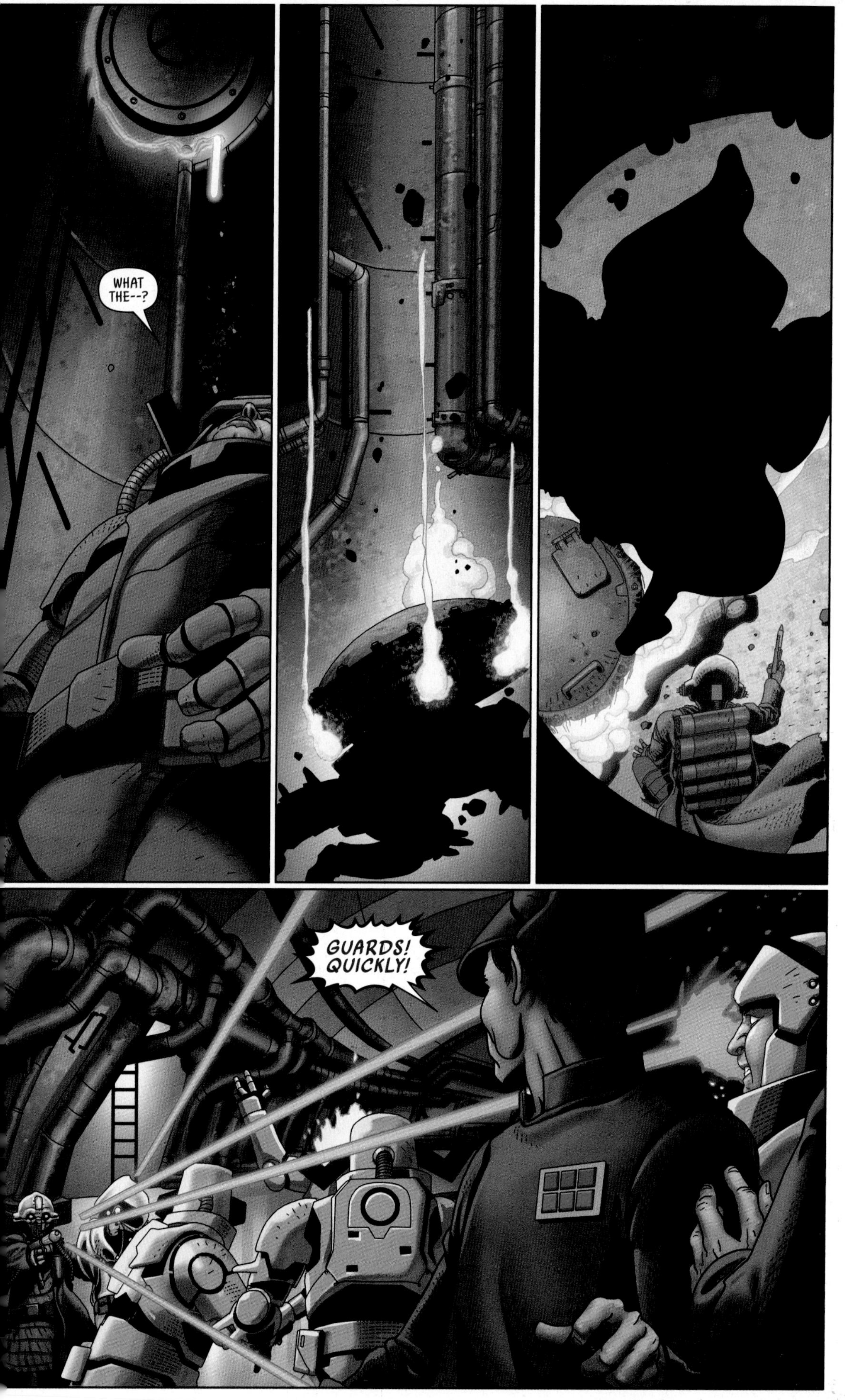
WHAT THE--?
GUARDS! QUICKLY!

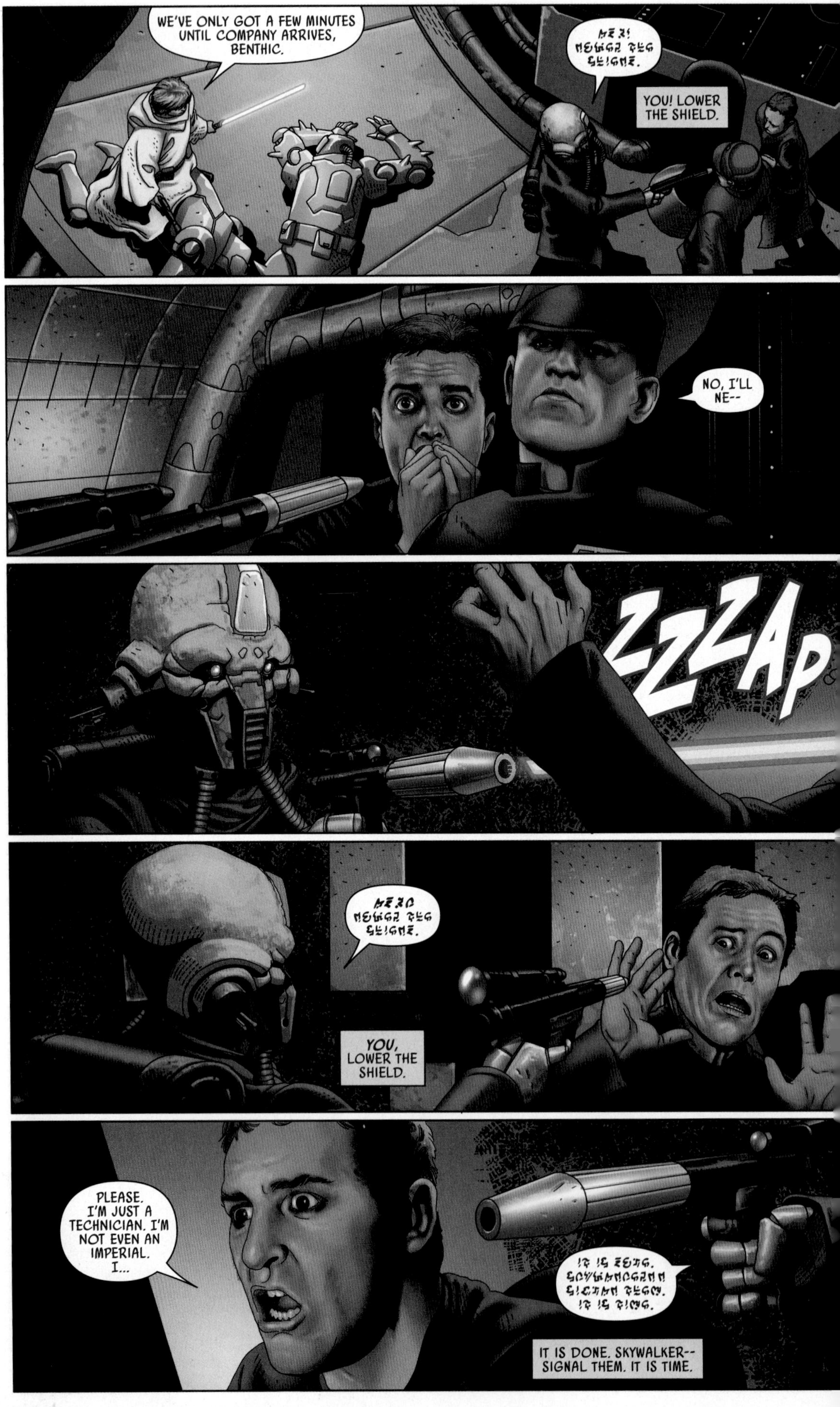
WE'VE ONLY GOT A FEW MINUTES UNTIL COMPANY ARRIVES, BENTHIC.
YOU! LOWER THE SHIELD.
NO, I'LL NE--
ZZZAP
YOU, LOWER THE SHIELD.
PLEASE. I'M JUST A TECHNICIAN. I'M NOT EVEN AN IMPERIAL. I...
IT IS DONE. SKYWALKER-- SIGNAL THEM. IT IS TIME.

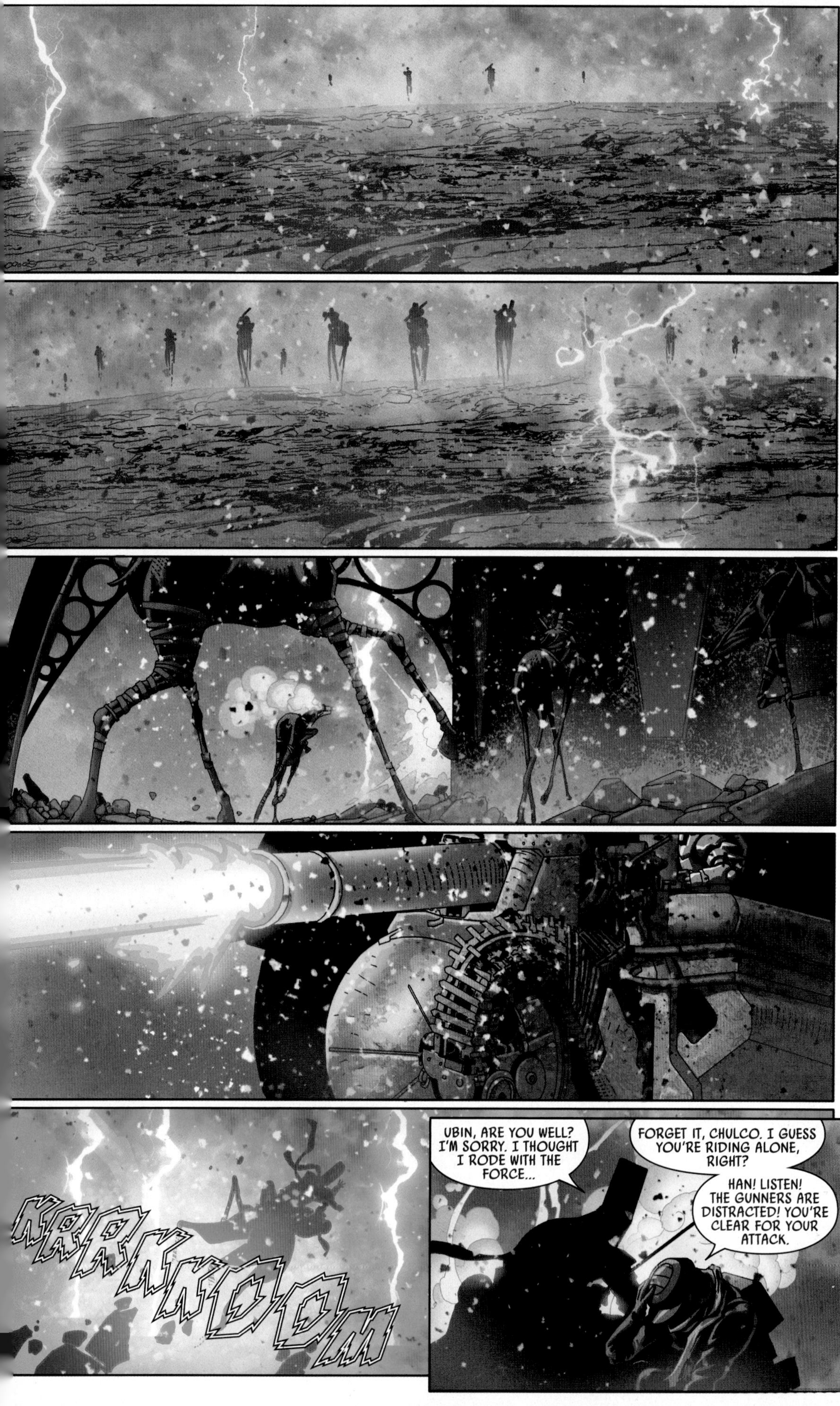
KRRNKOOM
UBIN, ARE YOU WELL? I'M SORRY. I THOUGHT I RODE WITH THE FORCE...
FORGET IT, CHULCO. I GUESS YOU'RE RIDING ALONE, RIGHT?
HAN! LISTEN! THE GUNNERS ARE DISTRACTED! YOU'RE CLEAR FOR YOUR ATTACK.

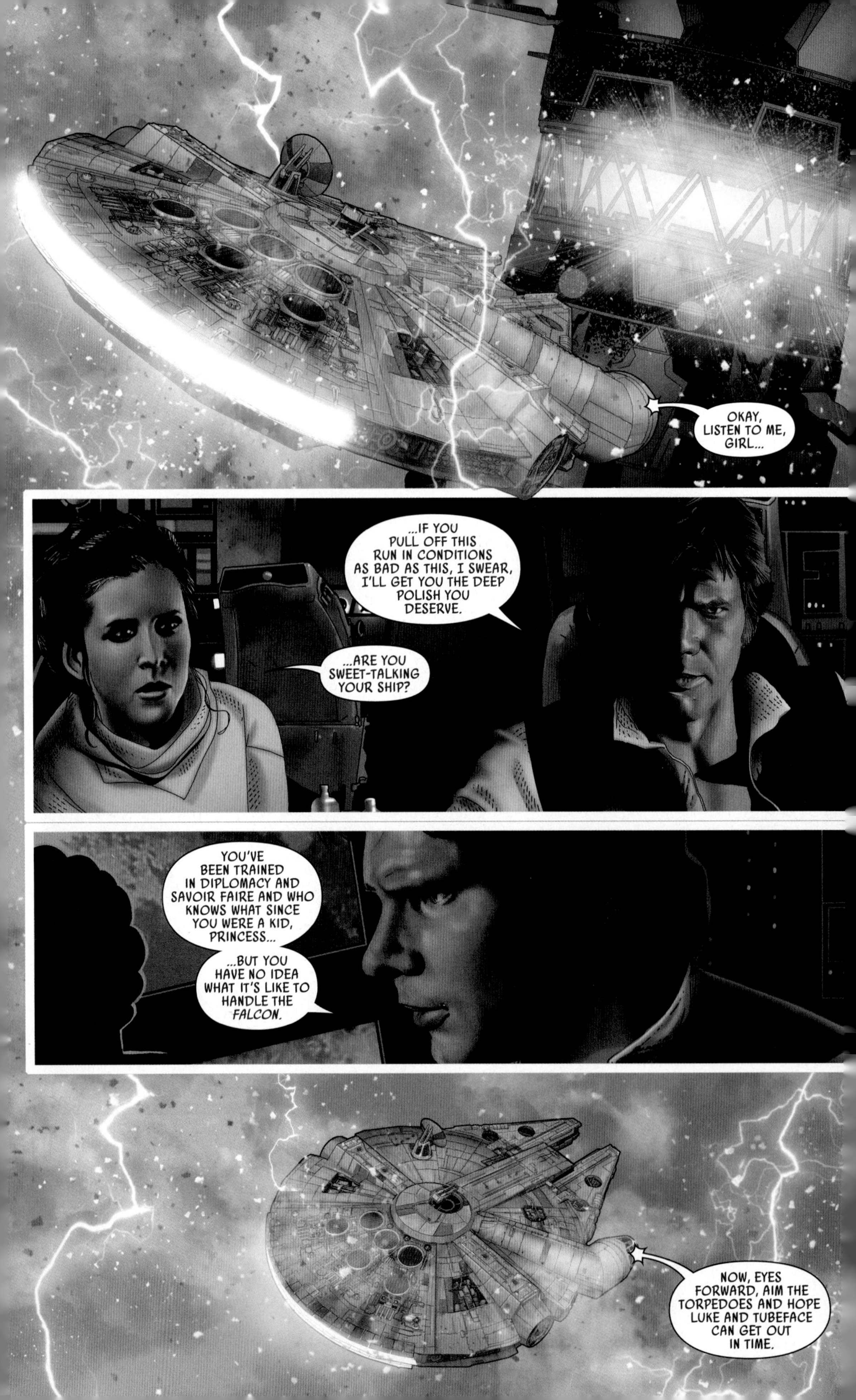
OKAY, LISTEN TO ME, GIRL...
...IF YOU PULL OFF THIS RUN IN CONDITIONS AS BAD AS THIS, I SWEAR, I'LL GET YOU THE DEEP POLISH YOU DESERVE.
...ARE YOU SWEET-TALKING YOUR SHIP?
YOU'VE BEEN TRAINED IN DIPLOMACY AND SAVOIR FAIRE AND WHO KNOWS WHAT SINCE YOU WERE A KID, PRINCESS...
...BUT YOU HAVE NO IDEA WHAT IT'S LIKE TO HANDLE THE *FALCON.*
NOW, EYES FORWARD, AIM THE TORPEDOES AND HOPE LUKE AND TUBEFACE CAN GET OUT IN TIME.

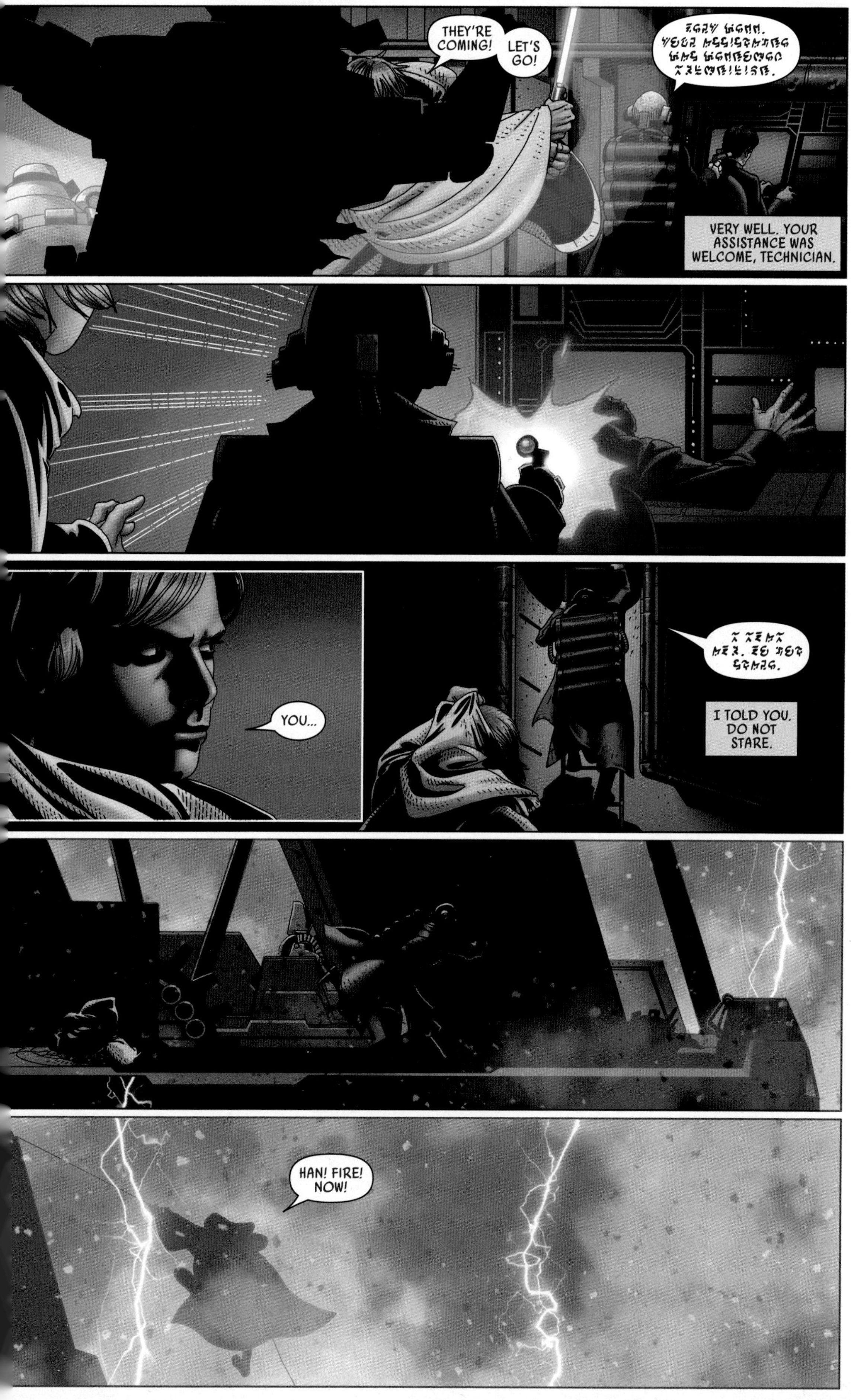
THEY'RE COMING!
LET'S GO!
VERY WELL. YOUR ASSISTANCE WAS WELCOME, TECHNICIAN.
YOU...
I TOLD YOU. DO NOT STARE.
HAN! FIRE! NOW!

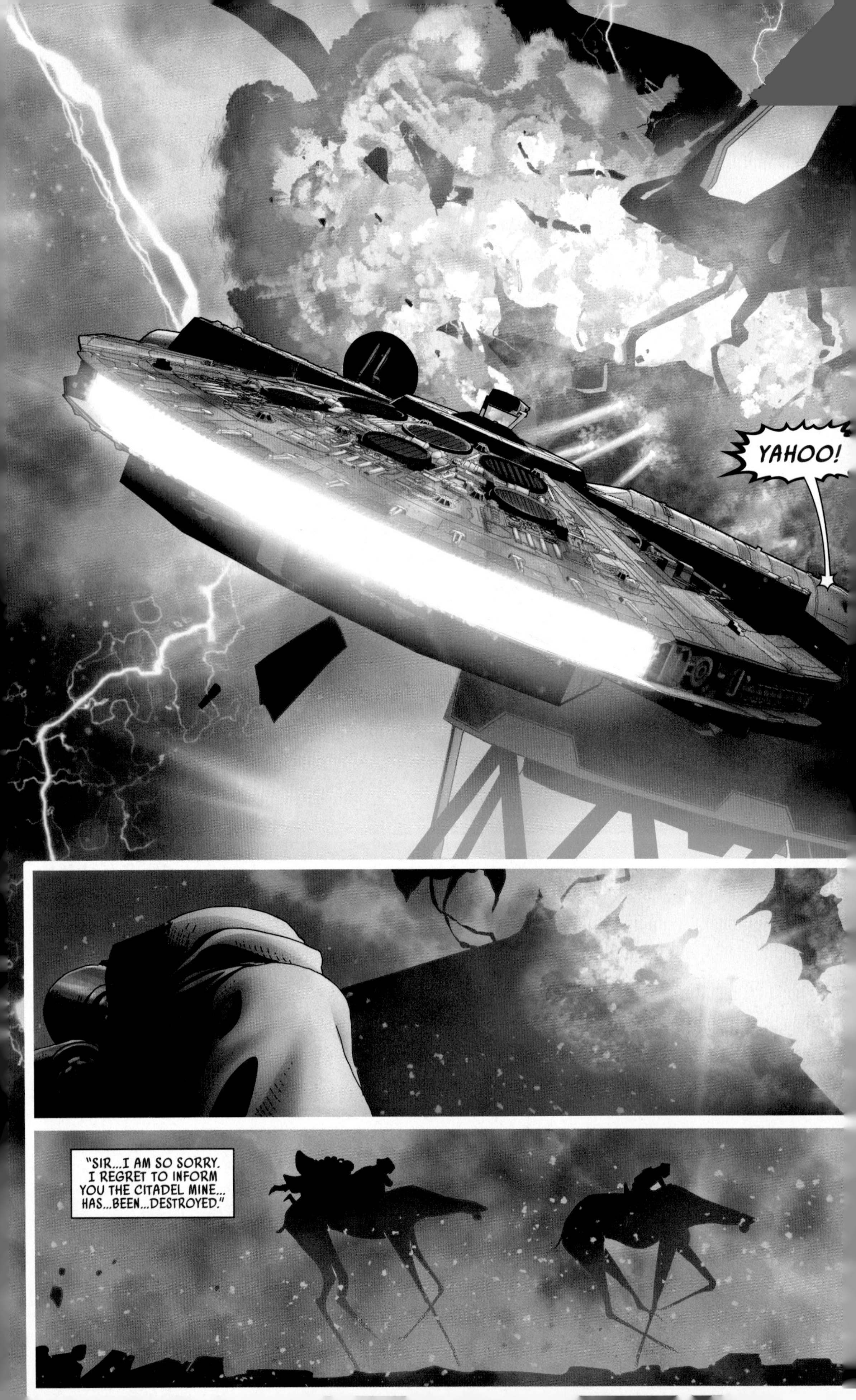
YAHOO!
"SIR...I AM SO SORRY. I REGRET TO INFORM YOU THE CITADEL MINE... HAS...BEEN...DESTROYED."

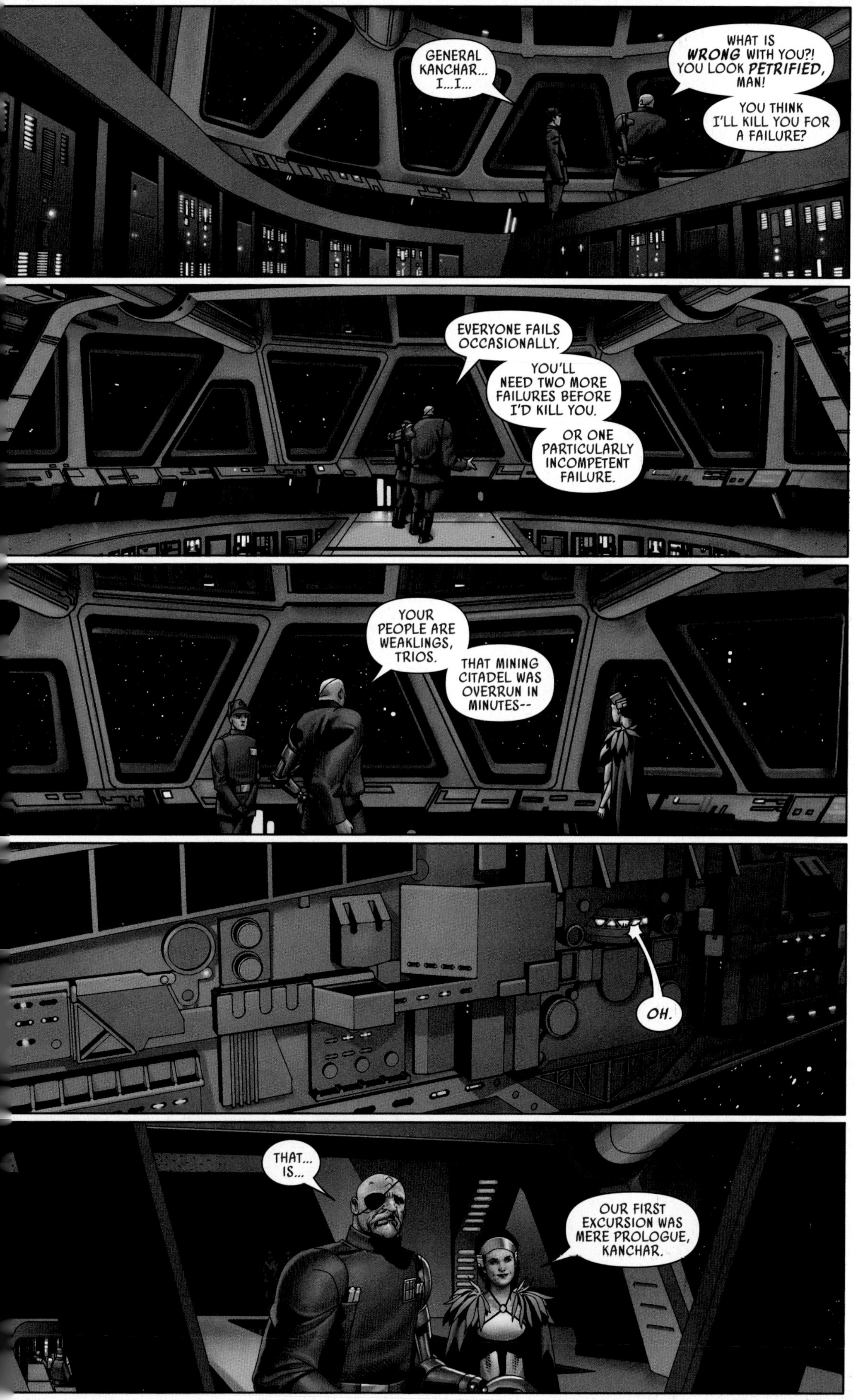
GENERAL KANCHAR... I...I...
WHAT IS **WRONG** WITH YOU?! YOU LOOK **PETRIFIED**, MAN!
YOU THINK I'LL KILL YOU FOR A FAILURE?
EVERYONE FAILS OCCASIONALLY.
YOU'LL NEED TWO MORE FAILURES BEFORE I'D KILL YOU.
OR ONE PARTICULARLY INCOMPETENT FAILURE.
YOUR PEOPLE ARE WEAKLINGS, TRIOS.
THAT MINING CITADEL WAS OVERRUN IN MINUTES--
OH.
THAT... IS...
OUR FIRST EXCURSION WAS MERE PROLOGUE, KANCHAR.

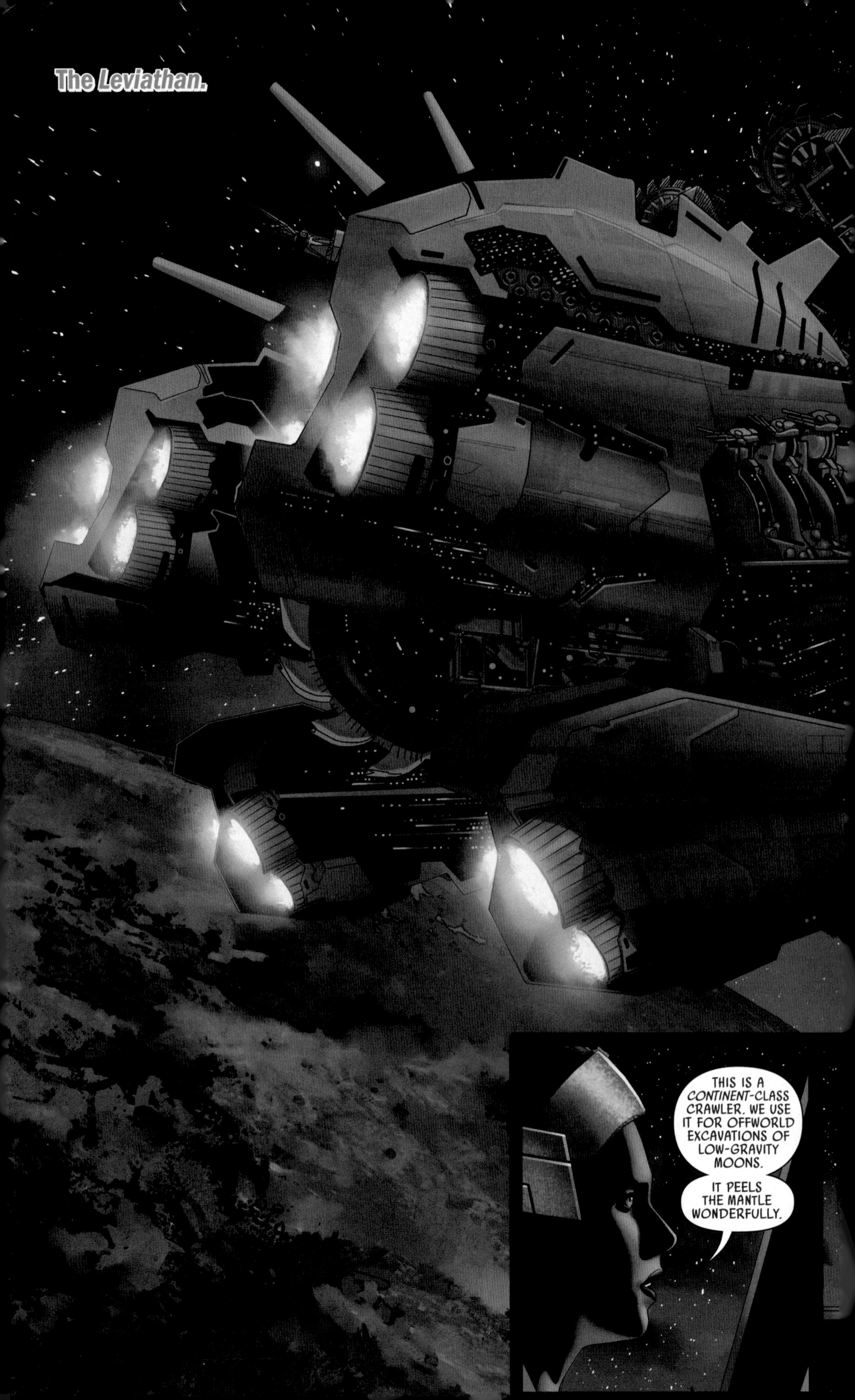
The Leviathan.
THIS IS A CONTINENT-CLASS CRAWLER. WE USE IT FOR OFFWORLD EXCAVATIONS OF LOW-GRAVITY MOONS.
IT PEELS THE MANTLE WONDERFULLY.

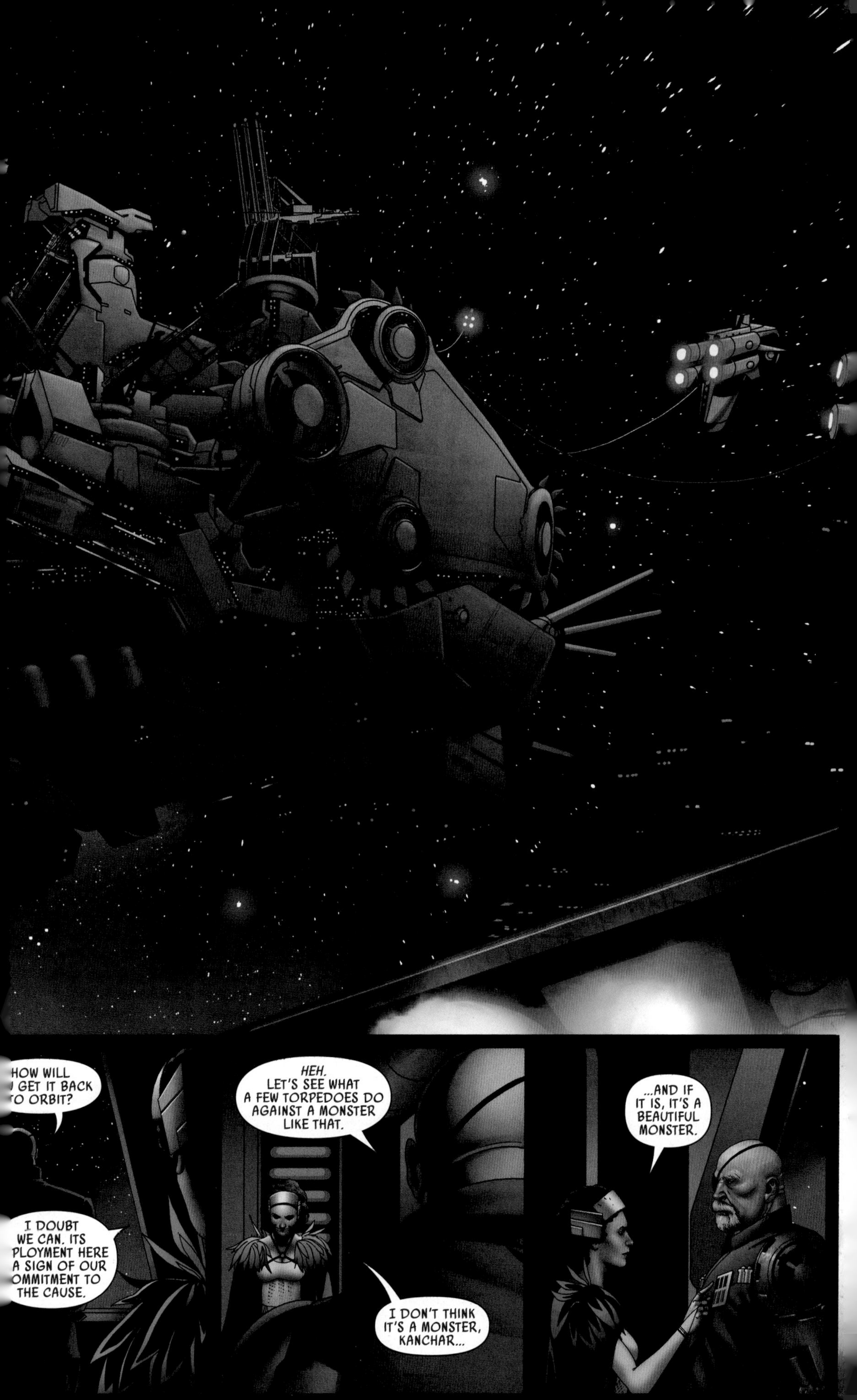

HOW WILL
GET IT BACK
O ORBIT?
I DOUBT
WE CAN. ITS
PLOYMENT HERE
A SIGN OF OUR
OMMITMENT TO
THE CAUSE.
HEH.
LET'S SEE WHAT
A FEW TORPEDOES DO
AGAINST A MONSTER
LIKE THAT.
I DON'T THINK
IT'S A MONSTER,
KANCHAR...
...AND IF
IT IS, IT'S A
BEAUTIFUL
MONSTER.

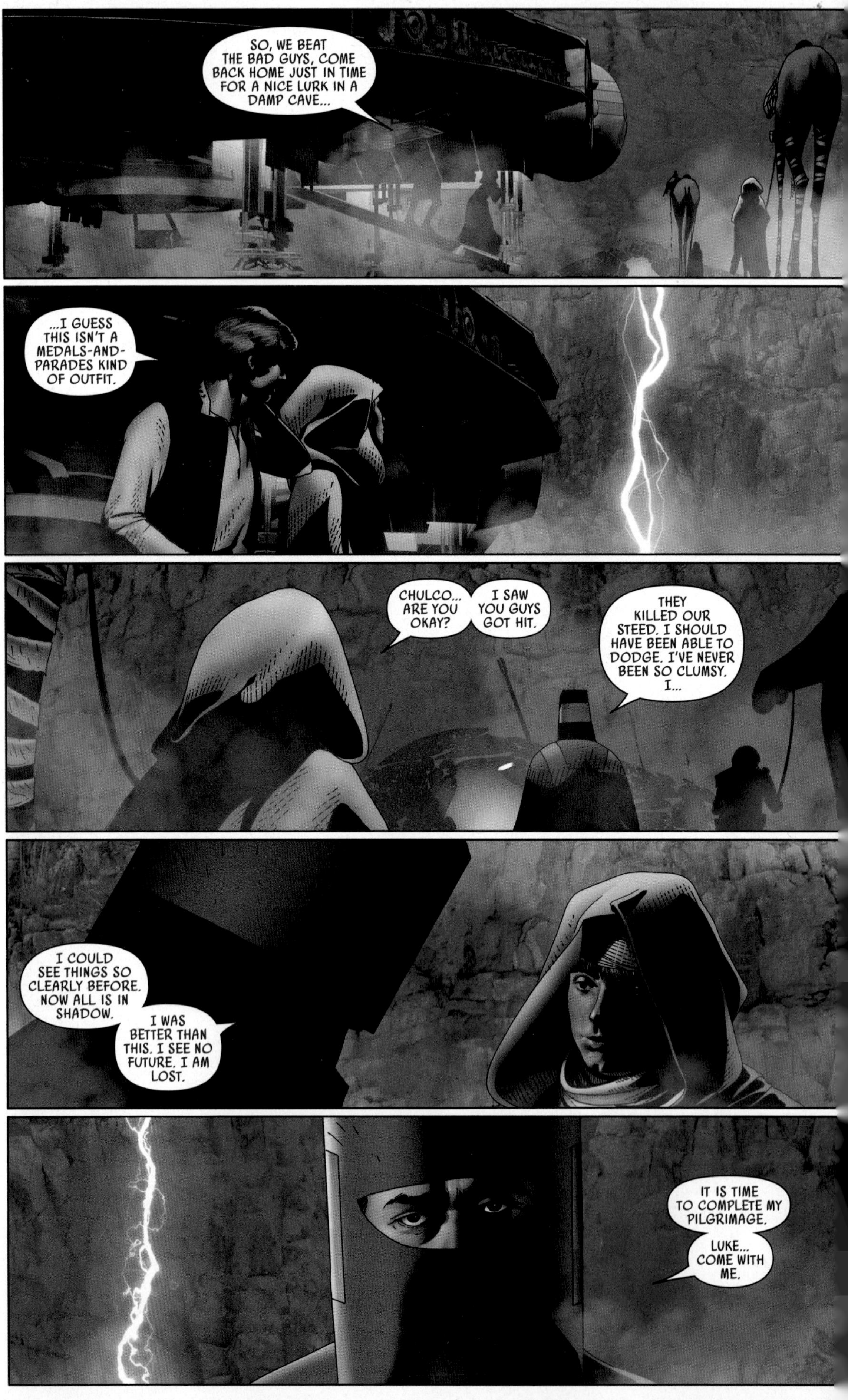
SO, WE BEAT THE BAD GUYS, COME BACK HOME JUST IN TIME FOR A NICE LURK IN A DAMP CAVE...
...I GUESS THIS ISN'T A MEDALS-AND-PARADES KIND OF OUTFIT.
CHULCO... ARE YOU OKAY?
I SAW YOU GUYS GOT HIT.
THEY KILLED OUR STEED. I SHOULD HAVE BEEN ABLE TO DODGE. I'VE NEVER BEEN SO CLUMSY. I...
I COULD SEE THINGS SO CLEARLY BEFORE. NOW ALL IS IN SHADOW.
I WAS BETTER THAN THIS. I SEE NO FUTURE. I AM LOST.
IT IS TIME TO COMPLETE MY PILGRIMAGE.
LUKE... COME WITH ME.

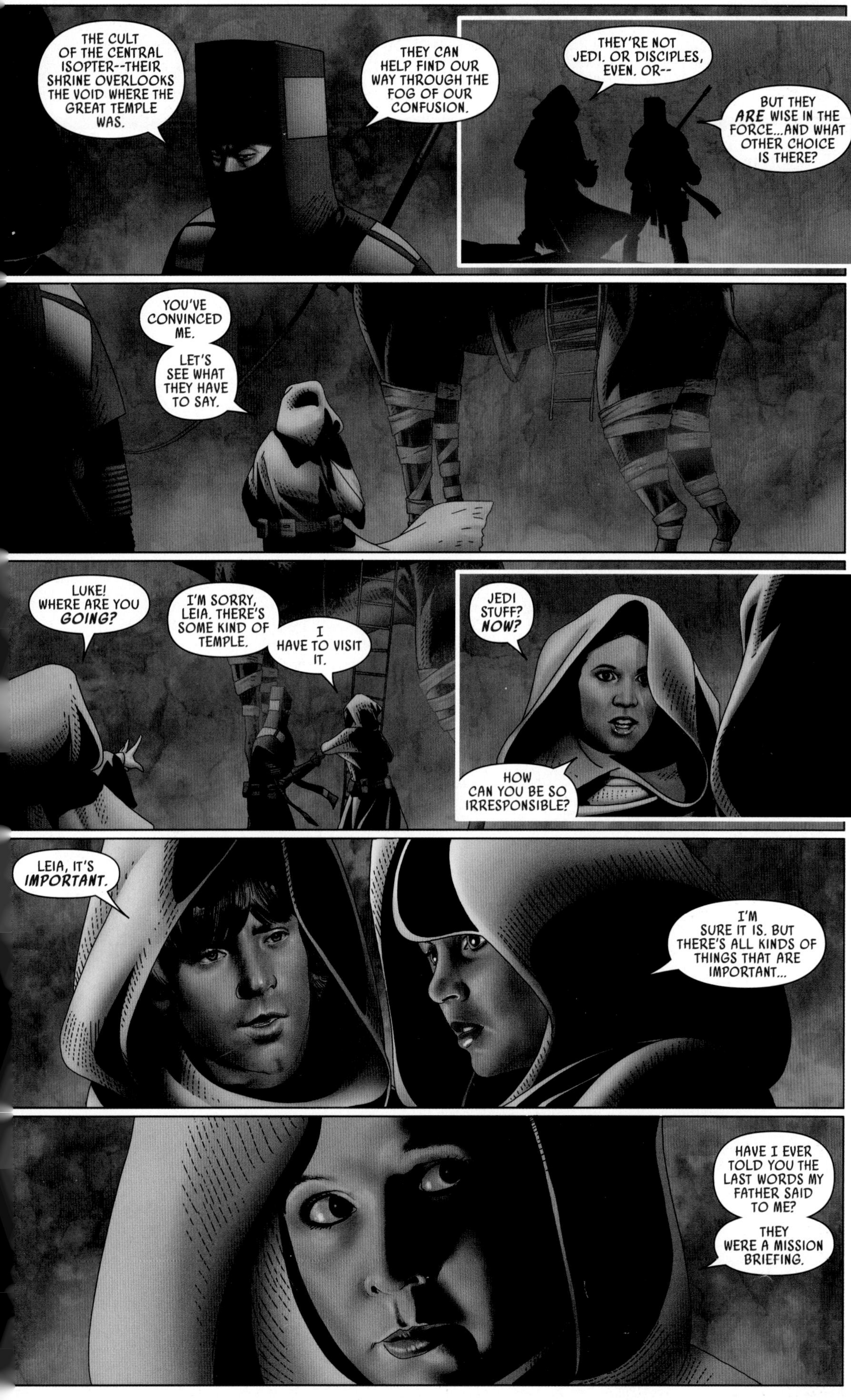
THE CULT OF THE CENTRAL ISOPTER--THEIR SHRINE OVERLOOKS THE VOID WHERE THE GREAT TEMPLE WAS.
THEY CAN HELP FIND OUR WAY THROUGH THE FOG OF OUR CONFUSION.
THEY'RE NOT JEDI. OR DISCIPLES, EVEN. OR--
BUT THEY *ARE* WISE IN THE FORCE...AND WHAT OTHER CHOICE IS THERE?
YOU'VE CONVINCED ME.
LET'S SEE WHAT THEY HAVE TO SAY.
LUKE! WHERE ARE YOU *GOING?*
I'M SORRY, LEIA. THERE'S SOME KIND OF TEMPLE.
I HAVE TO VISIT IT.
JEDI STUFF? *NOW?*
HOW CAN YOU BE SO IRRESPONSIBLE?
LEIA, IT'S *IMPORTANT.*
I'M SURE IT IS. BUT THERE'S ALL KINDS OF THINGS THAT ARE IMPORTANT...
HAVE I EVER TOLD YOU THE LAST WORDS MY FATHER SAID TO ME?
THEY WERE A MISSION BRIEFING.

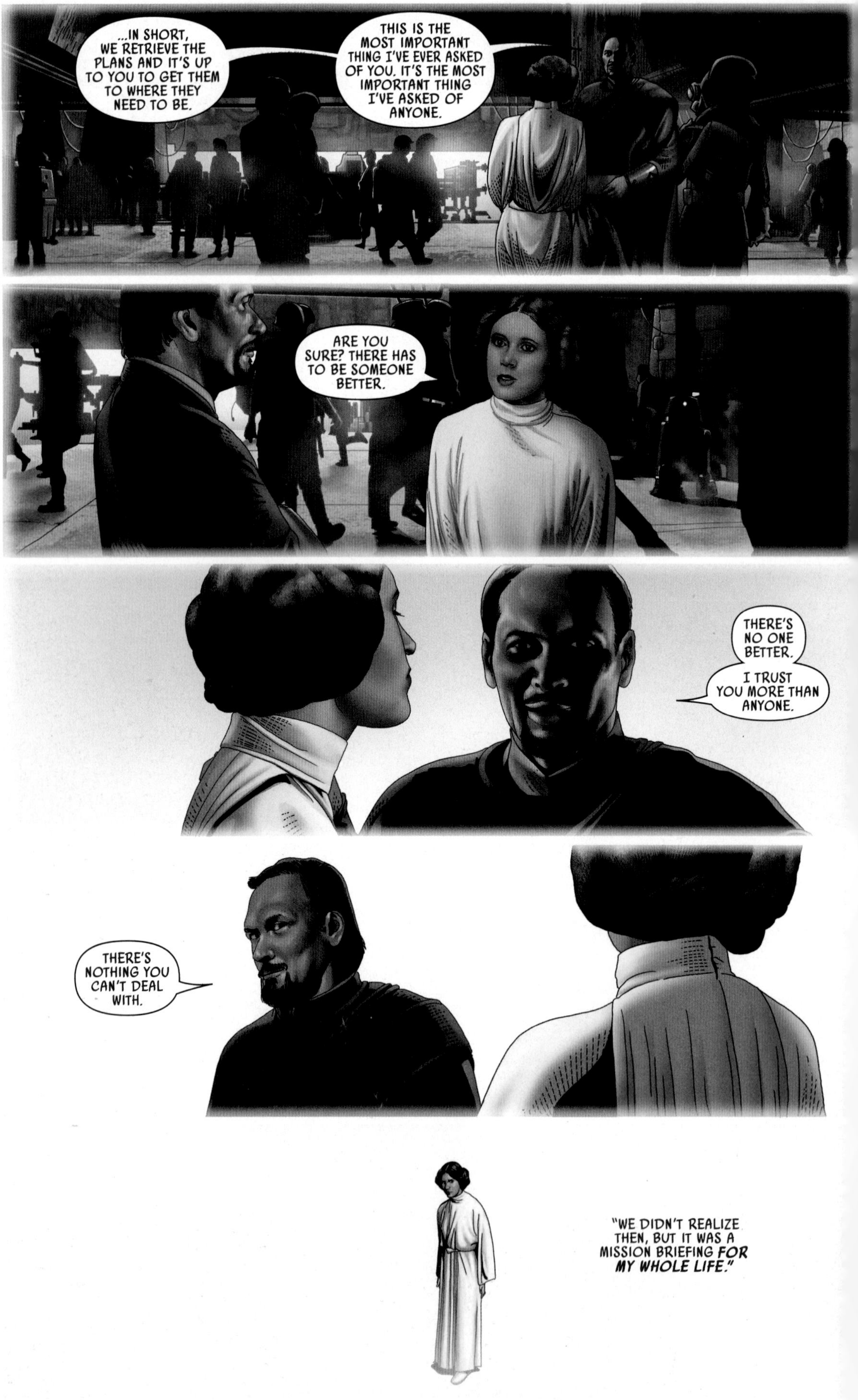
...IN SHORT, WE RETRIEVE THE PLANS AND IT'S UP TO YOU TO GET THEM TO WHERE THEY NEED TO BE.
THIS IS THE MOST IMPORTANT THING I'VE EVER ASKED OF YOU. IT'S THE MOST IMPORTANT THING I'VE ASKED OF ANYONE.
ARE YOU SURE? THERE HAS TO BE SOMEONE BETTER.
THERE'S NO ONE BETTER.
I TRUST YOU MORE THAN ANYONE.
THERE'S NOTHING YOU CAN'T DEAL WITH.
"WE DIDN'T REALIZE THEN, BUT IT WAS A MISSION BRIEFING *FOR MY WHOLE LIFE.*"

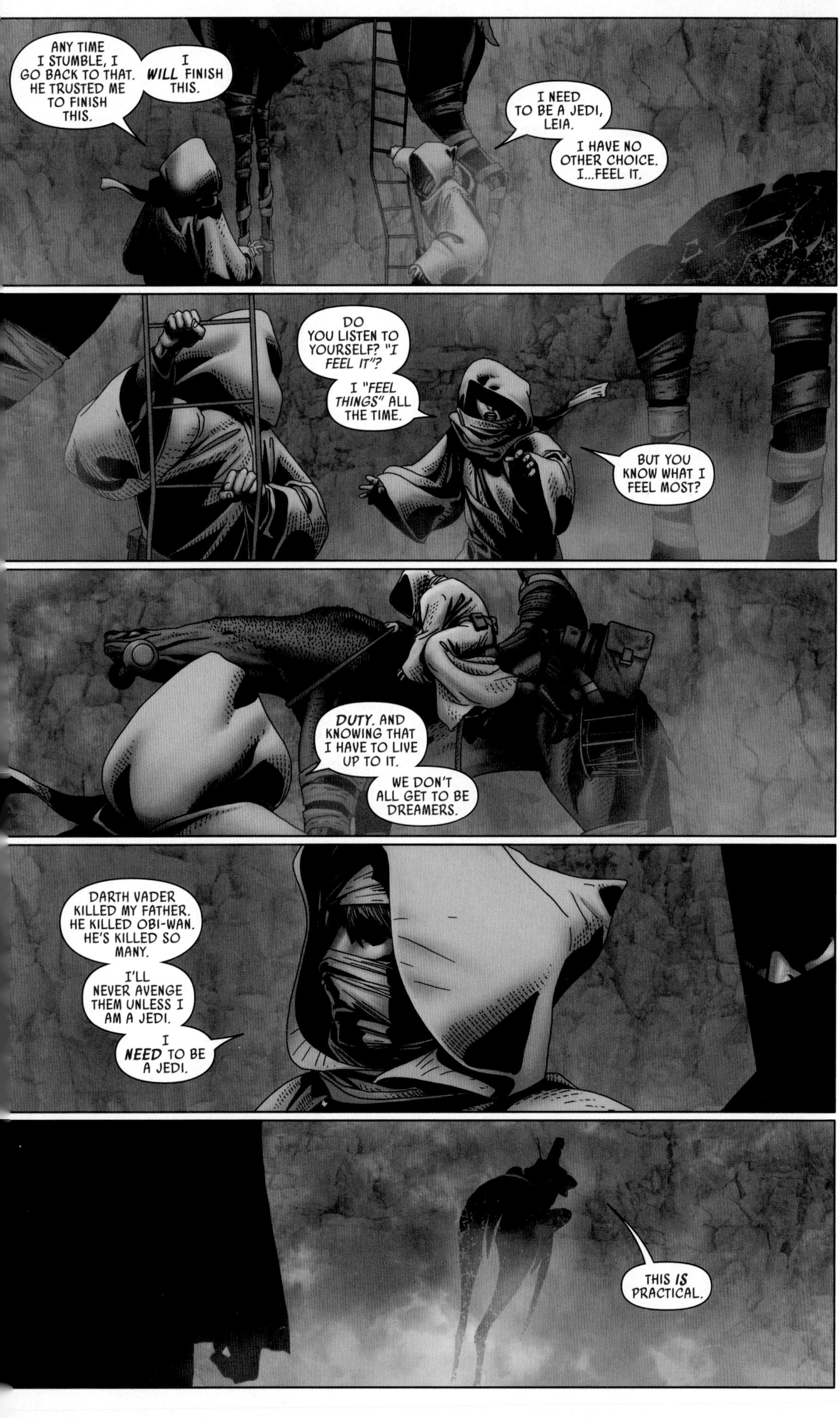
ANY TIME I STUMBLE, I GO BACK TO THAT. HE TRUSTED ME TO FINISH THIS.
I *WILL* FINISH THIS.
I NEED TO BE A JEDI, LEIA.
I HAVE NO OTHER CHOICE. I...FEEL IT.
DO YOU LISTEN TO YOURSELF? "I FEEL IT"?
I *"FEEL THINGS"* ALL THE TIME.
BUT YOU KNOW WHAT I FEEL MOST?
DUTY. AND KNOWING THAT I HAVE TO LIVE UP TO IT.
WE DON'T ALL GET TO BE DREAMERS.
DARTH VADER KILLED MY FATHER. HE KILLED OBI-WAN. HE'S KILLED SO MANY.
I'LL NEVER AVENGE THEM UNLESS I AM A JEDI.
I *NEED* TO BE A JEDI.
THIS *IS* PRACTICAL.

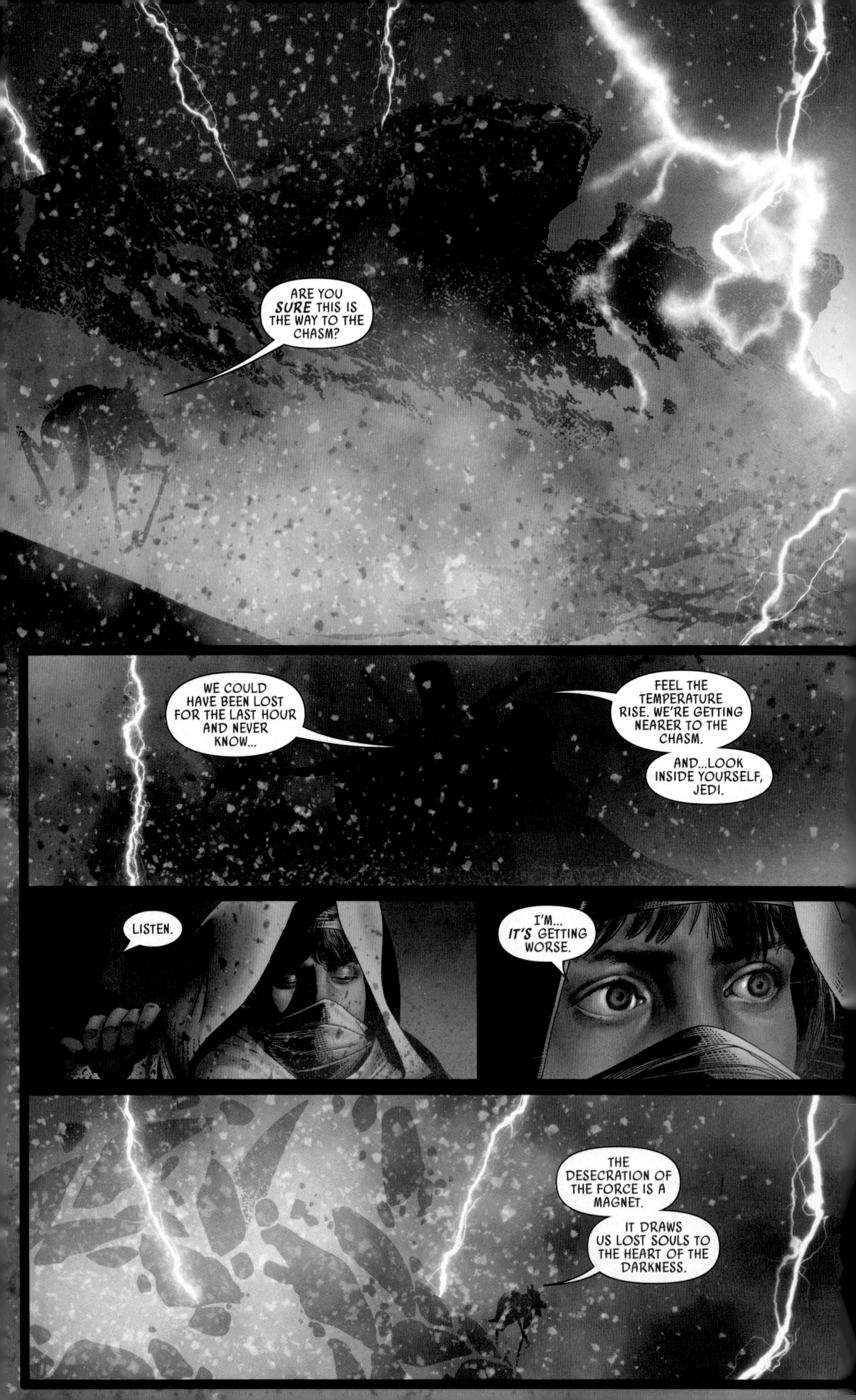

ARE YOU SURE THIS IS THE WAY TO THE CHASM?
WE COULD HAVE BEEN LOST FOR THE LAST HOUR AND NEVER KNOW...
FEEL THE TEMPERATURE RISE. WE'RE GETTING NEARER TO THE CHASM.
AND...LOOK INSIDE YOURSELF, JEDI.
LISTEN.
I'M... IT'S GETTING WORSE.
THE DESECRATION OF THE FORCE IS A MAGNET.
IT DRAWS US LOST SOULS TO THE HEART OF THE DARKNESS.

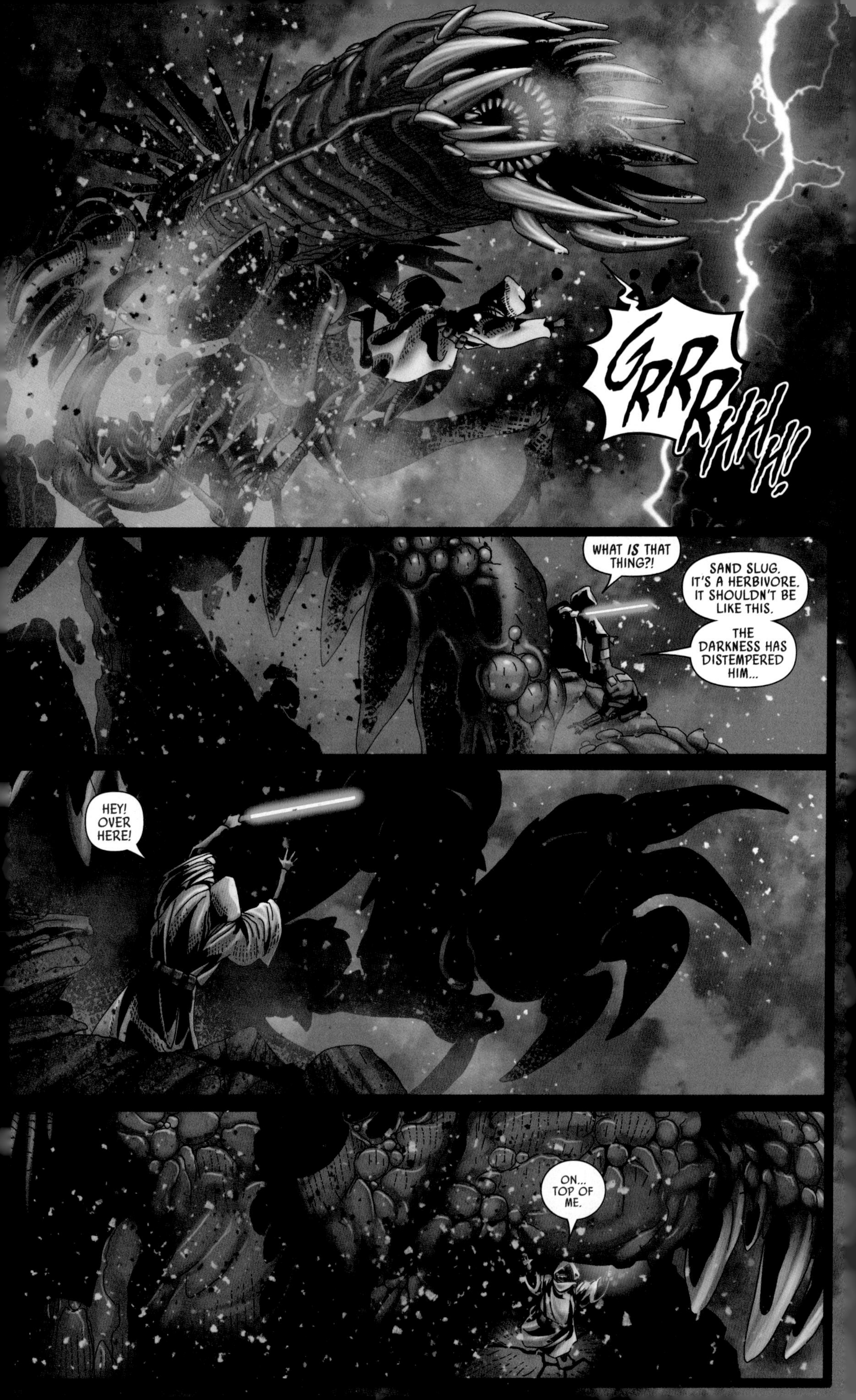
GRRRHHH!!
WHAT IS THAT THING?!
SAND SLUG. IT'S A HERBIVORE. IT SHOULDN'T BE LIKE THIS.
THE DARKNESS HAS DISTEMPERED HIM...
HEY! OVER HERE!
ON... TOP OF ME.

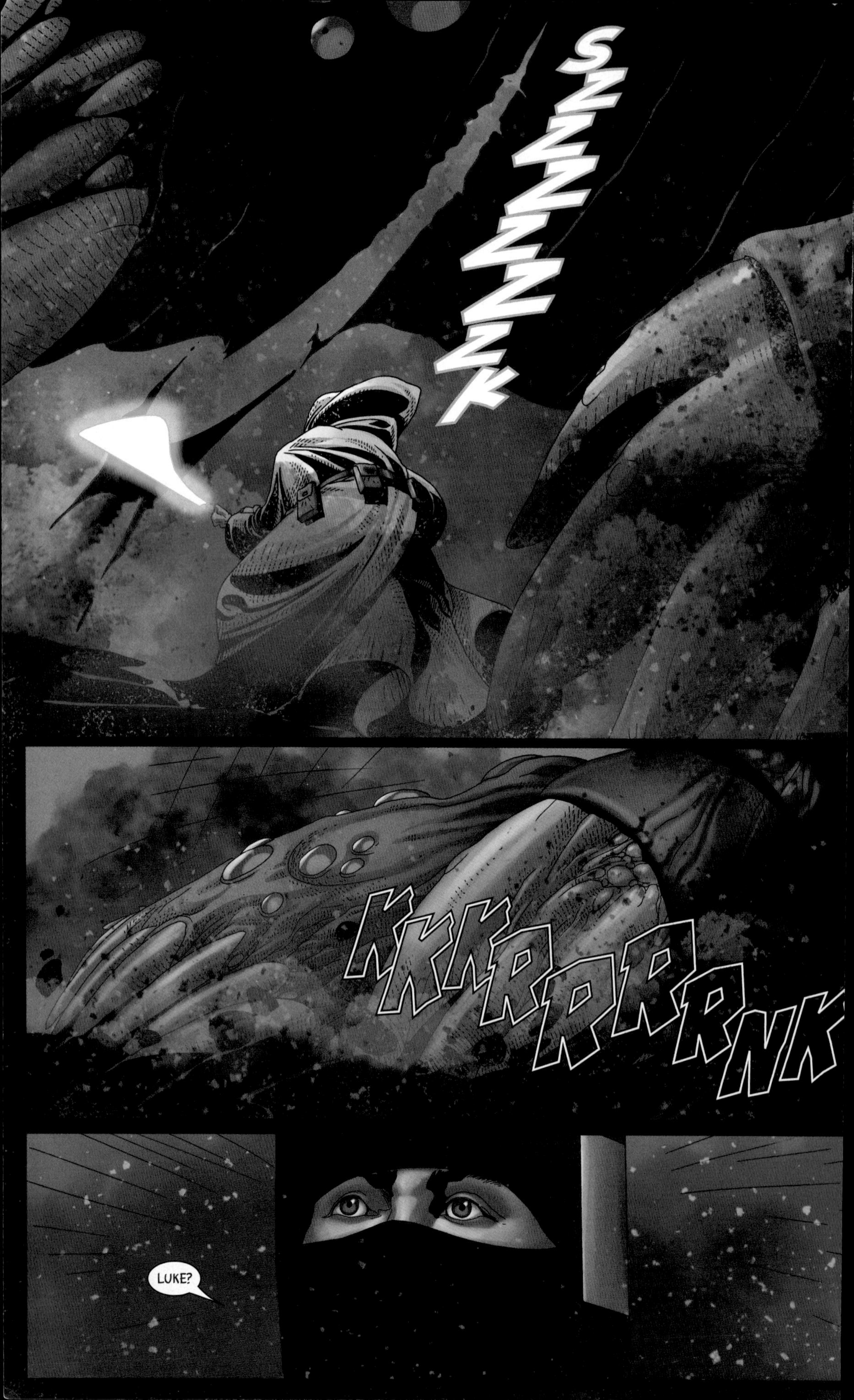
SZZZZZZK
KKKRRRRNK
LUKE?

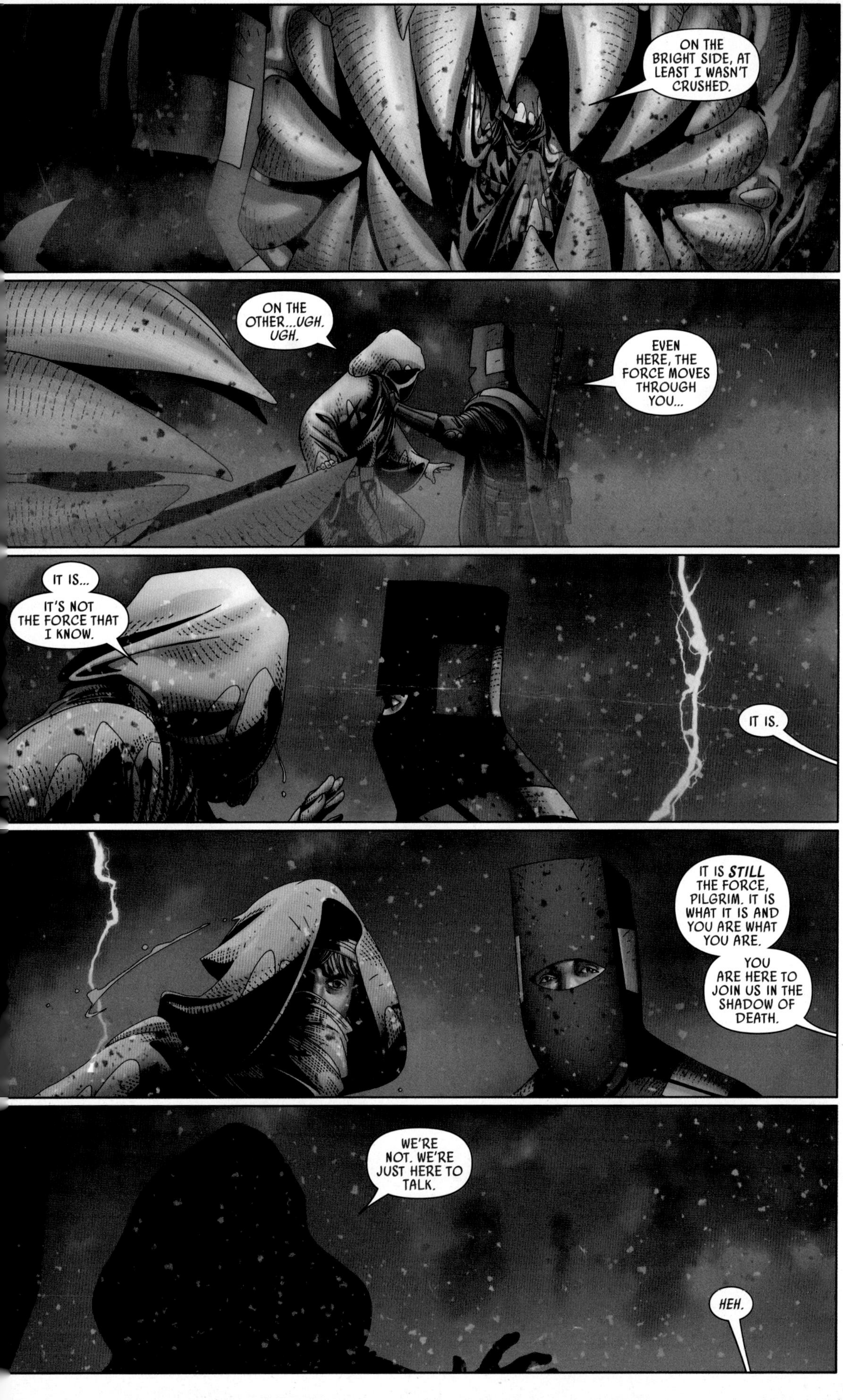
ON THE BRIGHT SIDE, AT LEAST I WASN'T CRUSHED.
ON THE OTHER...UGH. UGH.
EVEN HERE, THE FORCE MOVES THROUGH YOU...
IT IS...
IT'S NOT THE FORCE THAT I KNOW.
IT IS.
IT IS STILL THE FORCE, PILGRIM. IT IS WHAT IT IS AND YOU ARE WHAT YOU ARE.
YOU ARE HERE TO JOIN US IN THE SHADOW OF DEATH.
WE'RE NOT. WE'RE JUST HERE TO TALK.
HEH.

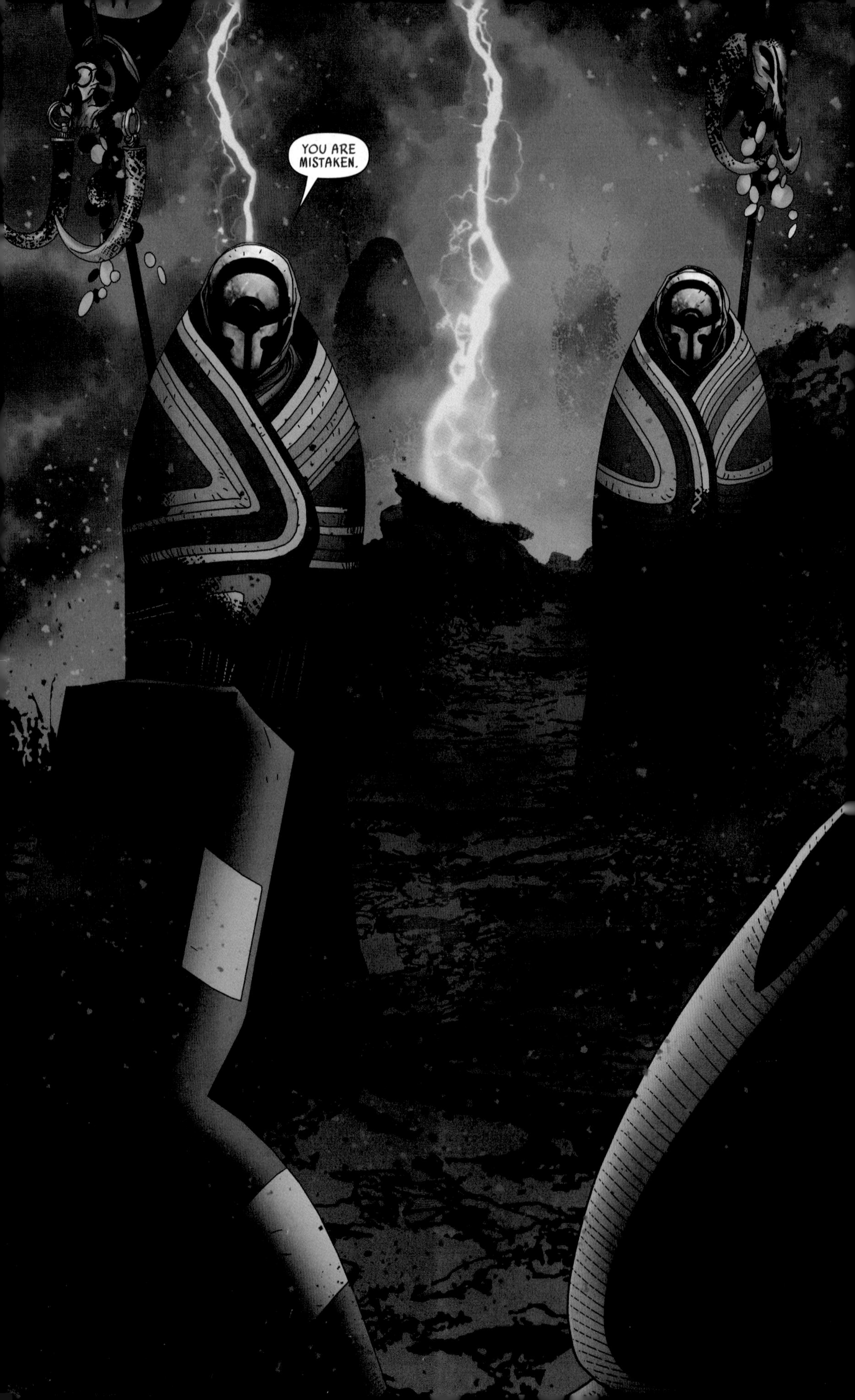
YOU ARE MISTAKEN.

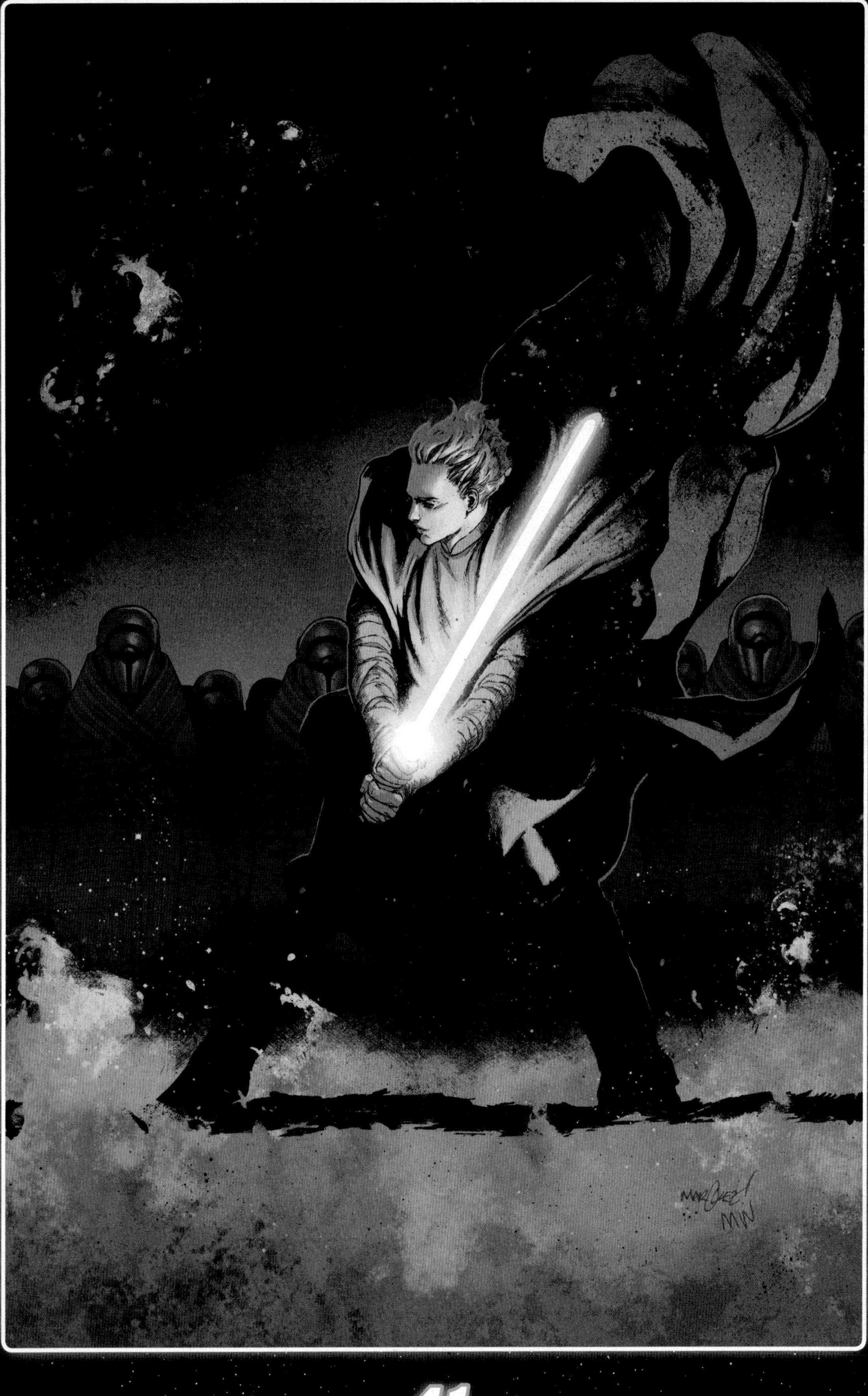

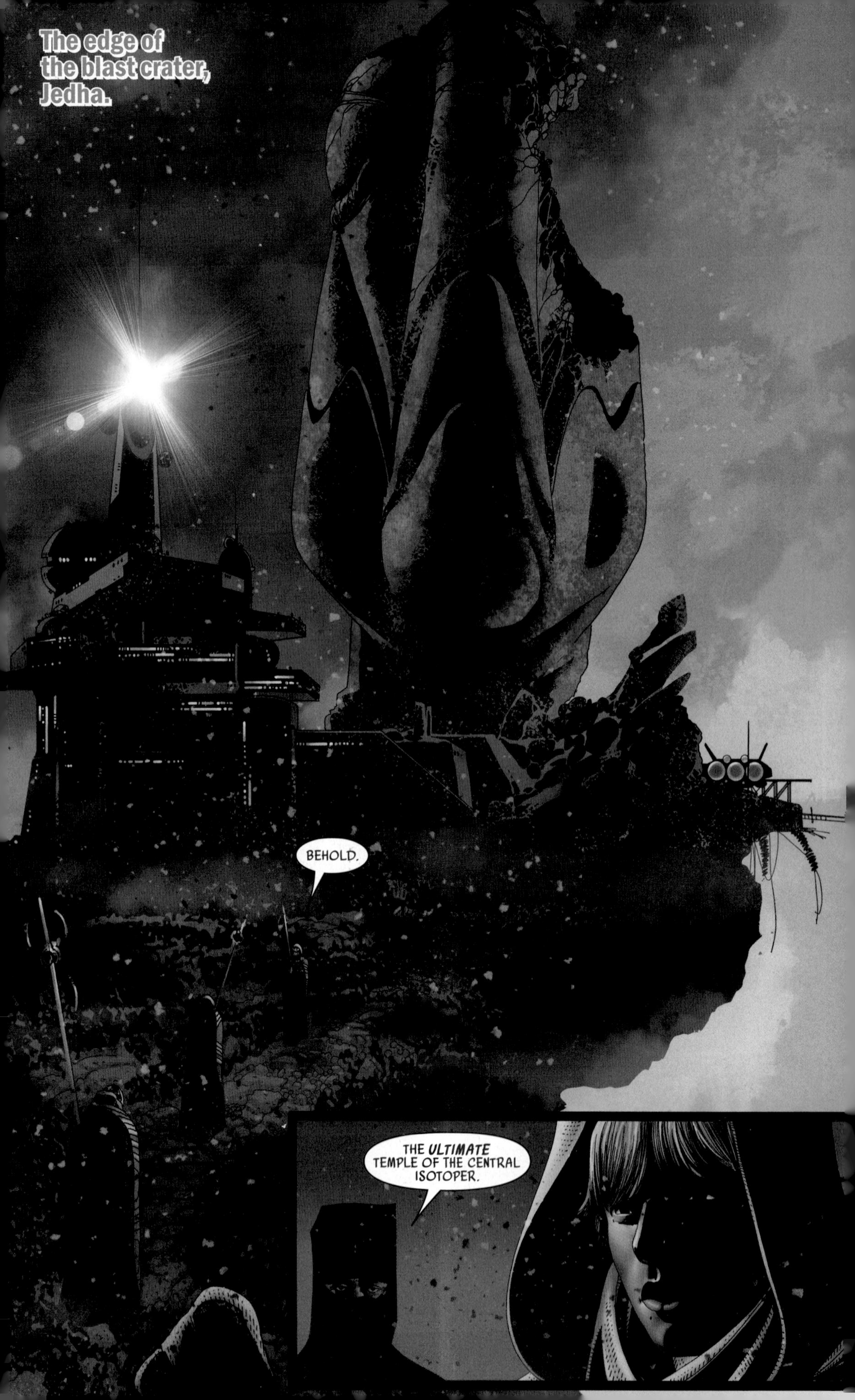
The edge of the blast crater, Jedha.
BEHOLD.
THE ULTIMATE TEMPLE OF THE CENTRAL ISOTOPER.

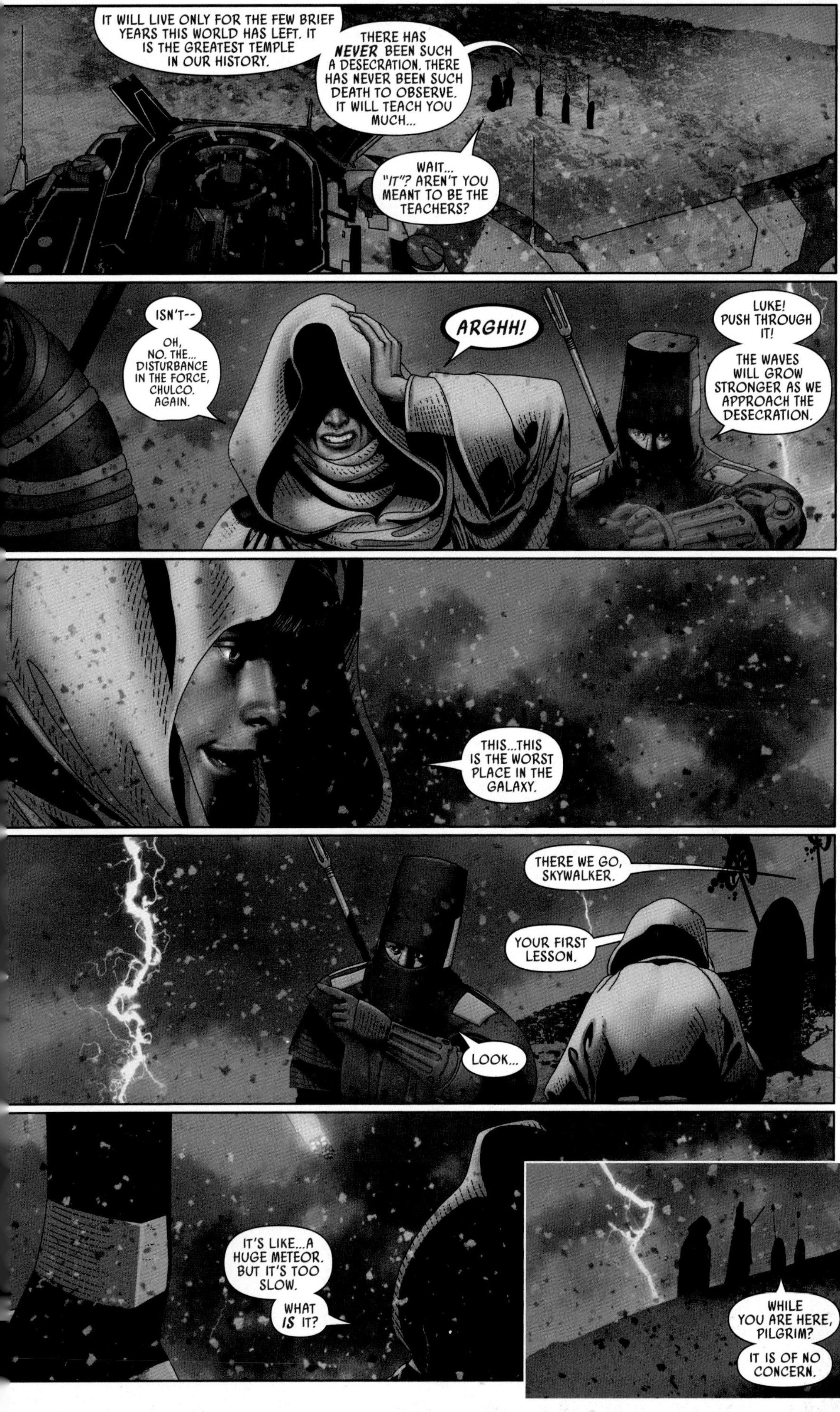

IT WILL LIVE ONLY FOR THE FEW BRIEF YEARS THIS WORLD HAS LEFT. IT IS THE GREATEST TEMPLE IN OUR HISTORY.
THERE HAS NEVER BEEN SUCH A DESECRATION. THERE HAS NEVER BEEN SUCH DEATH TO OBSERVE. IT WILL TEACH YOU MUCH...
WAIT... "IT"? AREN'T YOU MEANT TO BE THE TEACHERS?
ISN'T--
OH, NO. THE... DISTURBANCE IN THE FORCE, CHULCO. AGAIN.
ARGHH!
LUKE! PUSH THROUGH IT!
THE WAVES WILL GROW STRONGER AS WE APPROACH THE DESECRATION.
THIS...THIS IS THE WORST PLACE IN THE GALAXY.
THERE WE GO, SKYWALKER.
YOUR FIRST LESSON.
LOOK...
IT'S LIKE...A HUGE METEOR. BUT IT'S TOO SLOW.
WHAT IS IT?
WHILE YOU ARE HERE, PILGRIM?
IT IS OF NO CONCERN.

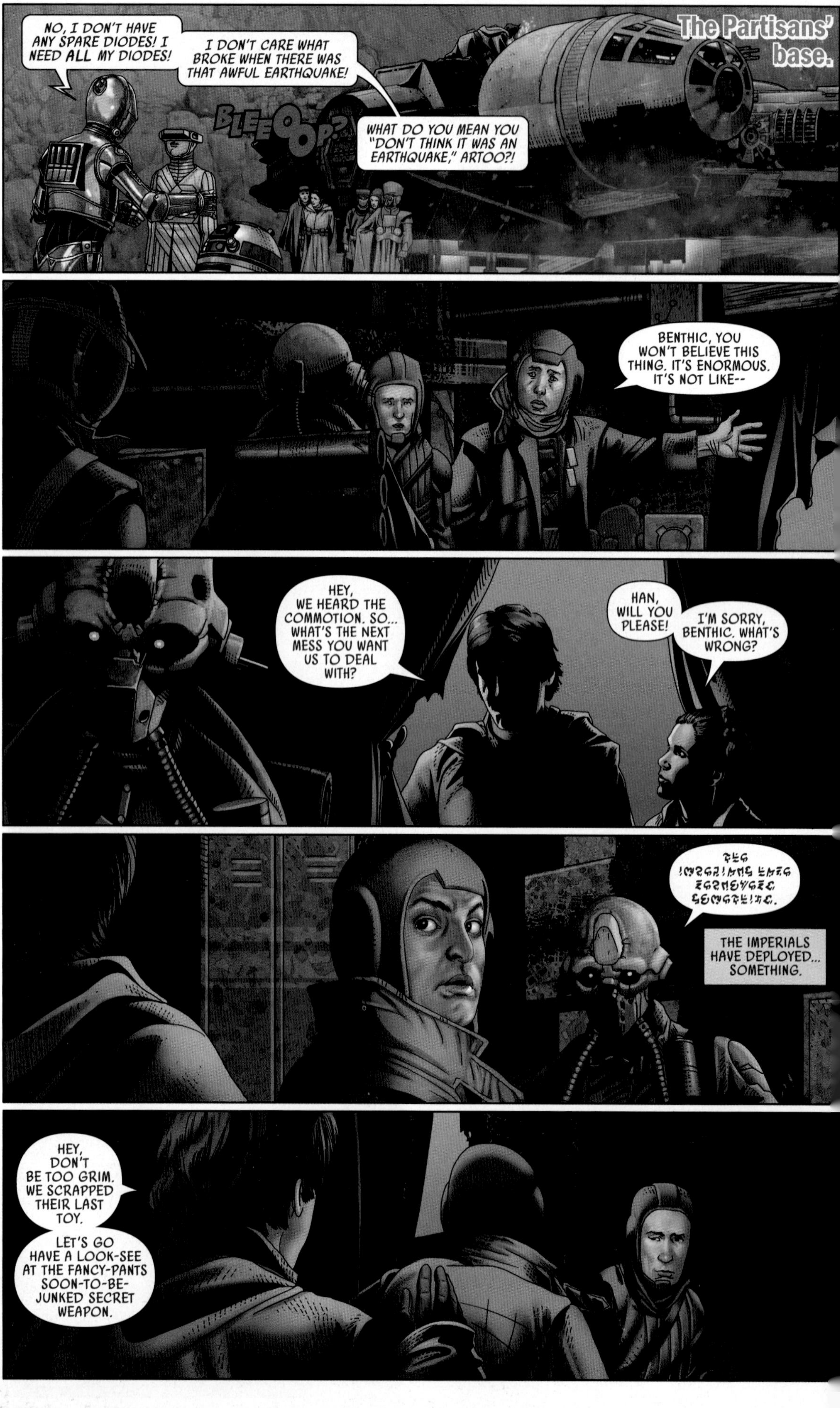

The Partisans' base.
NO, I DON'T HAVE ANY SPARE DIODES! I NEED ALL MY DIODES!
I DON'T CARE WHAT BROKE WHEN THERE WAS THAT AWFUL EARTHQUAKE!
BLEEOOP?
WHAT DO YOU MEAN YOU "DON'T THINK IT WAS AN EARTHQUAKE," ARTOO?!
BENTHIC, YOU WON'T BELIEVE THIS THING. IT'S ENORMOUS. IT'S NOT LIKE--
HEY, WE HEARD THE COMMOTION. SO... WHAT'S THE NEXT MESS YOU WANT US TO DEAL WITH?
HAN, WILL YOU PLEASE!
I'M SORRY, BENTHIC. WHAT'S WRONG?
THE IMPERIALS HAVE DEPLOYED... SOMETHING.
HEY, DON'T BE TOO GRIM. WE SCRAPPED THEIR LAST TOY.
LET'S GO HAVE A LOOK-SEE AT THE FANCY-PANTS SOON-TO-BE-JUNKED SECRET WEAPON.

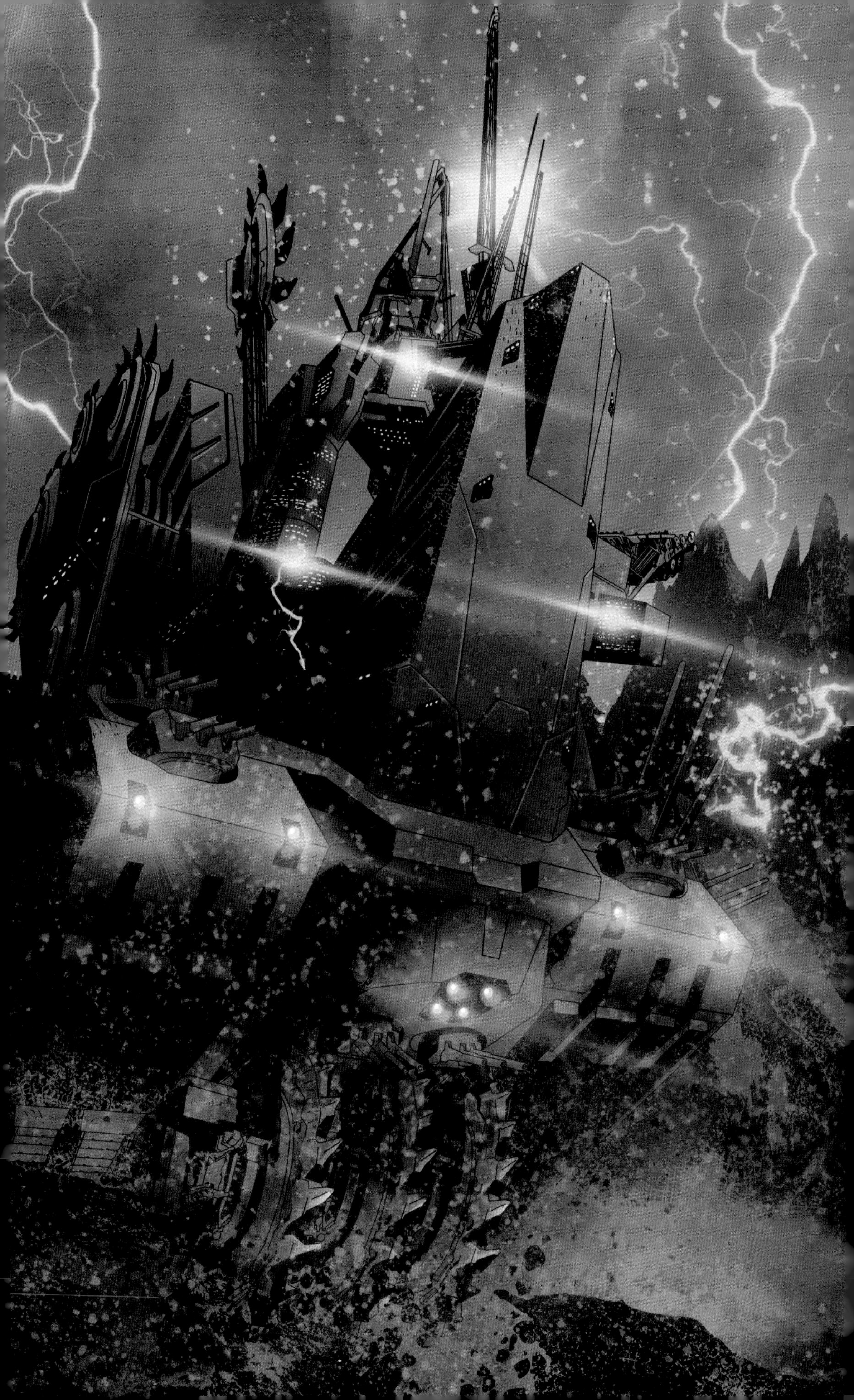

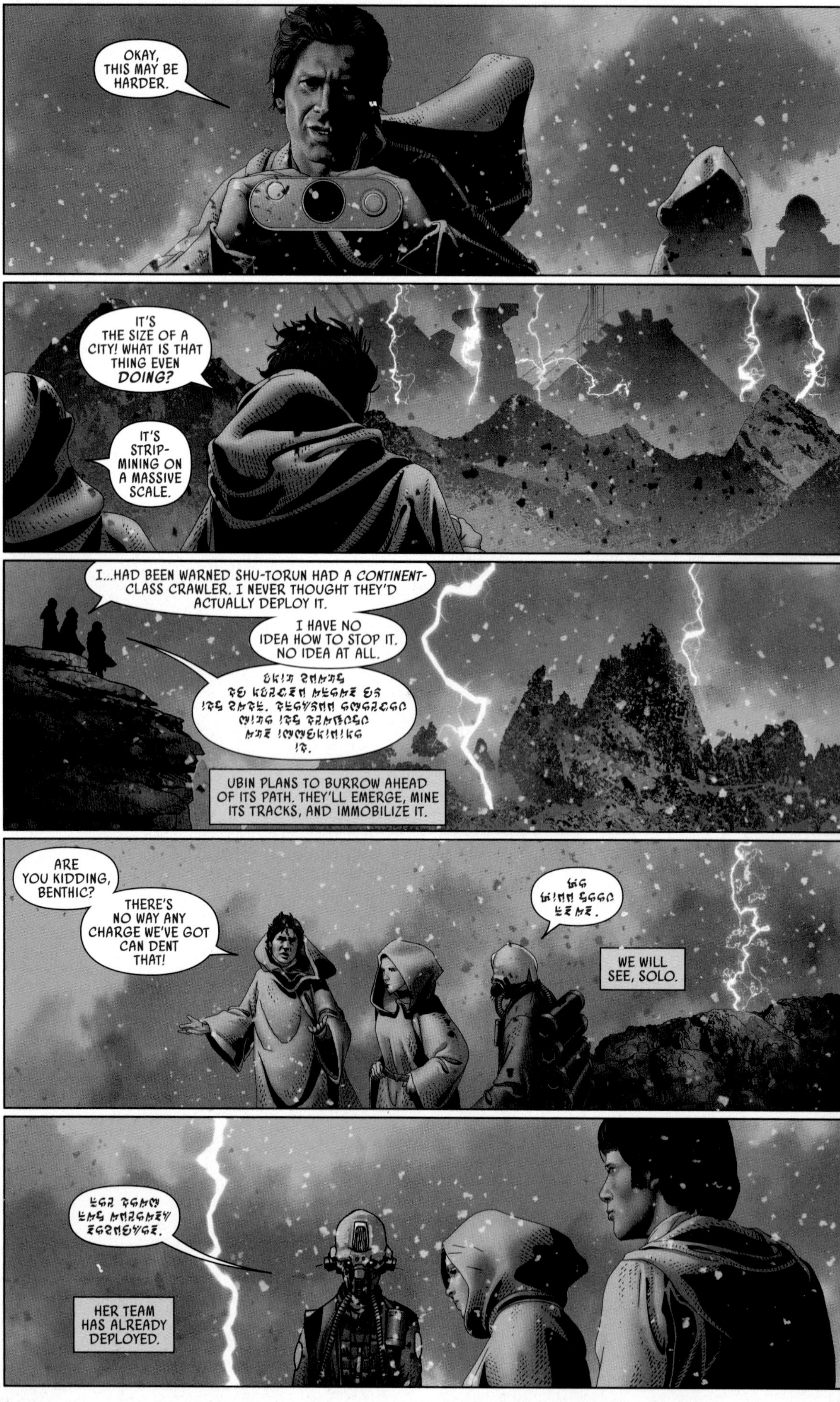
OKAY, THIS MAY BE HARDER.
IT'S THE SIZE OF A CITY! WHAT IS THAT THING EVEN *DOING?*
IT'S STRIP-MINING ON A MASSIVE SCALE.
I...HAD BEEN WARNED SHU-TORUN HAD A *CONTINENT*-CLASS CRAWLER. I NEVER THOUGHT THEY'D ACTUALLY DEPLOY IT.
I HAVE NO IDEA HOW TO STOP IT. NO IDEA AT ALL.
UBIN PLANS TO BURROW AHEAD OF ITS PATH. THEY'LL EMERGE, MINE ITS TRACKS, AND IMMOBILIZE IT.
ARE YOU KIDDING, BENTHIC?
THERE'S NO WAY ANY CHARGE WE'VE GOT CAN DENT THAT!
WE WILL SEE, SOLO.
HER TEAM HAS ALREADY DEPLOYED.

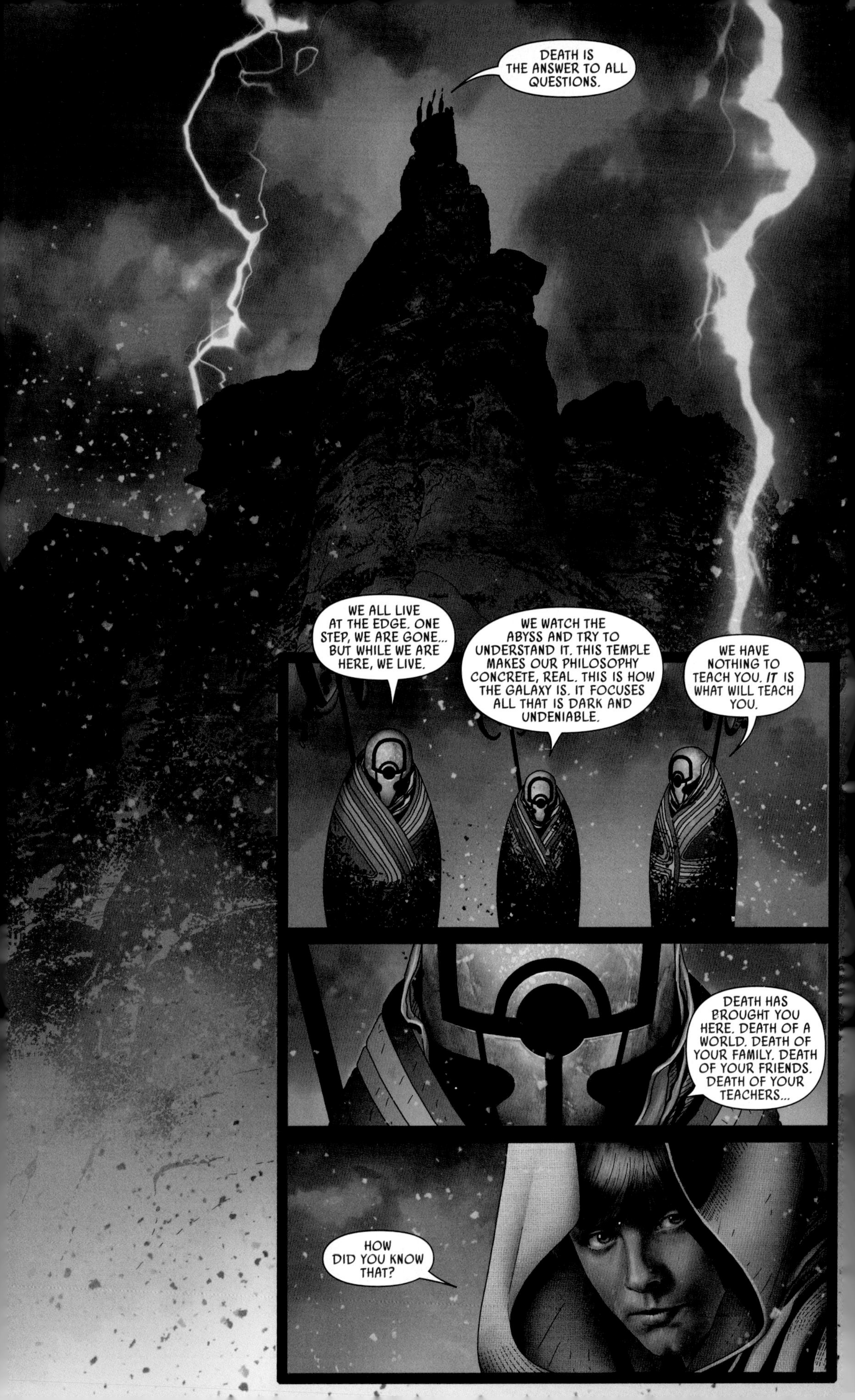
DEATH IS THE ANSWER TO ALL QUESTIONS.
WE ALL LIVE AT THE EDGE. ONE STEP, WE ARE GONE... BUT WHILE WE ARE HERE, WE LIVE.
WE WATCH THE ABYSS AND TRY TO UNDERSTAND IT. THIS TEMPLE MAKES OUR PHILOSOPHY CONCRETE, REAL. THIS IS HOW THE GALAXY IS. IT FOCUSES ALL THAT IS DARK AND UNDENIABLE.
WE HAVE NOTHING TO TEACH YOU. *IT* IS WHAT WILL TEACH YOU.
DEATH HAS BROUGHT YOU HERE. DEATH OF A WORLD. DEATH OF YOUR FAMILY. DEATH OF YOUR FRIENDS. DEATH OF YOUR TEACHERS...
HOW DID YOU KNOW THAT?

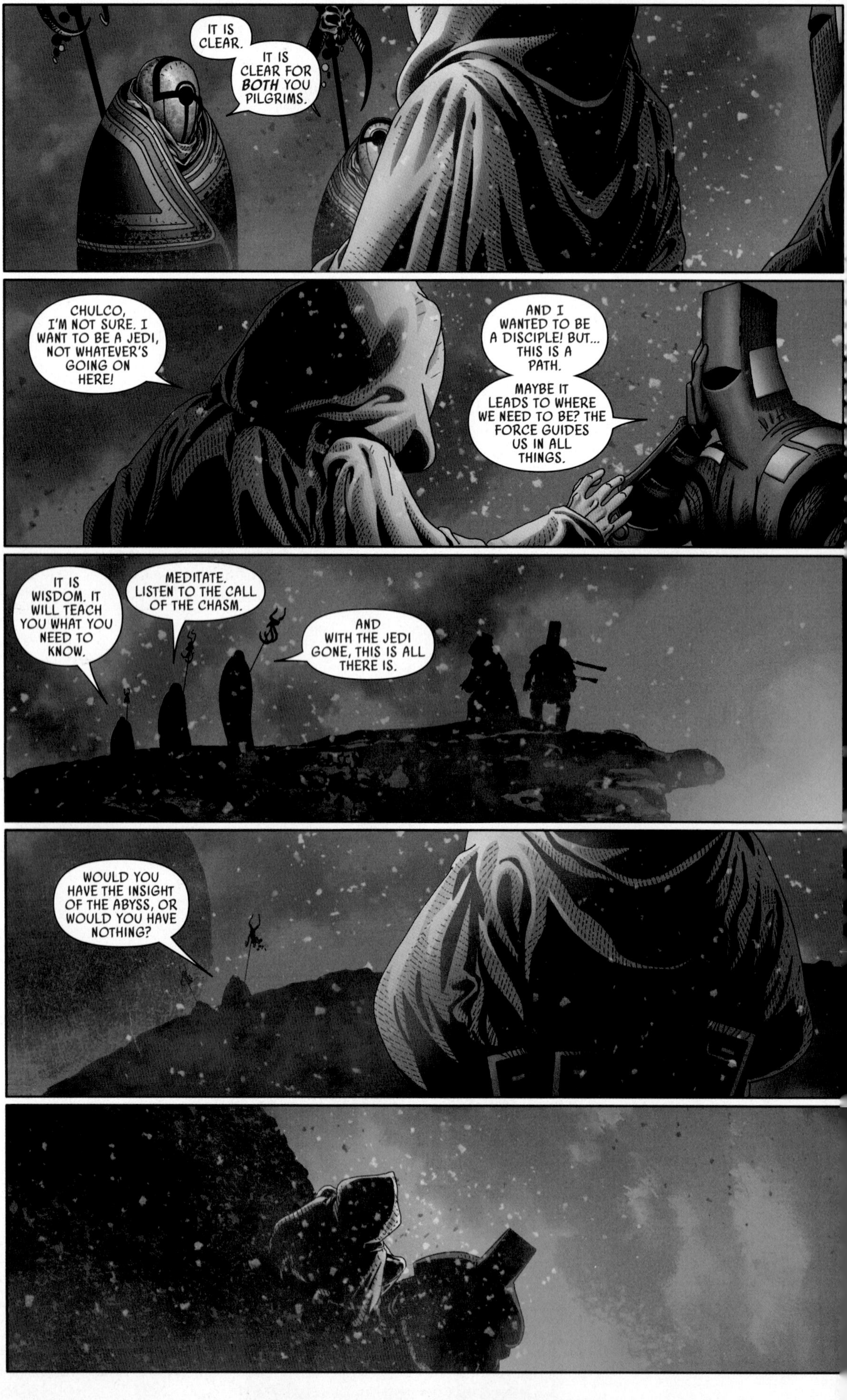
IT IS CLEAR.
IT IS CLEAR FOR *BOTH* YOU PILGRIMS.
CHULCO, I'M NOT SURE. I WANT TO BE A JEDI, NOT WHATEVER'S GOING ON HERE!
AND I WANTED TO BE A DISCIPLE! BUT... THIS IS A PATH.
MAYBE IT LEADS TO WHERE WE NEED TO BE? THE FORCE GUIDES US IN ALL THINGS.
IT IS WISDOM. IT WILL TEACH YOU WHAT YOU NEED TO KNOW.
MEDITATE. LISTEN TO THE CALL OF THE CHASM.
AND WITH THE JEDI GONE, THIS IS ALL THERE IS.
WOULD YOU HAVE THE INSIGHT OF THE ABYSS, OR WOULD YOU HAVE NOTHING?

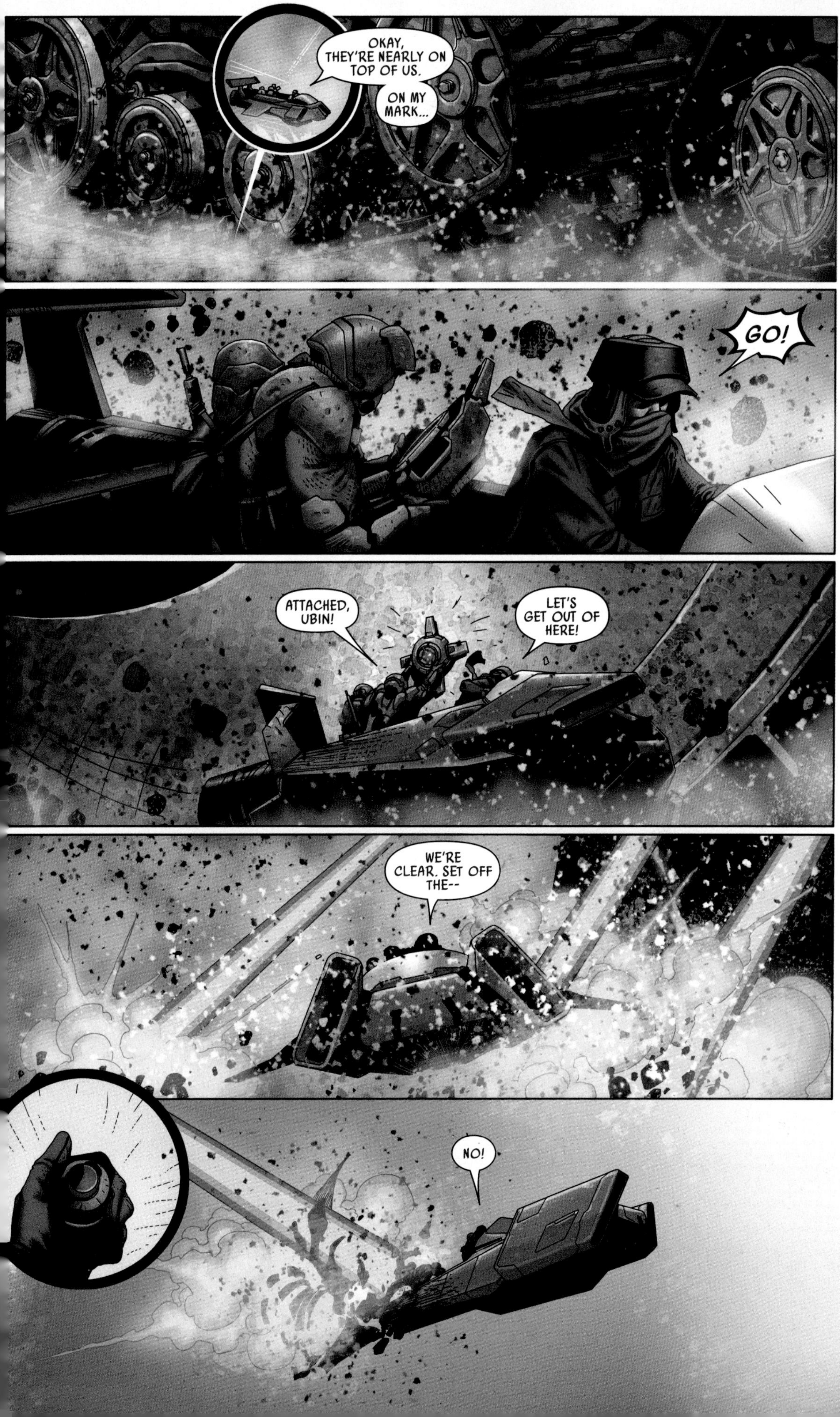
OKAY, THEY'RE NEARLY ON TOP OF US.
ON MY MARK...
GO!
ATTACHED, UBIN!
LET'S GET OUT OF HERE!
WE'RE CLEAR. SET OFF THE--
NO!

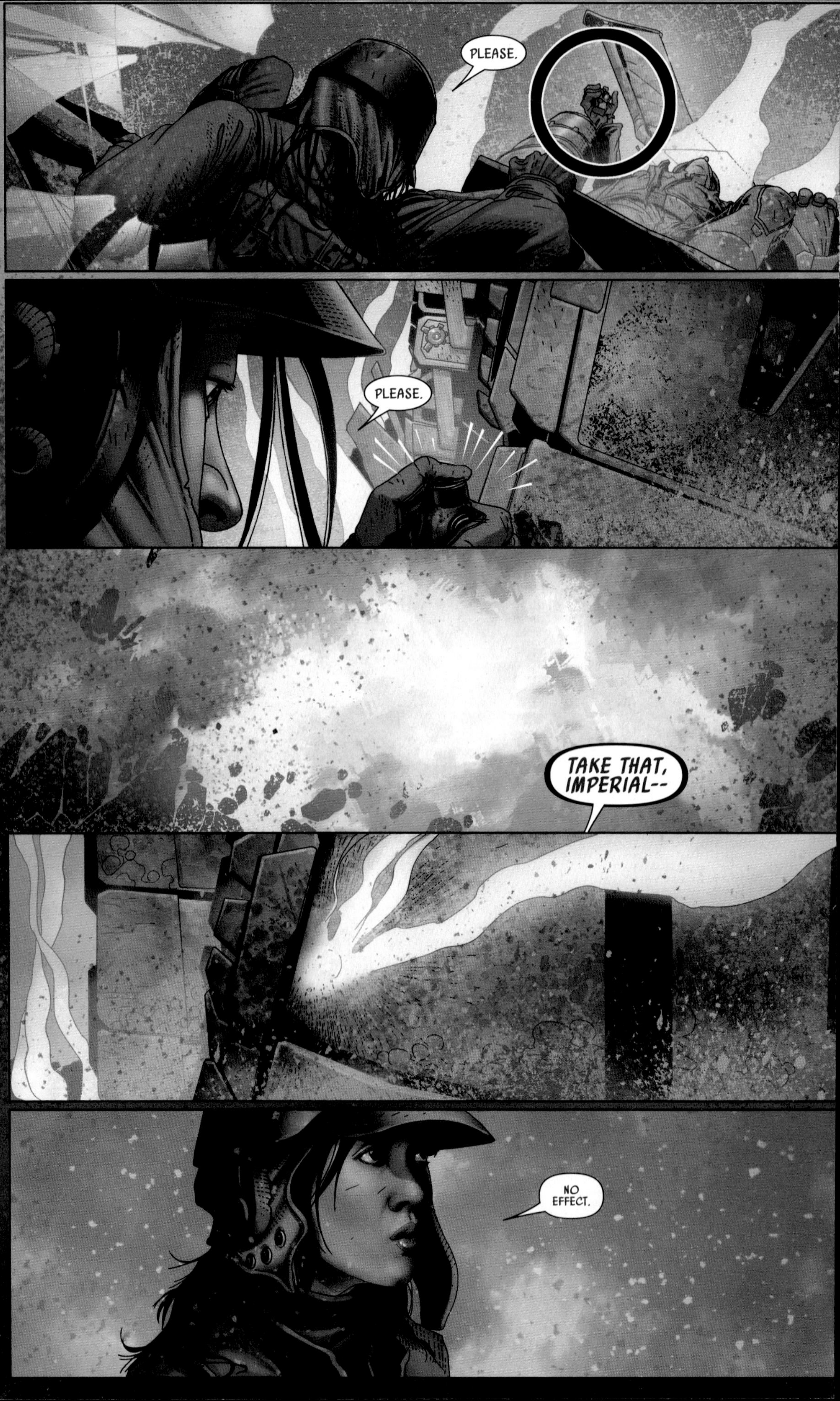
PLEASE.
PLEASE.
TAKE THAT, IMPERIAL--
NO EFFECT.

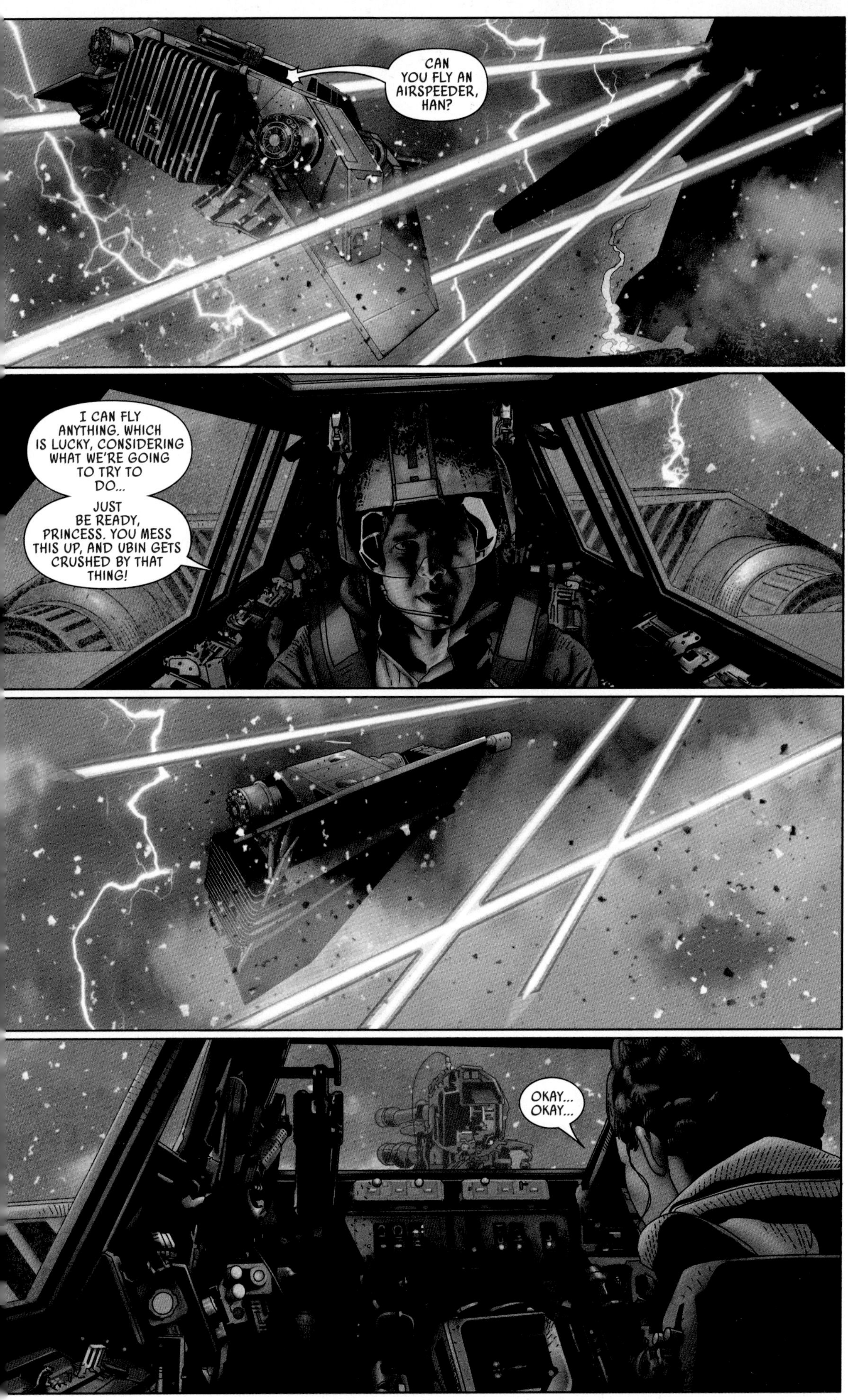
CAN YOU FLY AN AIRSPEEDER, HAN?
I CAN FLY ANYTHING. WHICH IS LUCKY, CONSIDERING WHAT WE'RE GOING TO TRY TO DO...
JUST BE READY, PRINCESS. YOU MESS THIS UP, AND UBIN GETS CRUSHED BY THAT THING!
OKAY... OKAY...

KLLNK

GOT HER.

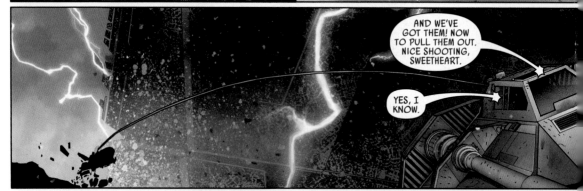

AND WE'VE GOT THEM! NOW TO PULL THEM OUT. NICE SHOOTING, SWEETHEART.

YES, I KNOW.

KRRRRNNNK

OKAY, WE'RE CLEAR, HAN. YOU SURE YOU CAN ACTUALLY GET THEM DOWN SAFELY?

I'D BETTER. RISKING OUR LIVES JUST TO KILL UBIN'S TEAM WOULD BE PLAIN PERVERSE.

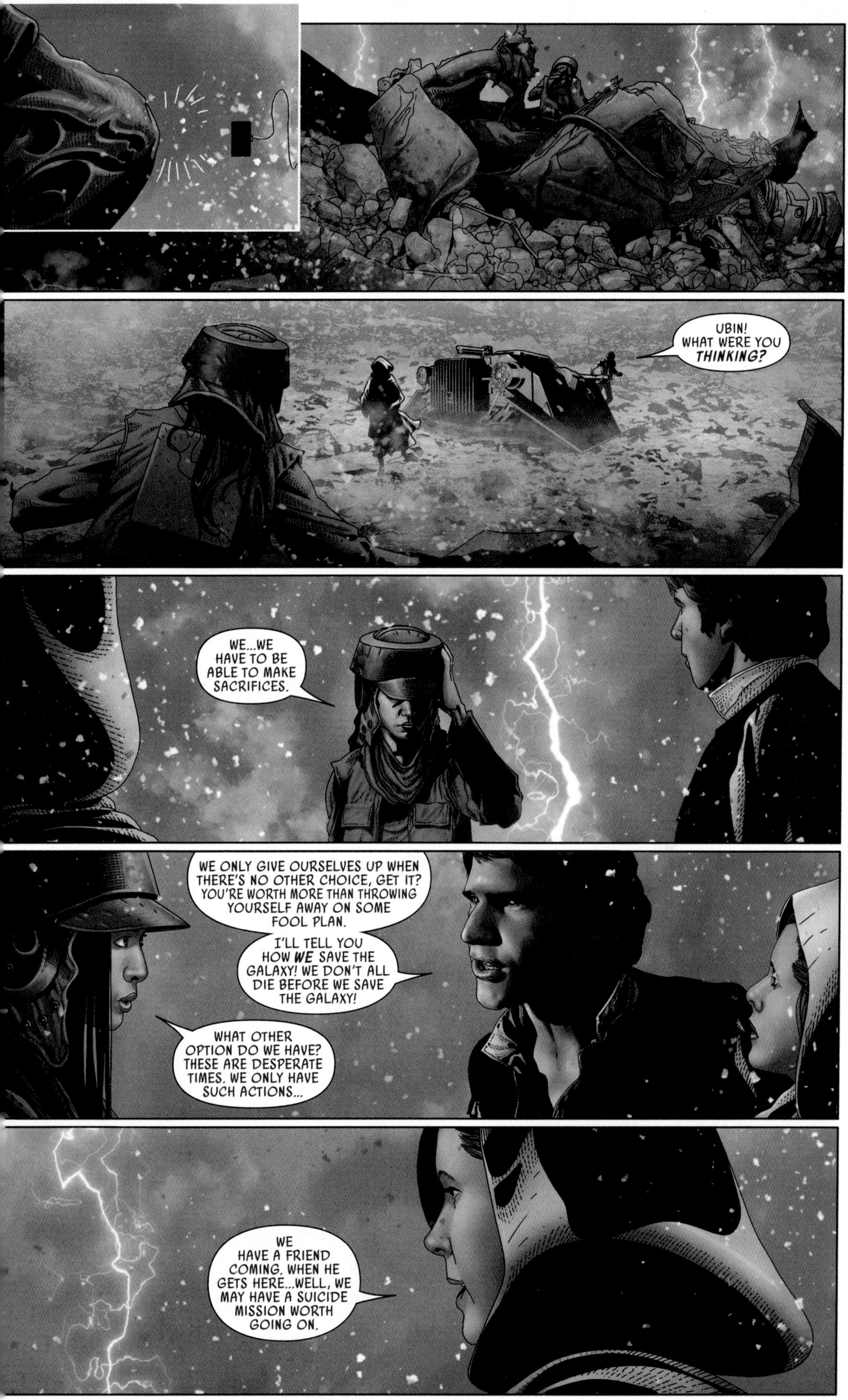
UBIN! WHAT WERE YOU *THINKING?*
WE...WE HAVE TO BE ABLE TO MAKE SACRIFICES.
WE ONLY GIVE OURSELVES UP WHEN THERE'S NO OTHER CHOICE, GET IT? YOU'RE WORTH MORE THAN THROWING YOURSELF AWAY ON SOME FOOL PLAN.
I'LL TELL YOU HOW *WE* SAVE THE GALAXY! WE DON'T ALL DIE BEFORE WE SAVE THE GALAXY!
WHAT OTHER OPTION DO WE HAVE? THESE ARE DESPERATE TIMES. WE ONLY HAVE SUCH ACTIONS...
WE HAVE A FRIEND COMING. WHEN HE GETS HERE...WELL, WE MAY HAVE A SUICIDE MISSION WORTH GOING ON.

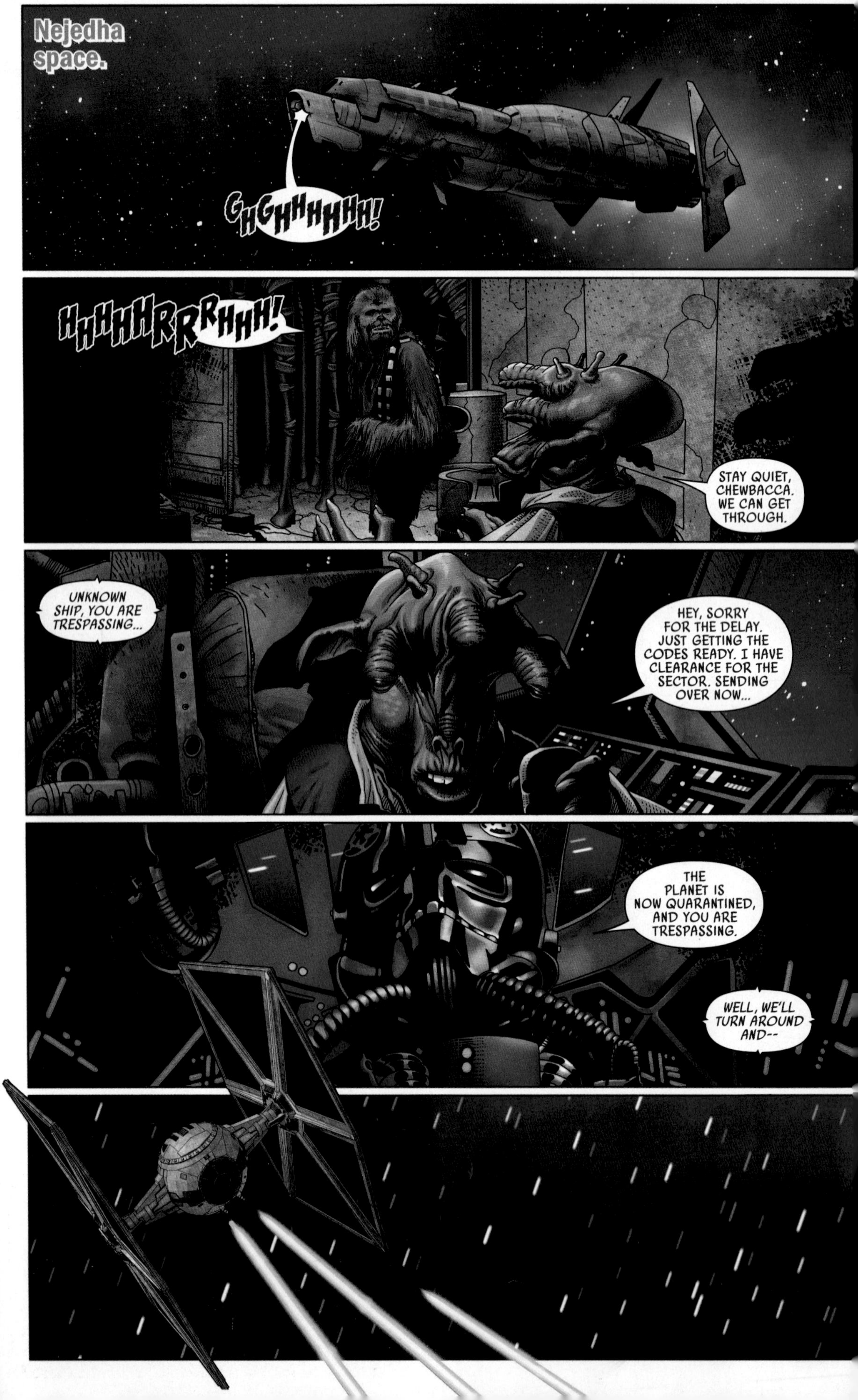
Nejedha space.
GHGHHHHHH!
HHHHHRRRHHH!
STAY QUIET, CHEWBACCA. WE CAN GET THROUGH.
UNKNOWN SHIP, YOU ARE TRESPASSING...
HEY, SORRY FOR THE DELAY. JUST GETTING THE CODES READY. I HAVE CLEARANCE FOR THE SECTOR. SENDING OVER NOW...
THE PLANET IS NOW QUARANTINED, AND YOU ARE TRESPASSING.
WELL, WE'LL TURN AROUND AND--

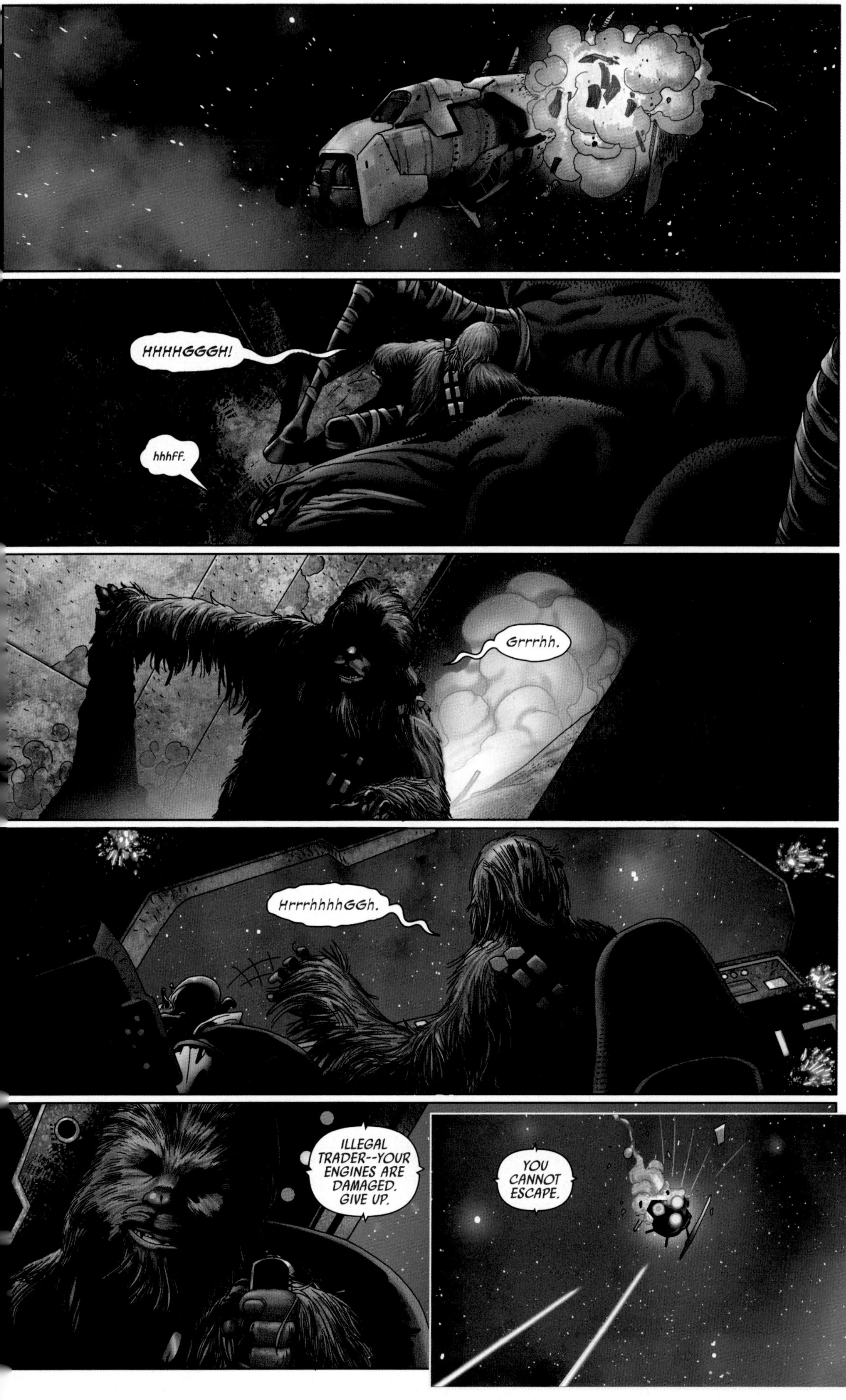
HHHHGGGH!
hhhff.
Grrrhh.
HrrrhhhhGGh.
ILLEGAL TRADER--YOUR ENGINES ARE DAMAGED. GIVE UP.
YOU CANNOT ESCAPE.

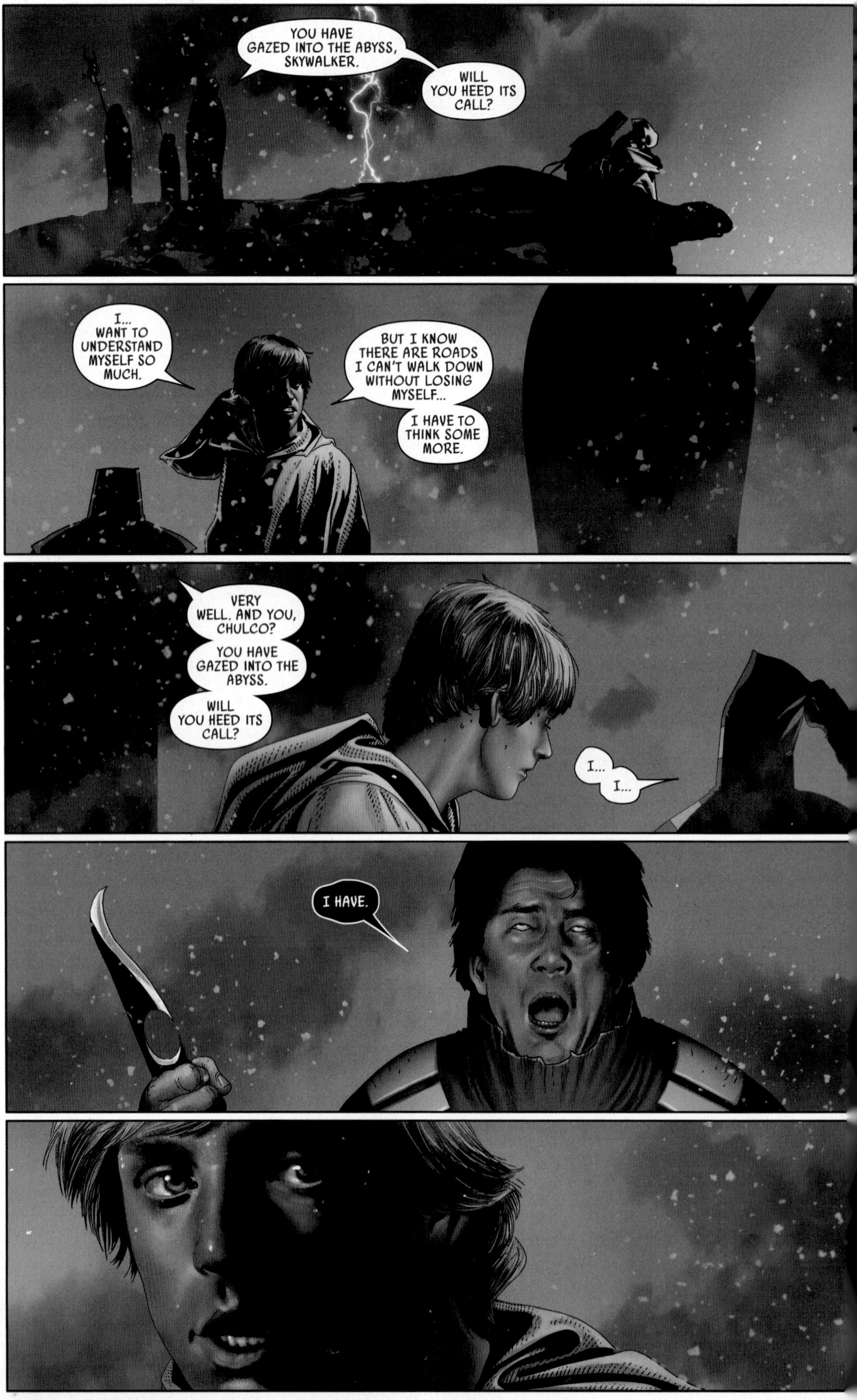
YOU HAVE GAZED INTO THE ABYSS, SKYWALKER.
WILL YOU HEED ITS CALL?
I... WANT TO UNDERSTAND MYSELF SO MUCH.
BUT I KNOW THERE ARE ROADS I CAN'T WALK DOWN WITHOUT LOSING MYSELF...
I HAVE TO THINK SOME MORE.
VERY WELL. AND YOU, CHULCO?
YOU HAVE GAZED INTO THE ABYSS.
WILL YOU HEED ITS CALL?
I...
I...
I HAVE.

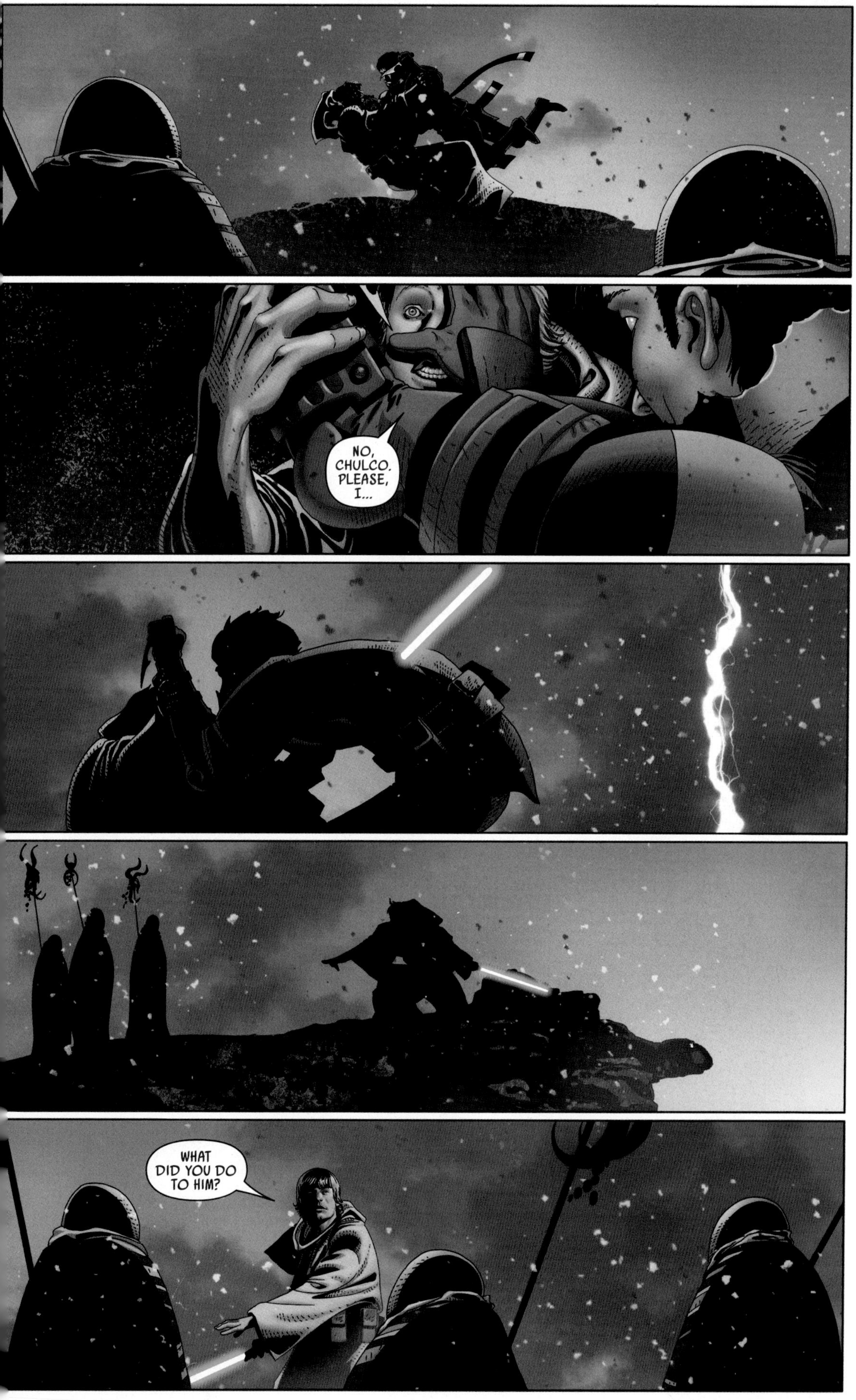
NO, CHULCO. PLEASE, I...
WHAT DID YOU DO TO HIM?

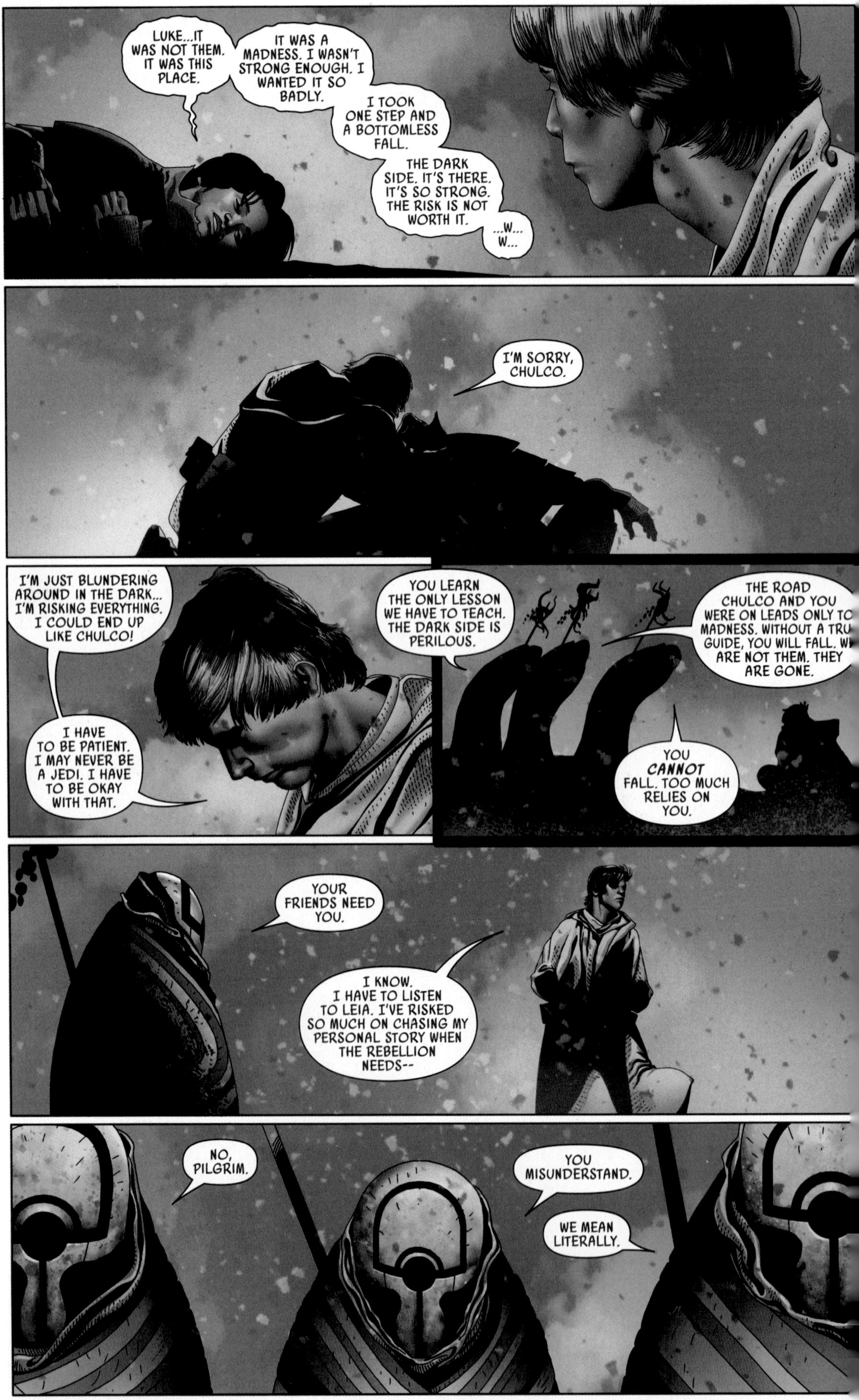

LUKE...IT WAS NOT THEM. IT WAS THIS PLACE.
IT WAS A MADNESS. I WASN'T STRONG ENOUGH. I WANTED IT SO BADLY.
I TOOK ONE STEP AND A BOTTOMLESS FALL.
THE DARK SIDE. IT'S THERE. IT'S SO STRONG. THE RISK IS NOT WORTH IT.
...W... W...
I'M SORRY, CHULCO.
I'M JUST BLUNDERING AROUND IN THE DARK... I'M RISKING EVERYTHING. I COULD END UP LIKE CHULCO!
I HAVE TO BE PATIENT. I MAY NEVER BE A JEDI. I HAVE TO BE OKAY WITH THAT.
YOU LEARN THE ONLY LESSON WE HAVE TO TEACH. THE DARK SIDE IS PERILOUS.
YOU CANNOT FALL. TOO MUCH RELIES ON YOU.
YOUR FRIENDS NEED YOU.
I KNOW. I HAVE TO LISTEN TO LEIA. I'VE RISKED SO MUCH ON CHASING MY PERSONAL STORY WHEN THE REBELLION NEEDS--
NO, PILGRIM.
YOU MISUNDERSTAND.
WE MEAN LITERALLY.

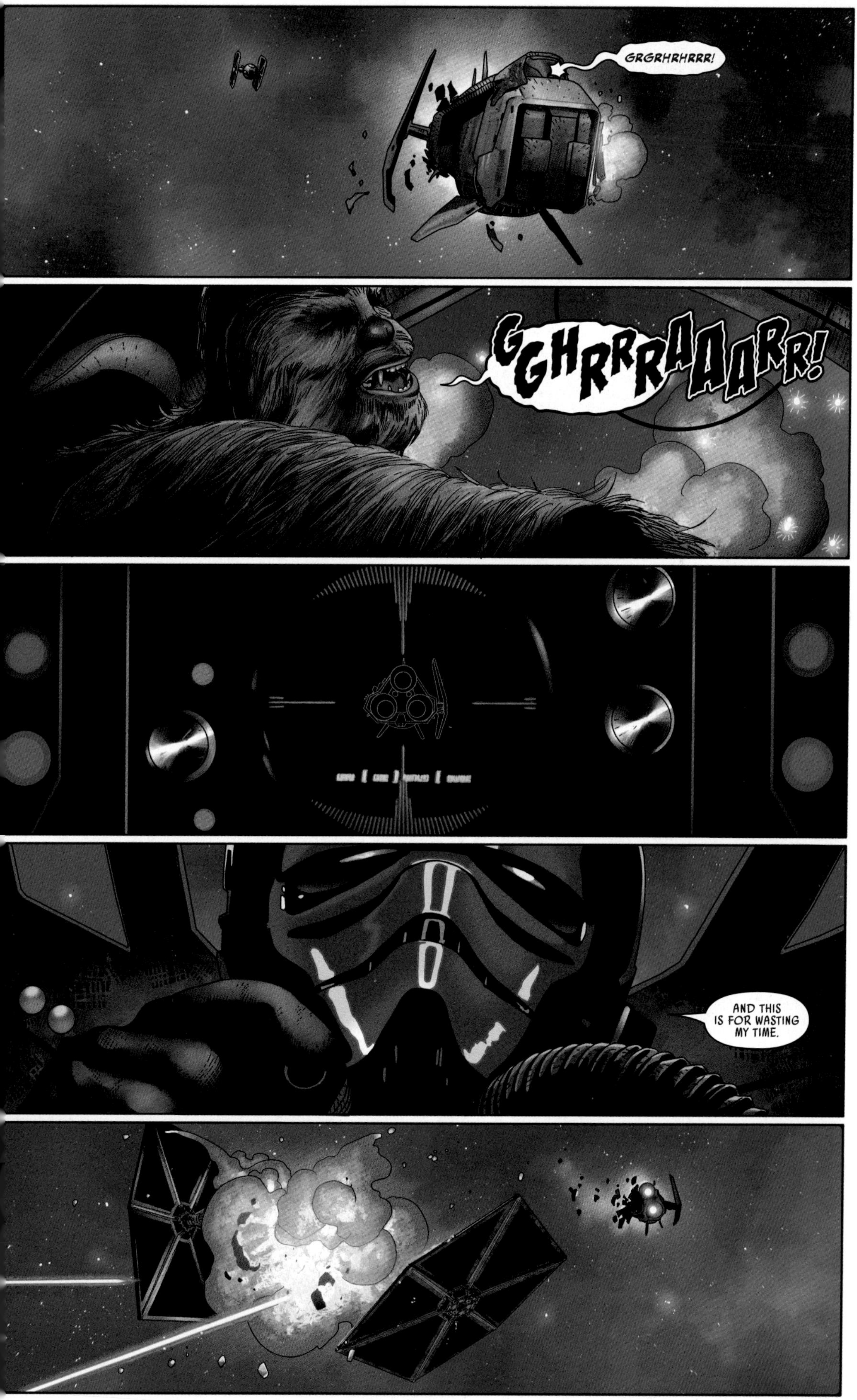
GRGRHRHRRR!
GGHRRRAAARRR!
AND THIS IS FOR WASTING MY TIME.

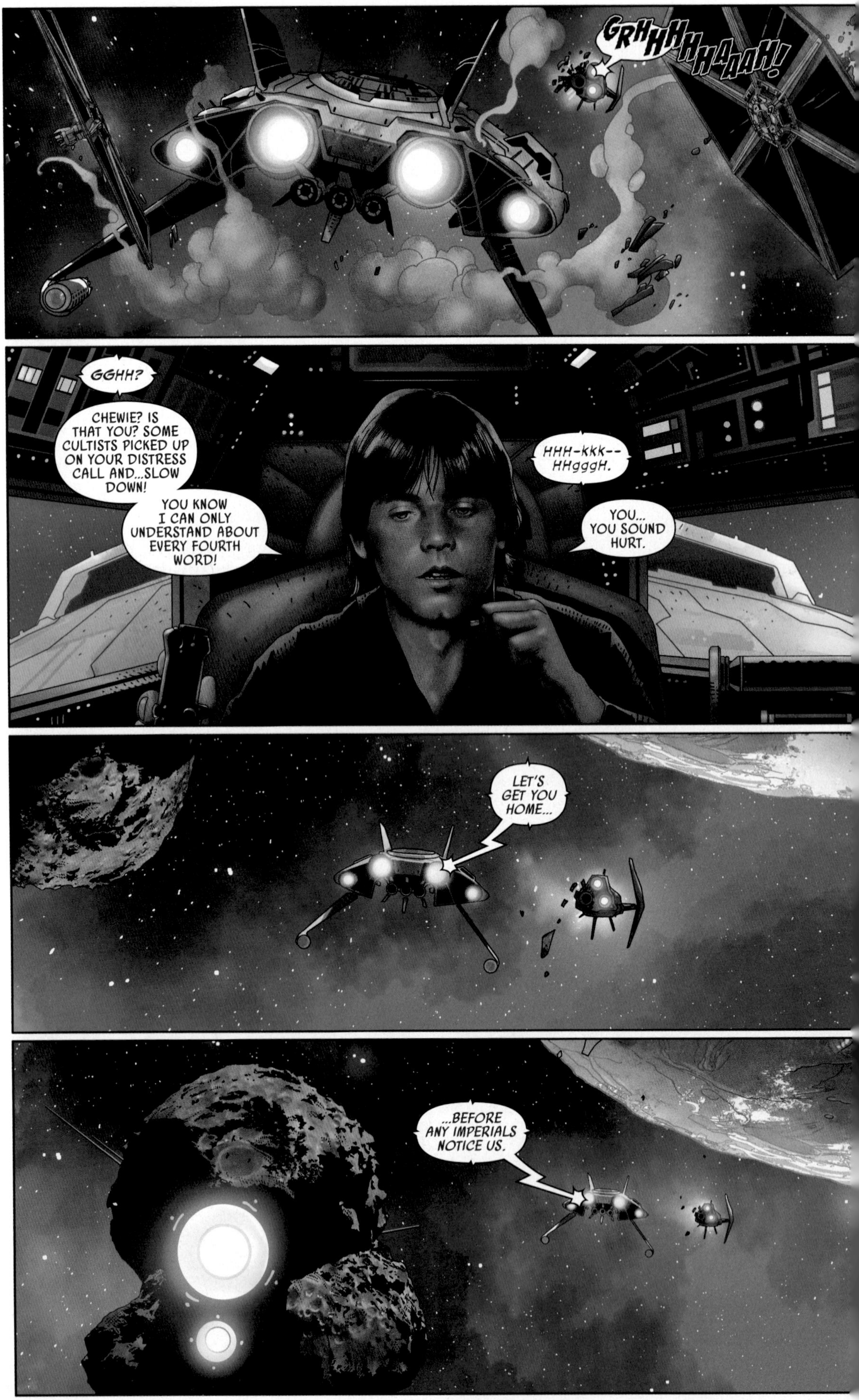
GRHHHHHAAAH!
GGHH?
CHEWIE? IS THAT YOU? SOME CULTISTS PICKED UP ON YOUR DISTRESS CALL AND...SLOW DOWN!
YOU KNOW I CAN ONLY UNDERSTAND ABOUT EVERY FOURTH WORD!
HHH-kkk--HHgggH.
YOU... YOU SOUND HURT.
LET'S GET YOU HOME...
...BEFORE ANY IMPERIALS NOTICE US.

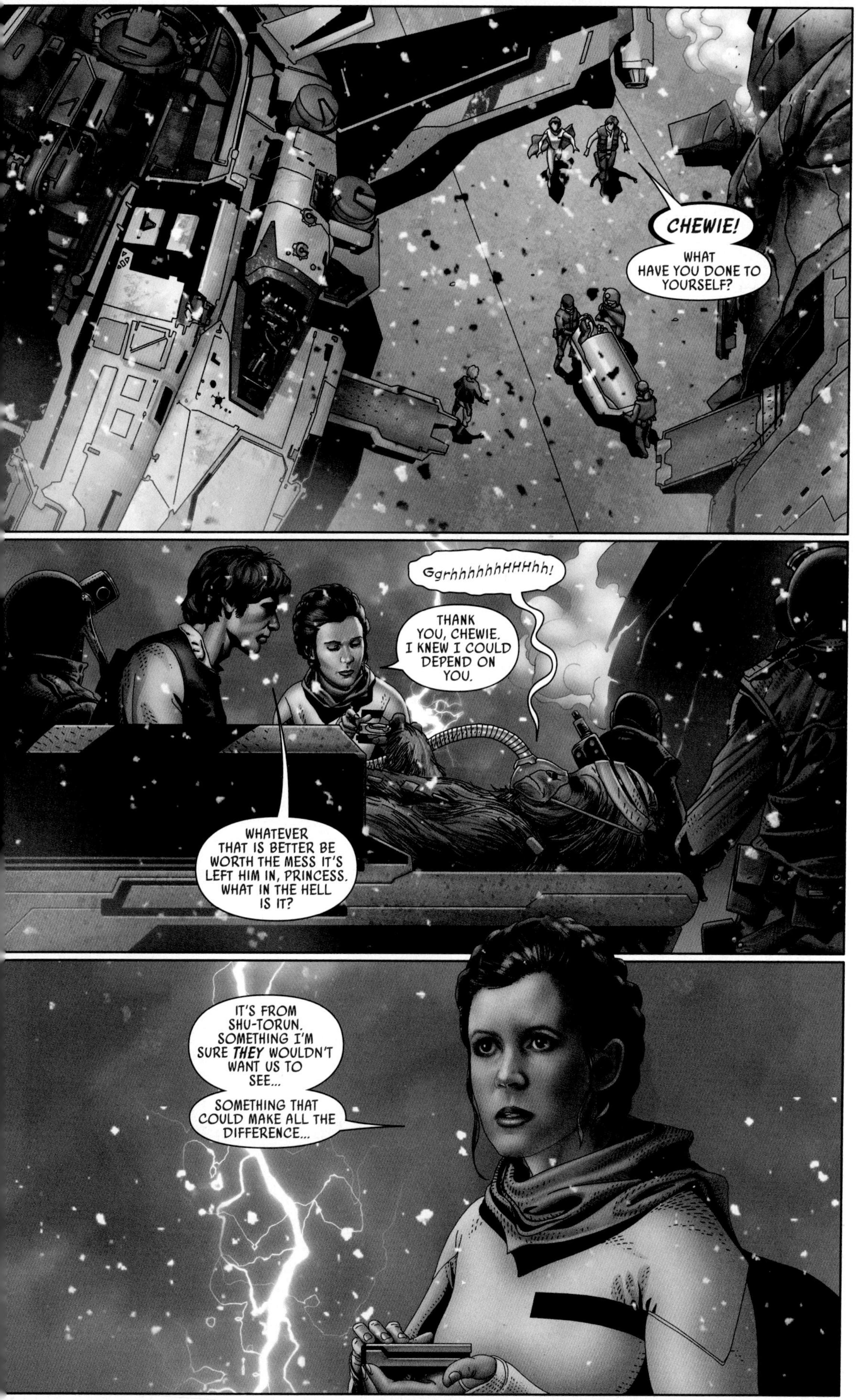
CHEWIE!
WHAT HAVE YOU DONE TO YOURSELF?
Ggrhhhhhhhhhh!
THANK YOU, CHEWIE. I KNEW I COULD DEPEND ON YOU.
WHATEVER THAT IS BETTER BE WORTH THE MESS IT'S LEFT HIM IN, PRINCESS. WHAT IN THE HELL IS IT?
IT'S FROM SHU-TORUN. SOMETHING I'M SURE *THEY* WOULDN'T WANT US TO SEE...
SOMETHING THAT COULD MAKE ALL THE DIFFERENCE...

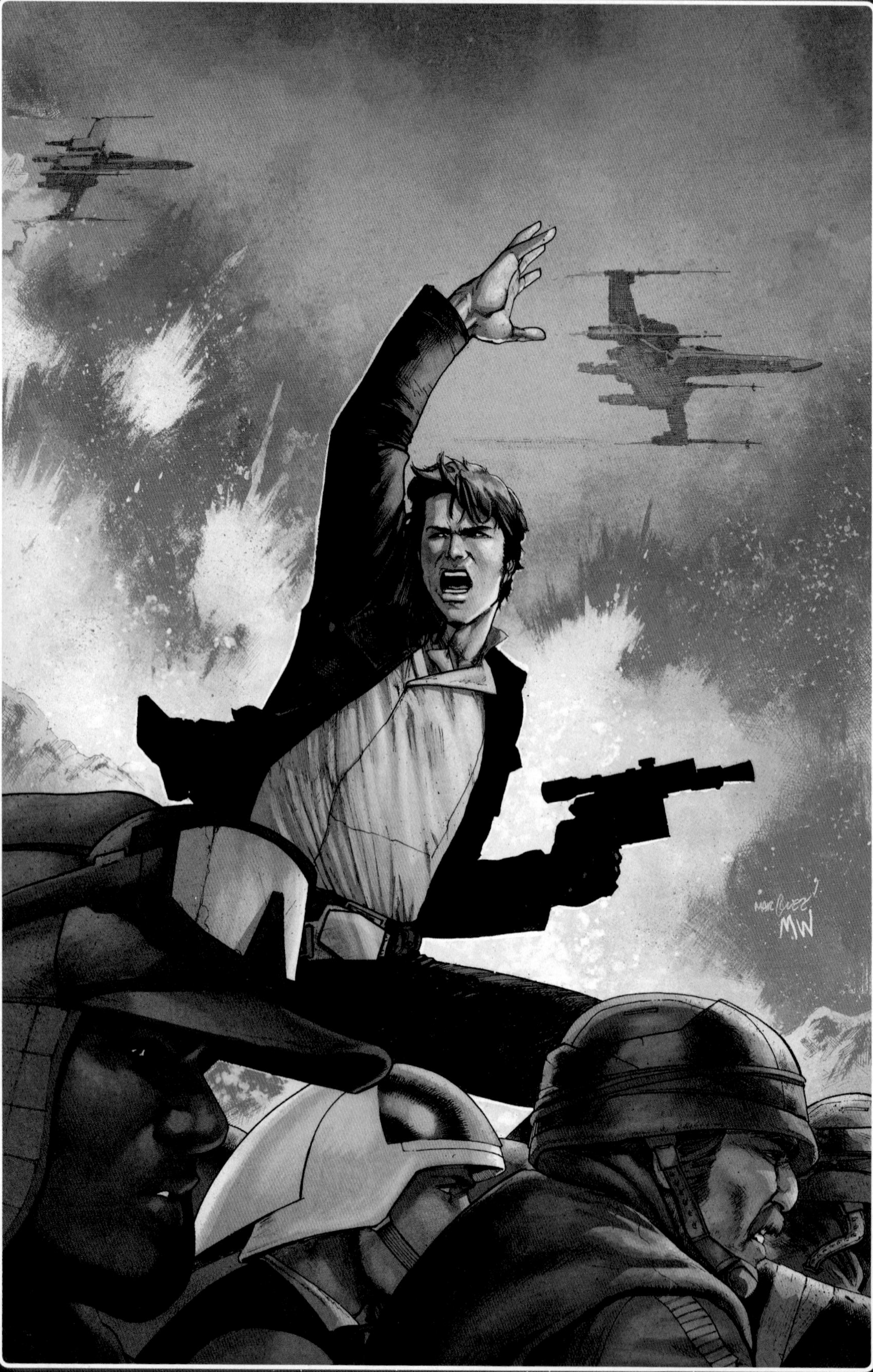

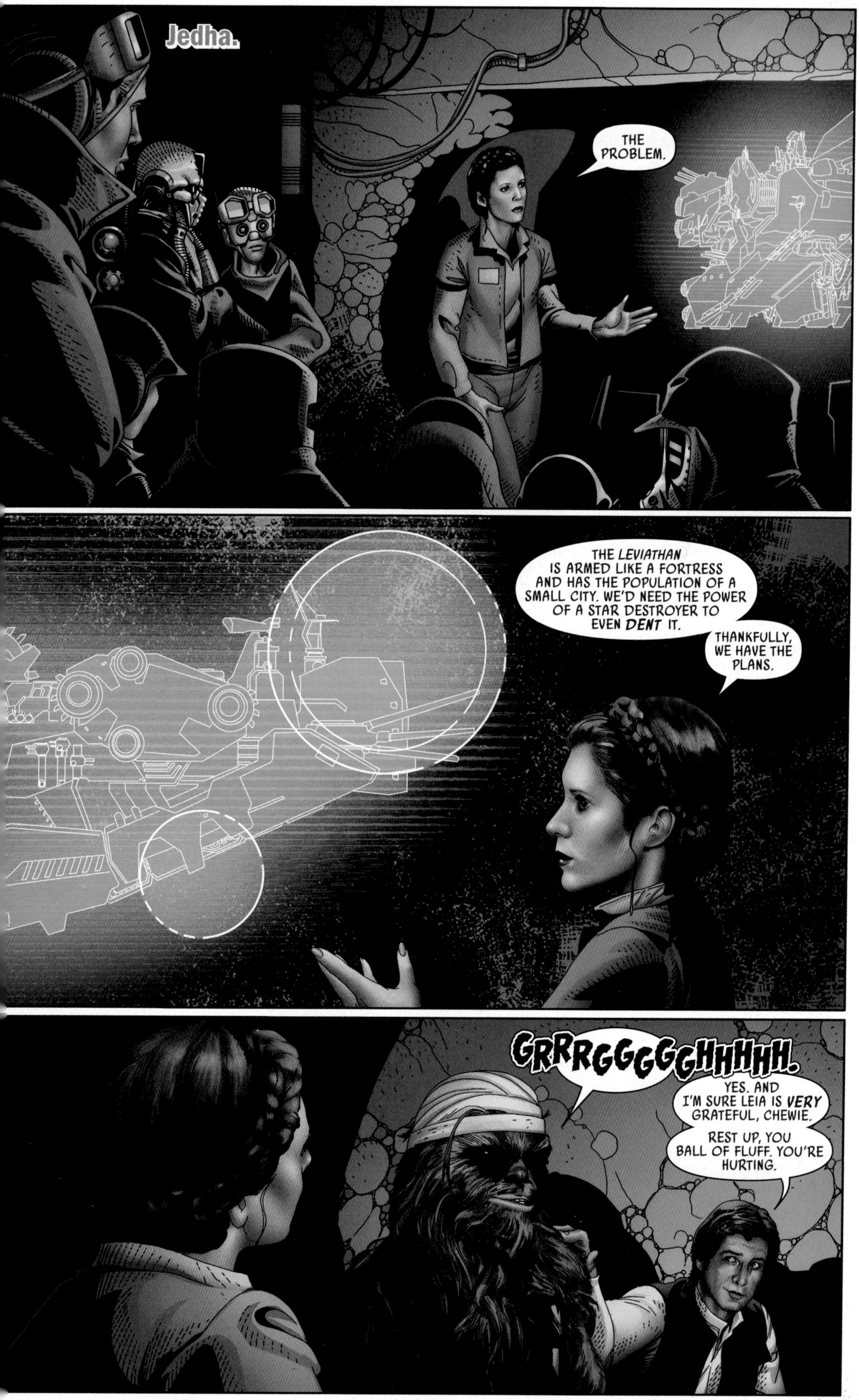
Jedha.
THE PROBLEM.
THE *LEVIATHAN* IS ARMED LIKE A FORTRESS AND HAS THE POPULATION OF A SMALL CITY. WE'D NEED THE POWER OF A STAR DESTROYER TO EVEN ***DENT*** IT.
THANKFULLY, WE HAVE THE PLANS.
GRRRGGGGGHHHHH.
YES. AND I'M SURE LEIA IS ***VERY*** GRATEFUL, CHEWIE.
REST UP, YOU BALL OF FLUFF. YOU'RE HURTING.

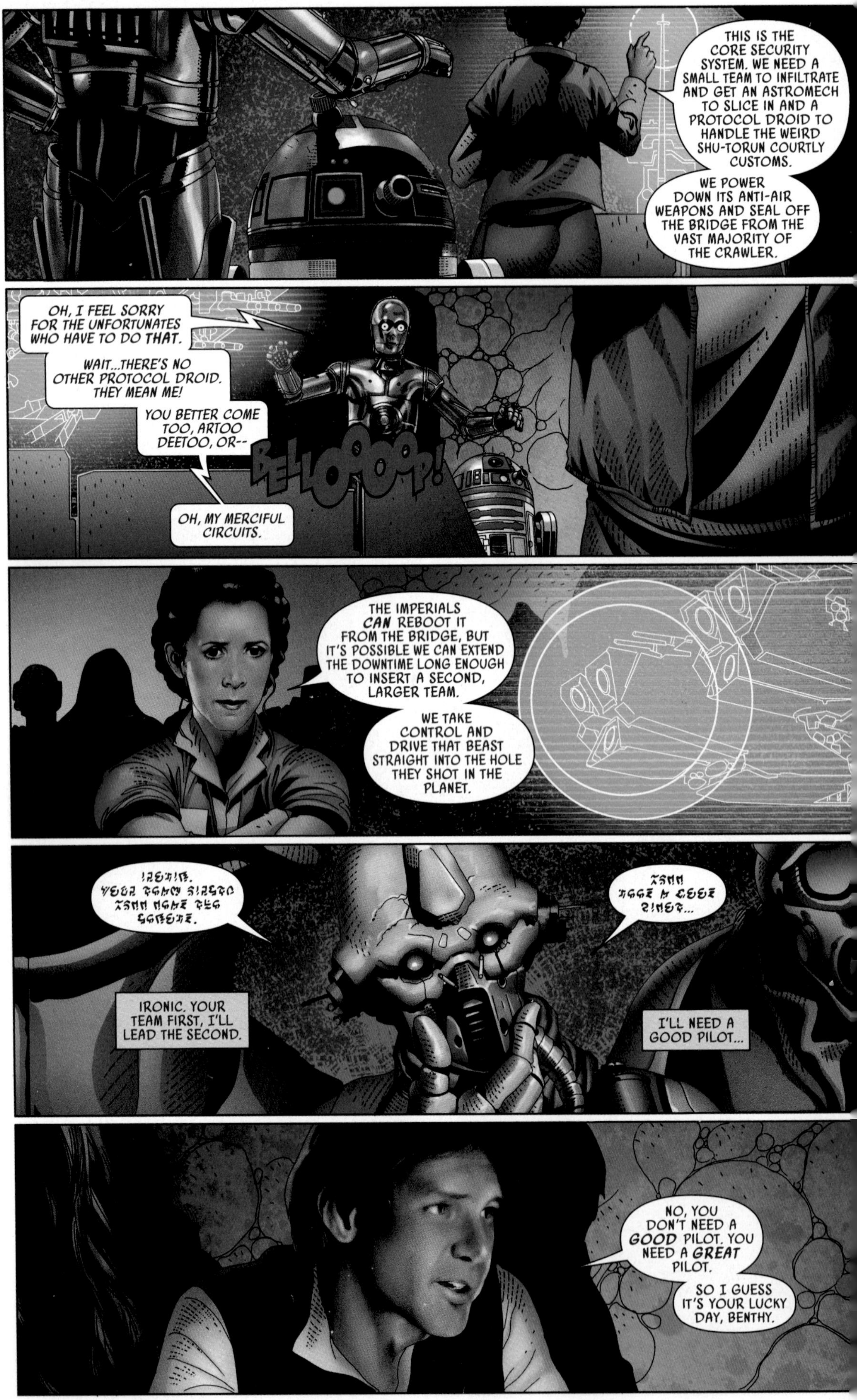
THIS IS THE CORE SECURITY SYSTEM. WE NEED A SMALL TEAM TO INFILTRATE AND GET AN ASTROMECH TO SLICE IN AND A PROTOCOL DROID TO HANDLE THE WEIRD SHU-TORUN COURTLY CUSTOMS.
WE POWER DOWN ITS ANTI-AIR WEAPONS AND SEAL OFF THE BRIDGE FROM THE VAST MAJORITY OF THE CRAWLER.
OH, I FEEL SORRY FOR THE UNFORTUNATES WHO HAVE TO DO THAT.
WAIT...THERE'S NO OTHER PROTOCOL DROID. THEY MEAN ME!
YOU BETTER COME TOO, ARTOO DEETOO, OR--
BELLOOOOP!
OH, MY MERCIFUL CIRCUITS.
THE IMPERIALS CAN REBOOT IT FROM THE BRIDGE, BUT IT'S POSSIBLE WE CAN EXTEND THE DOWNTIME LONG ENOUGH TO INSERT A SECOND, LARGER TEAM.
WE TAKE CONTROL AND DRIVE THAT BEAST STRAIGHT INTO THE HOLE THEY SHOT IN THE PLANET.
IRONIC. YOUR TEAM FIRST, I'LL LEAD THE SECOND.
I'LL NEED A GOOD PILOT...
NO, YOU DON'T NEED A GOOD PILOT. YOU NEED A GREAT PILOT.
SO I GUESS IT'S YOUR LUCKY DAY, BENTHY.

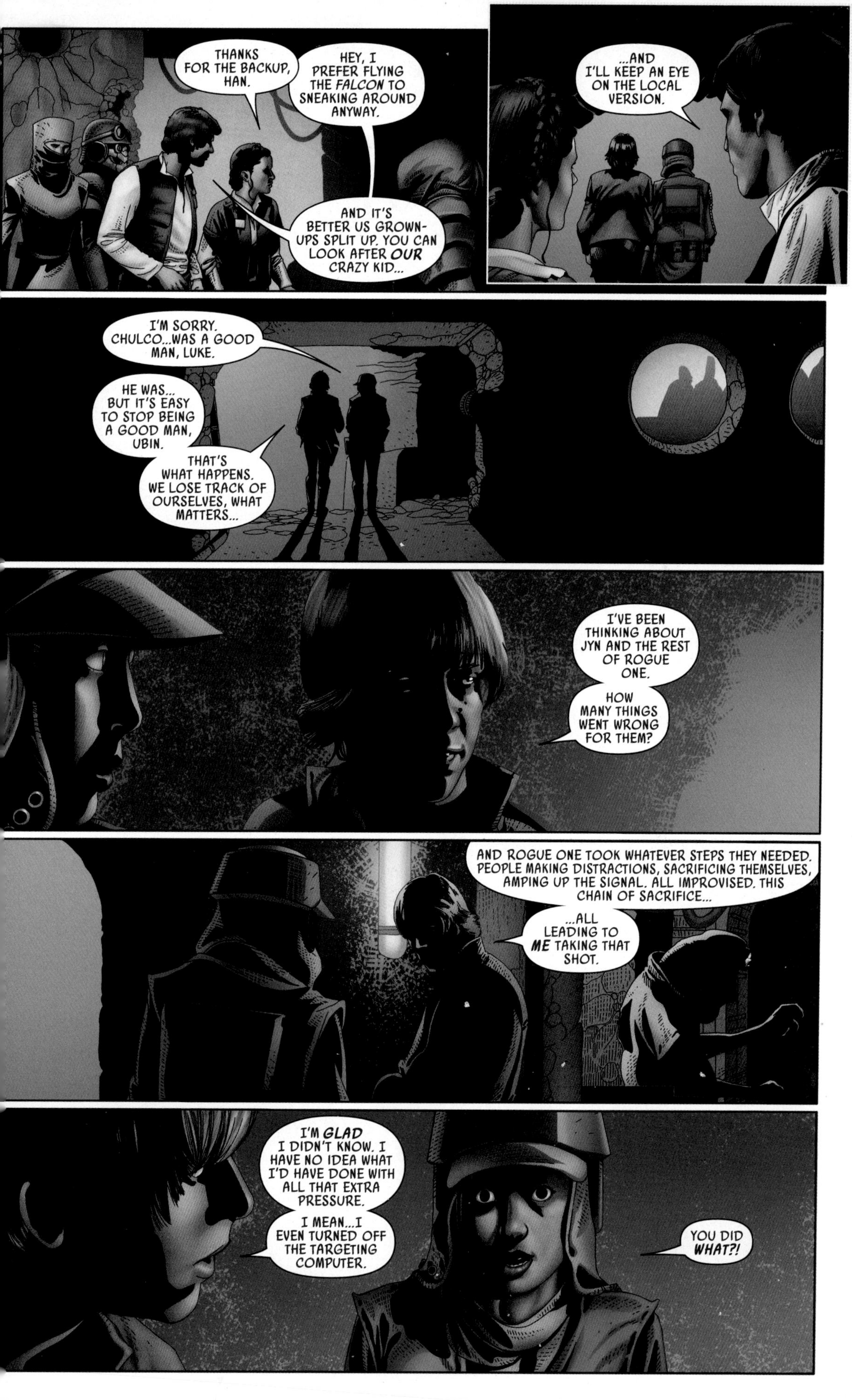
THANKS FOR THE BACKUP, HAN.
HEY, I PREFER FLYING THE FALCON TO SNEAKING AROUND ANYWAY.
AND IT'S BETTER US GROWN-UPS SPLIT UP. YOU CAN LOOK AFTER OUR CRAZY KID...
...AND I'LL KEEP AN EYE ON THE LOCAL VERSION.
I'M SORRY. CHULCO...WAS A GOOD MAN, LUKE.
HE WAS... BUT IT'S EASY TO STOP BEING A GOOD MAN, UBIN.
THAT'S WHAT HAPPENS. WE LOSE TRACK OF OURSELVES, WHAT MATTERS...
I'VE BEEN THINKING ABOUT JYN AND THE REST OF ROGUE ONE.
HOW MANY THINGS WENT WRONG FOR THEM?
AND ROGUE ONE TOOK WHATEVER STEPS THEY NEEDED. PEOPLE MAKING DISTRACTIONS, SACRIFICING THEMSELVES, AMPING UP THE SIGNAL. ALL IMPROVISED. THIS CHAIN OF SACRIFICE...
...ALL LEADING TO ME TAKING THAT SHOT.
I'M GLAD I DIDN'T KNOW. I HAVE NO IDEA WHAT I'D HAVE DONE WITH ALL THAT EXTRA PRESSURE.
I MEAN...I EVEN TURNED OFF THE TARGETING COMPUTER.
YOU DID WHAT?!

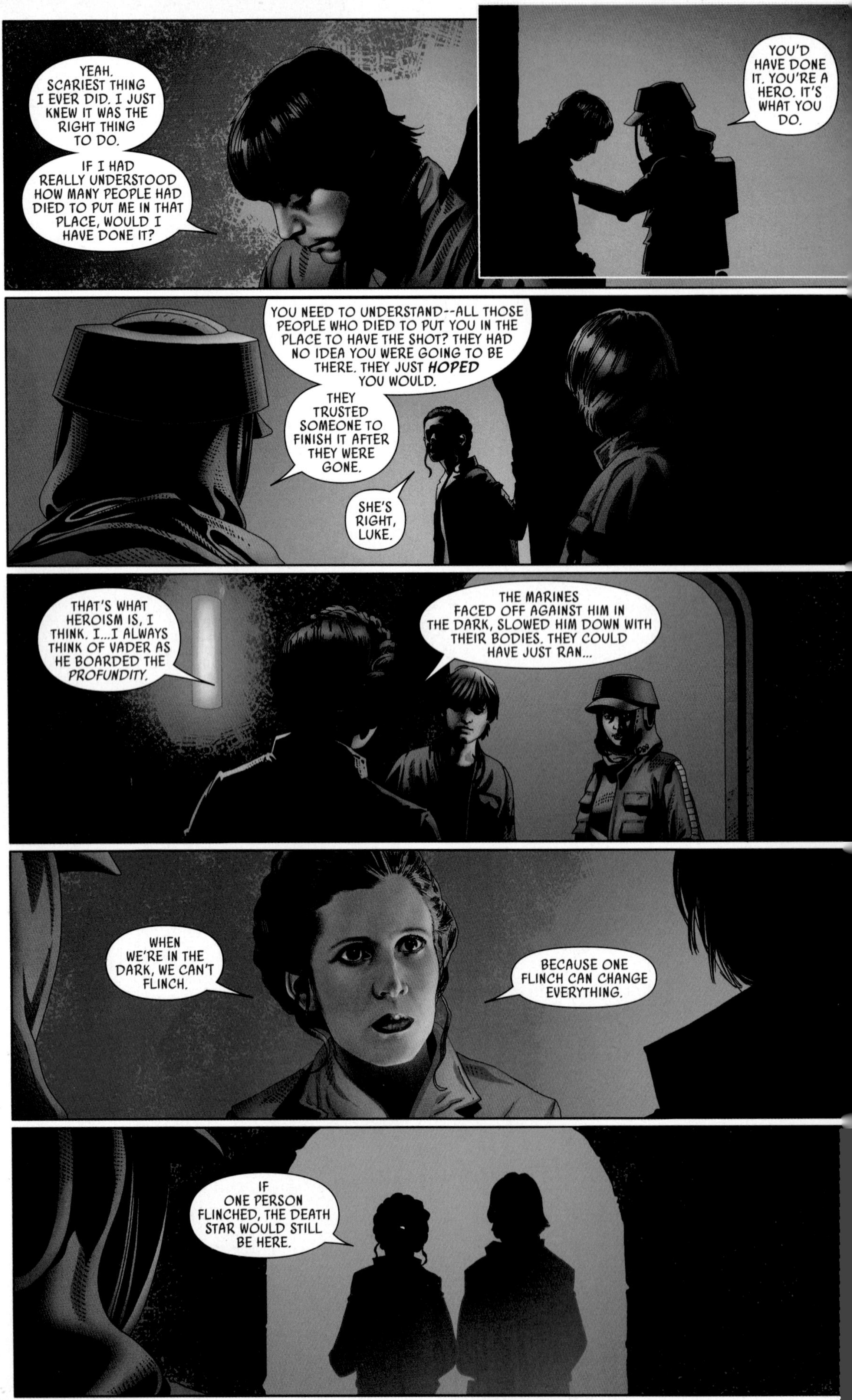
YEAH. SCARIEST THING I EVER DID. I JUST KNEW IT WAS THE RIGHT THING TO DO.
IF I HAD REALLY UNDERSTOOD HOW MANY PEOPLE HAD DIED TO PUT ME IN THAT PLACE, WOULD I HAVE DONE IT?
YOU'D HAVE DONE IT. YOU'RE A HERO. IT'S WHAT YOU DO.
YOU NEED TO UNDERSTAND--ALL THOSE PEOPLE WHO DIED TO PUT YOU IN THE PLACE TO HAVE THE SHOT? THEY HAD NO IDEA YOU WERE GOING TO BE THERE. THEY JUST **HOPED** YOU WOULD.
THEY TRUSTED SOMEONE TO FINISH IT AFTER THEY WERE GONE.
SHE'S RIGHT, LUKE.
THAT'S WHAT HEROISM IS, I THINK. I...I ALWAYS THINK OF VADER AS HE BOARDED THE *PROFUNDITY.*
THE MARINES FACED OFF AGAINST HIM IN THE DARK, SLOWED HIM DOWN WITH THEIR BODIES. THEY COULD HAVE JUST RAN...
WHEN WE'RE IN THE DARK, WE CAN'T FLINCH.
BECAUSE ONE FLINCH CAN CHANGE EVERYTHING.
IF ONE PERSON FLINCHED, THE DEATH STAR WOULD STILL BE HERE.

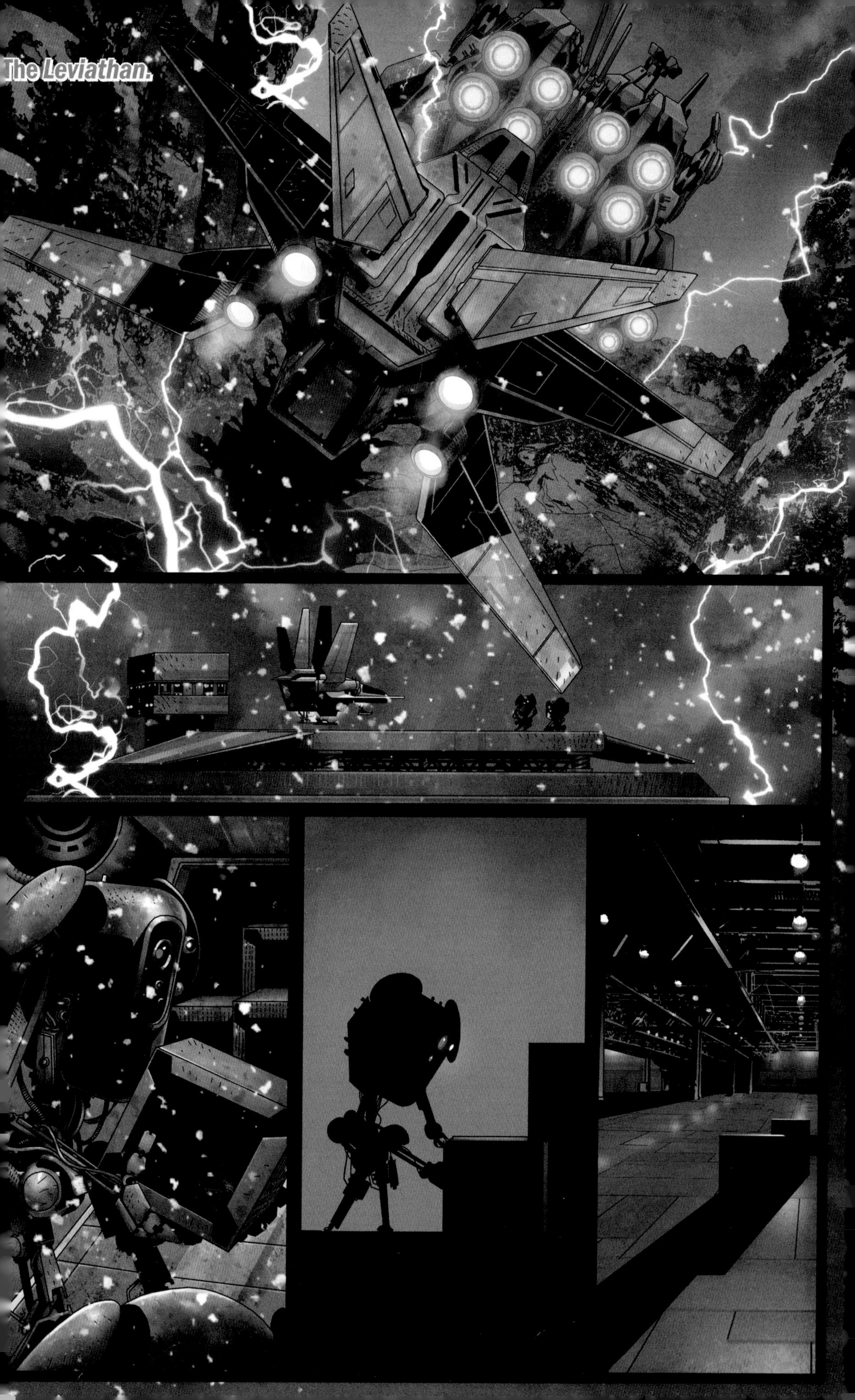
The Leviathan.

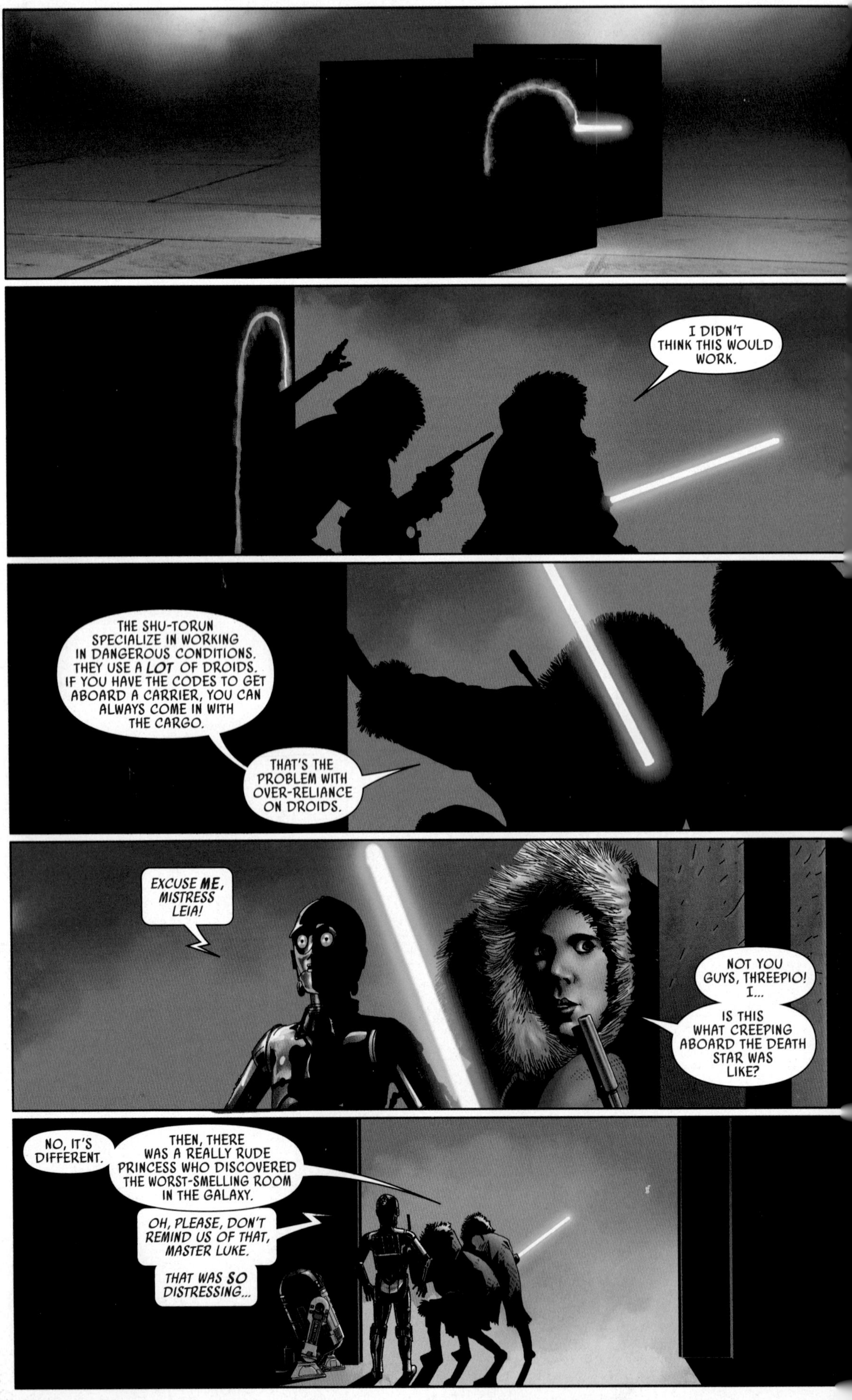
I DIDN'T THINK THIS WOULD WORK.
THE SHU-TORUN SPECIALIZE IN WORKING IN DANGEROUS CONDITIONS. THEY USE A LOT OF DROIDS. IF YOU HAVE THE CODES TO GET ABOARD A CARRIER, YOU CAN ALWAYS COME IN WITH THE CARGO.
THAT'S THE PROBLEM WITH OVER-RELIANCE ON DROIDS.
EXCUSE ME, MISTRESS LEIA!
NOT YOU GUYS, THREEPIO! I...
IS THIS WHAT CREEPING ABOARD THE DEATH STAR WAS LIKE?
NO, IT'S DIFFERENT.
THEN, THERE WAS A REALLY RUDE PRINCESS WHO DISCOVERED THE WORST-SMELLING ROOM IN THE GALAXY.
OH, PLEASE, DON'T REMIND US OF THAT, MASTER LUKE.
THAT WAS SO DISTRESSING...

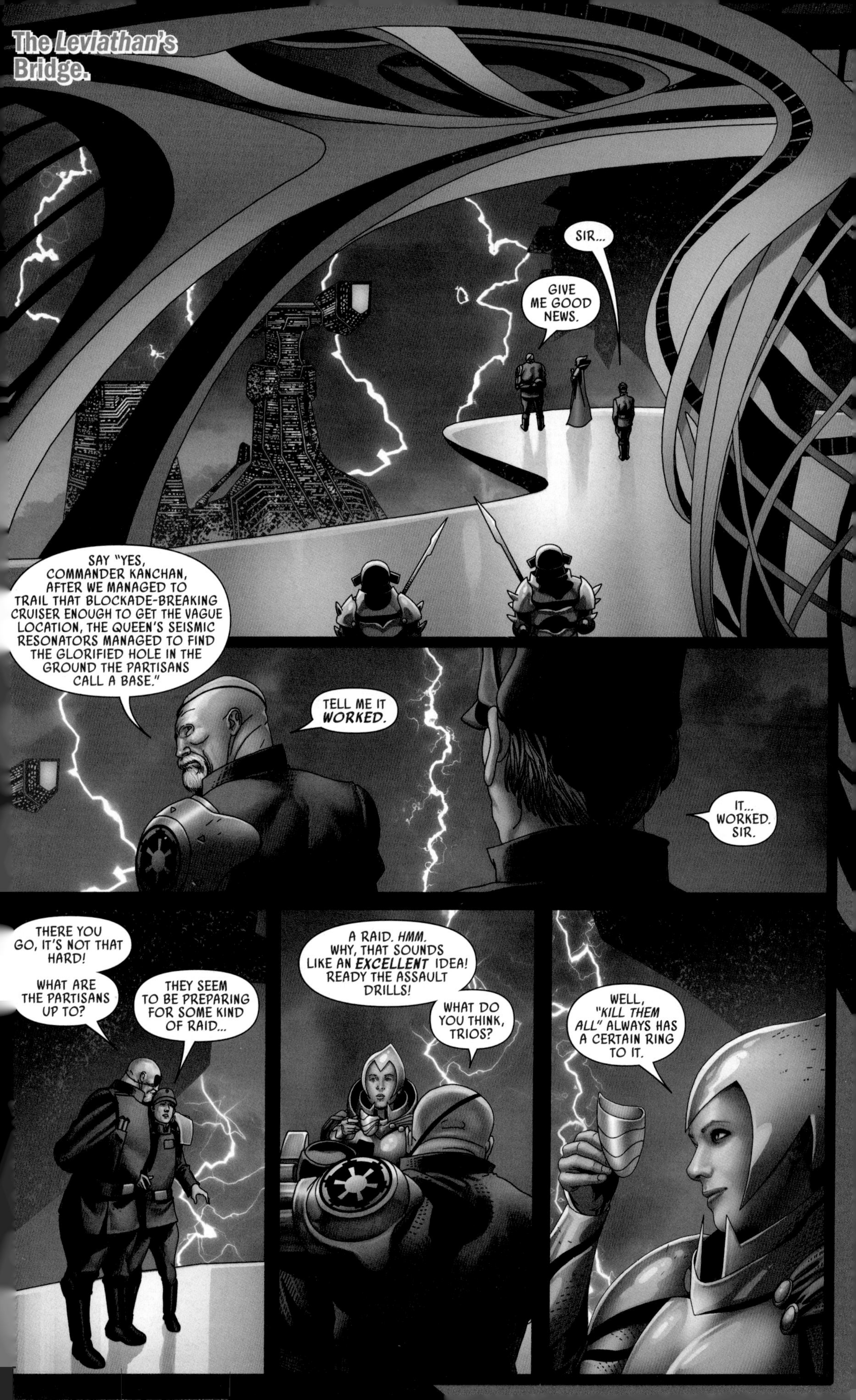
The Leviathan's Bridge.
SIR...
GIVE ME GOOD NEWS.
SAY "YES, COMMANDER KANCHAN, AFTER WE MANAGED TO TRAIL THAT BLOCKADE-BREAKING CRUISER ENOUGH TO GET THE VAGUE LOCATION, THE QUEEN'S SEISMIC RESONATORS MANAGED TO FIND THE GLORIFIED HOLE IN THE GROUND THE PARTISANS CALL A BASE."
TELL ME IT WORKED.
IT... WORKED. SIR.
THERE YOU GO, IT'S NOT THAT HARD!
WHAT ARE THE PARTISANS UP TO?
THEY SEEM TO BE PREPARING FOR SOME KIND OF RAID...
A RAID. HMM. WHY, THAT SOUNDS LIKE AN EXCELLENT IDEA! READY THE ASSAULT DRILLS!
WHAT DO YOU THINK, TRIOS?
WELL, "KILL THEM ALL" ALWAYS HAS A CERTAIN RING TO IT.

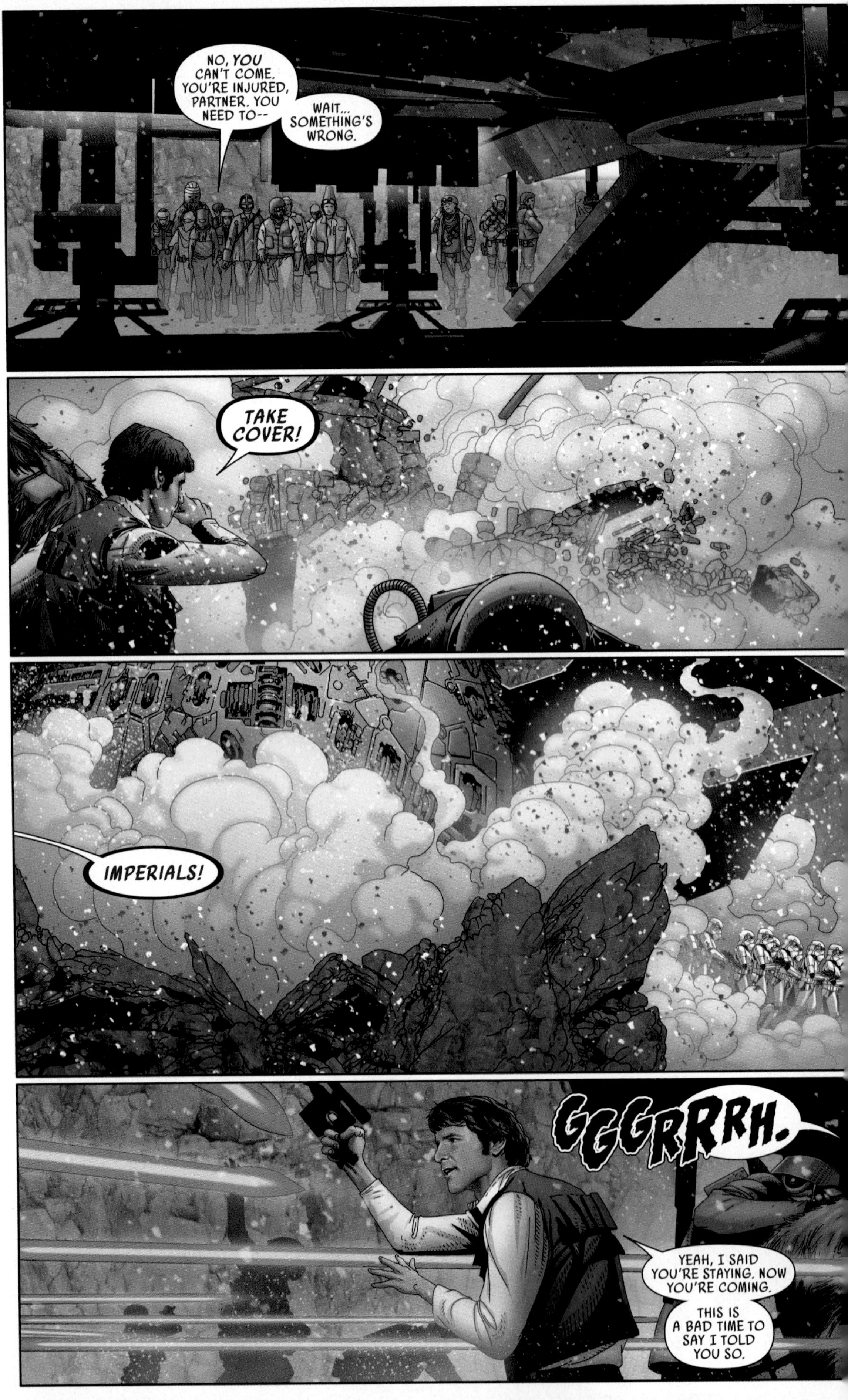

NO, YOU CAN'T COME. YOU'RE INJURED, PARTNER. YOU NEED TO--
WAIT... SOMETHING'S WRONG.
TAKE COVER!
IMPERIALS!
GGGRRRH.
YEAH, I SAID YOU'RE STAYING. NOW YOU'RE COMING.
THIS IS A BAD TIME TO SAY I TOLD YOU SO.

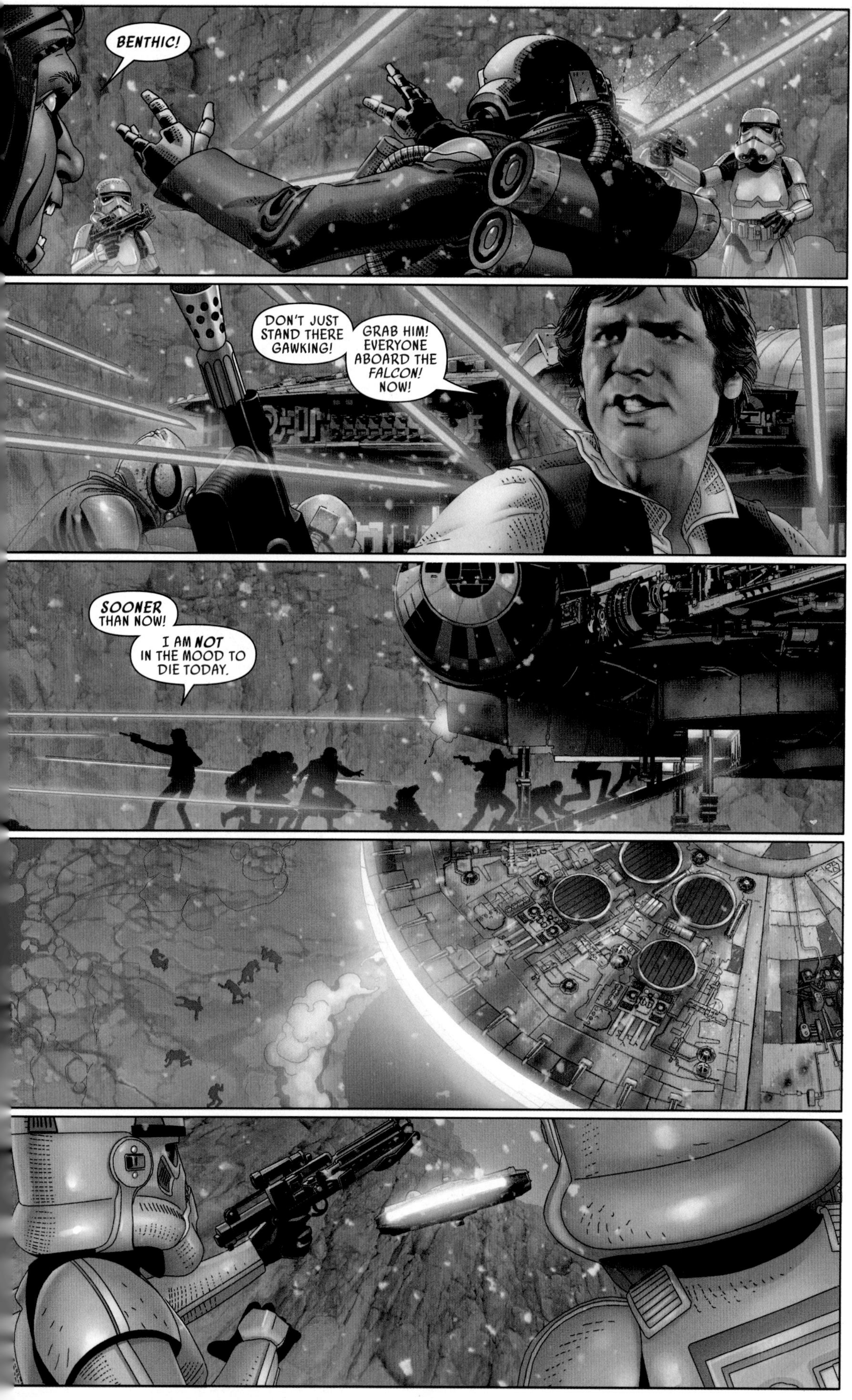
BENTHIC!
DON'T JUST STAND THERE GAWKING!
GRAB HIM! EVERYONE ABOARD THE FALCON! NOW!
SOONER THAN NOW!
I AM NOT IN THE MOOD TO DIE TODAY.

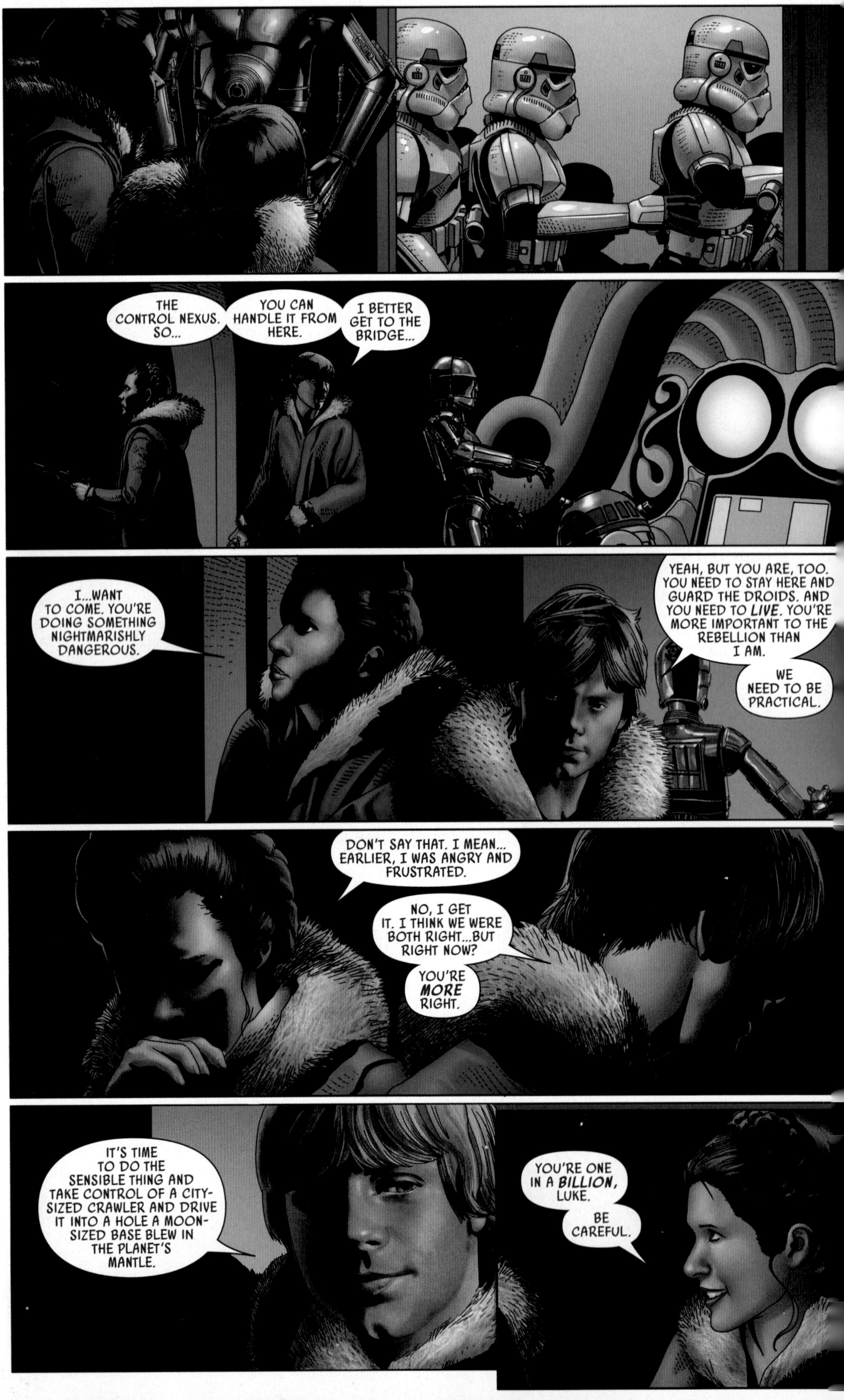
THE CONTROL NEXUS. SO...
YOU CAN HANDLE IT FROM HERE.
I BETTER GET TO THE BRIDGE...
I...WANT TO COME. YOU'RE DOING SOMETHING NIGHTMARISHLY DANGEROUS.
YEAH, BUT YOU ARE, TOO. YOU NEED TO STAY HERE AND GUARD THE DROIDS. AND YOU NEED TO LIVE. YOU'RE MORE IMPORTANT TO THE REBELLION THAN I AM.
WE NEED TO BE PRACTICAL.
DON'T SAY THAT. I MEAN... EARLIER, I WAS ANGRY AND FRUSTRATED.
NO, I GET IT. I THINK WE WERE BOTH RIGHT...BUT RIGHT NOW?
YOU'RE MORE RIGHT.
IT'S TIME TO DO THE SENSIBLE THING AND TAKE CONTROL OF A CITY-SIZED CRAWLER AND DRIVE IT INTO A HOLE A MOON-SIZED BASE BLEW IN THE PLANET'S MANTLE.
YOU'RE ONE IN A BILLION, LUKE.
BE CAREFUL.

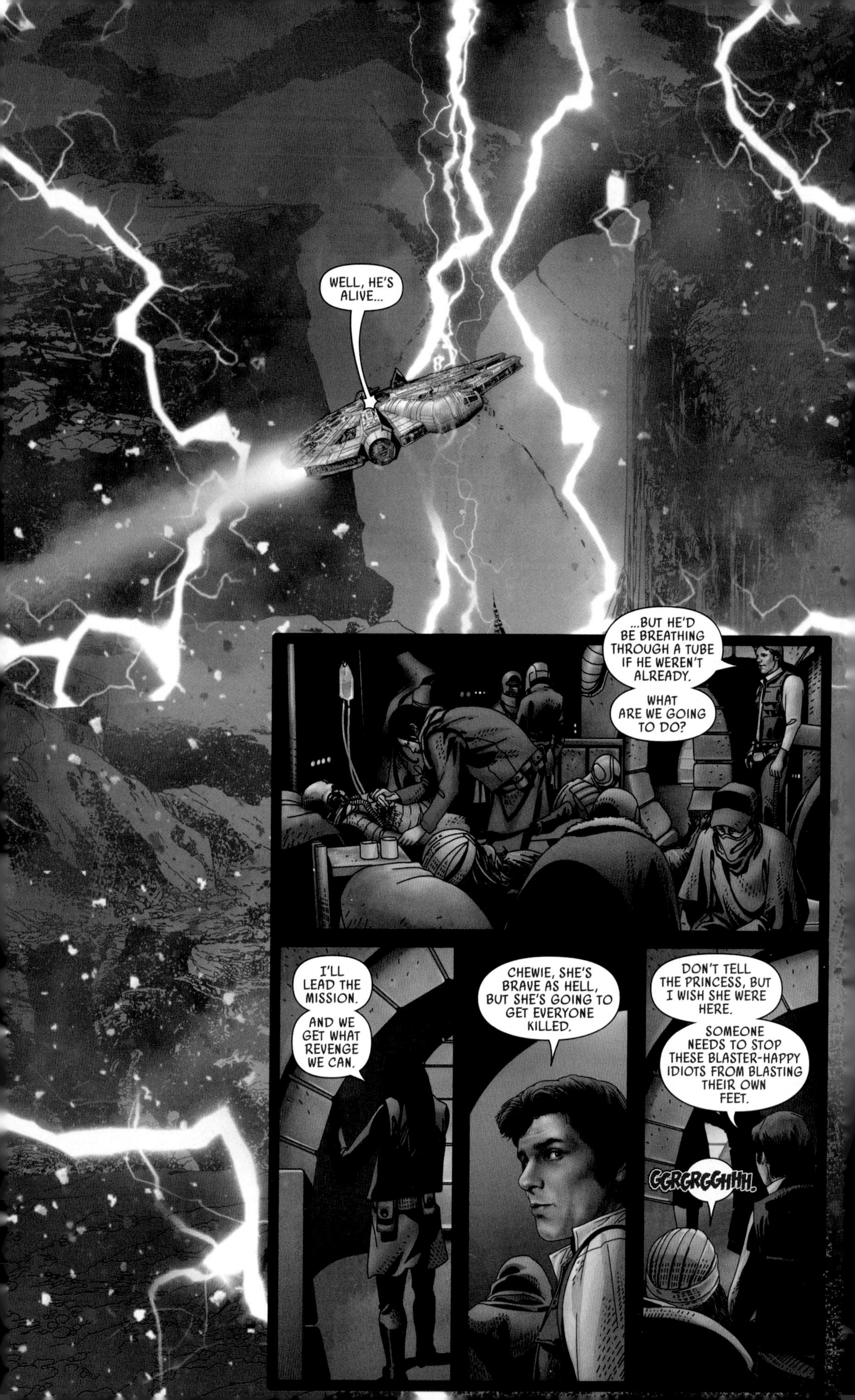
WELL, HE'S ALIVE...
...BUT HE'D BE BREATHING THROUGH A TUBE IF HE WEREN'T ALREADY.
WHAT ARE WE GOING TO DO?
I'LL LEAD THE MISSION.
AND WE GET WHAT REVENGE WE CAN.
CHEWIE, SHE'S BRAVE AS HELL, BUT SHE'S GOING TO GET EVERYONE KILLED.
DON'T TELL THE PRINCESS, BUT I WISH SHE WERE HERE.
SOMEONE NEEDS TO STOP THESE BLASTER-HAPPY IDIOTS FROM BLASTING THEIR OWN FEET.
GGRGRGGHHH.

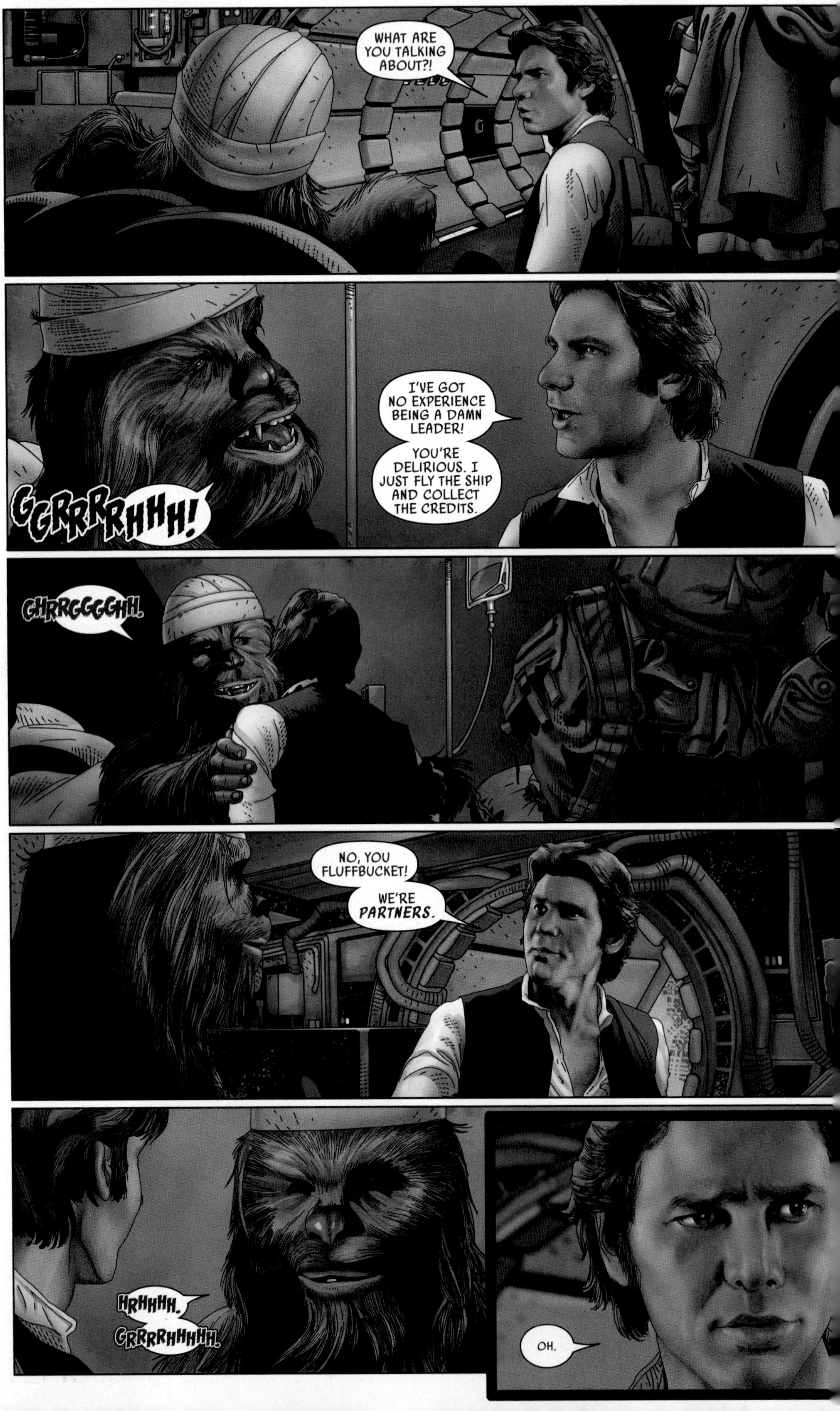
WHAT ARE YOU TALKING ABOUT?!
GGRRRRHHHH!
I'VE GOT NO EXPERIENCE BEING A DAMN LEADER!
YOU'RE DELIRIOUS. I JUST FLY THE SHIP AND COLLECT THE CREDITS.
GHRRGGGGHH.
NO, YOU FLUFFBUCKET!
WE'RE PARTNERS.
HRHHHH.
GRRRRHHHHH.
OH.

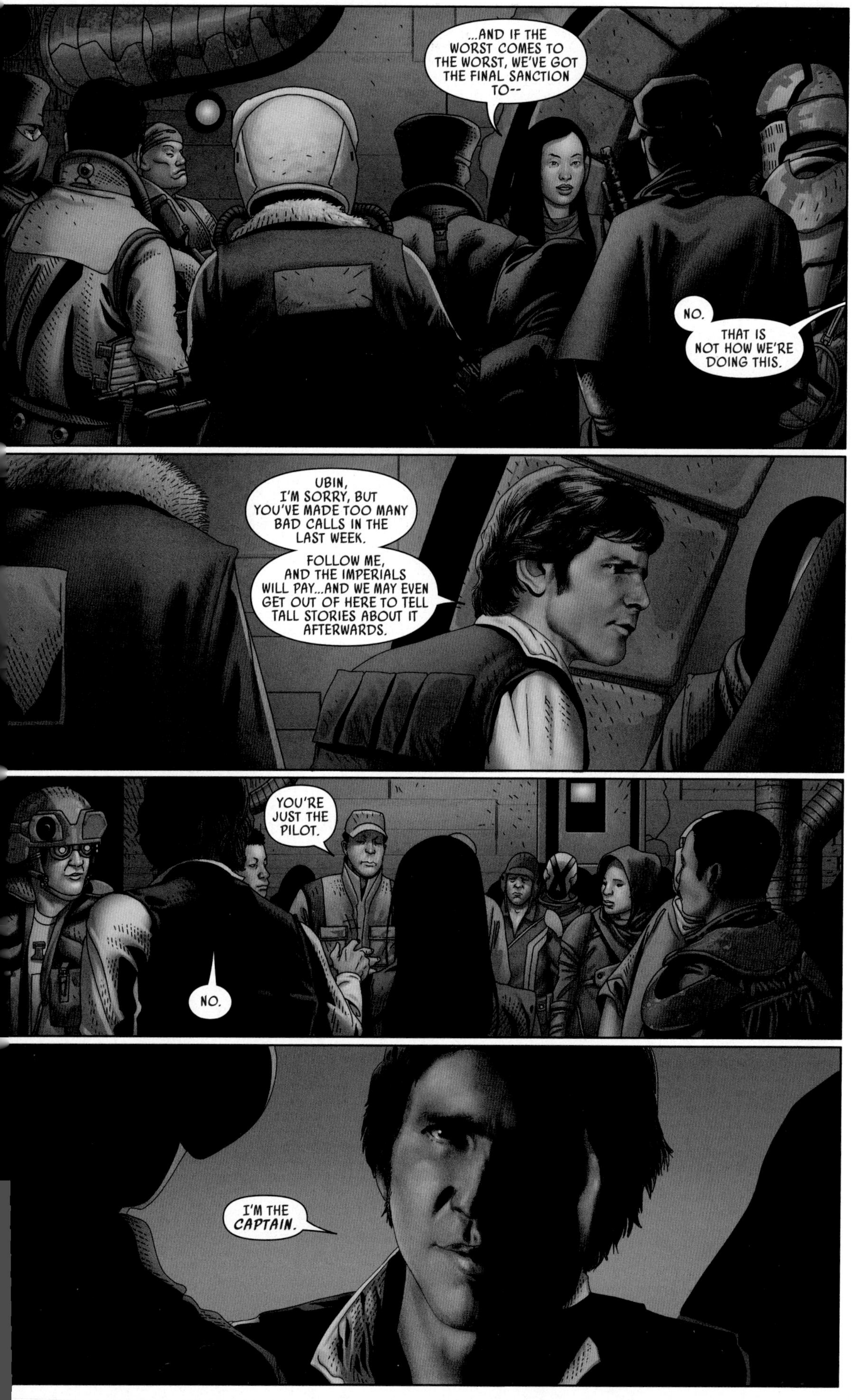
...AND IF THE WORST COMES TO THE WORST, WE'VE GOT THE FINAL SANCTION TO--
NO.
THAT IS NOT HOW WE'RE DOING THIS.
UBIN, I'M SORRY, BUT YOU'VE MADE TOO MANY BAD CALLS IN THE LAST WEEK.
FOLLOW ME, AND THE IMPERIALS WILL PAY...AND WE MAY EVEN GET OUT OF HERE TO TELL TALL STORIES ABOUT IT AFTERWARDS.
YOU'RE JUST THE PILOT.
NO.
I'M THE *CAPTAIN*.

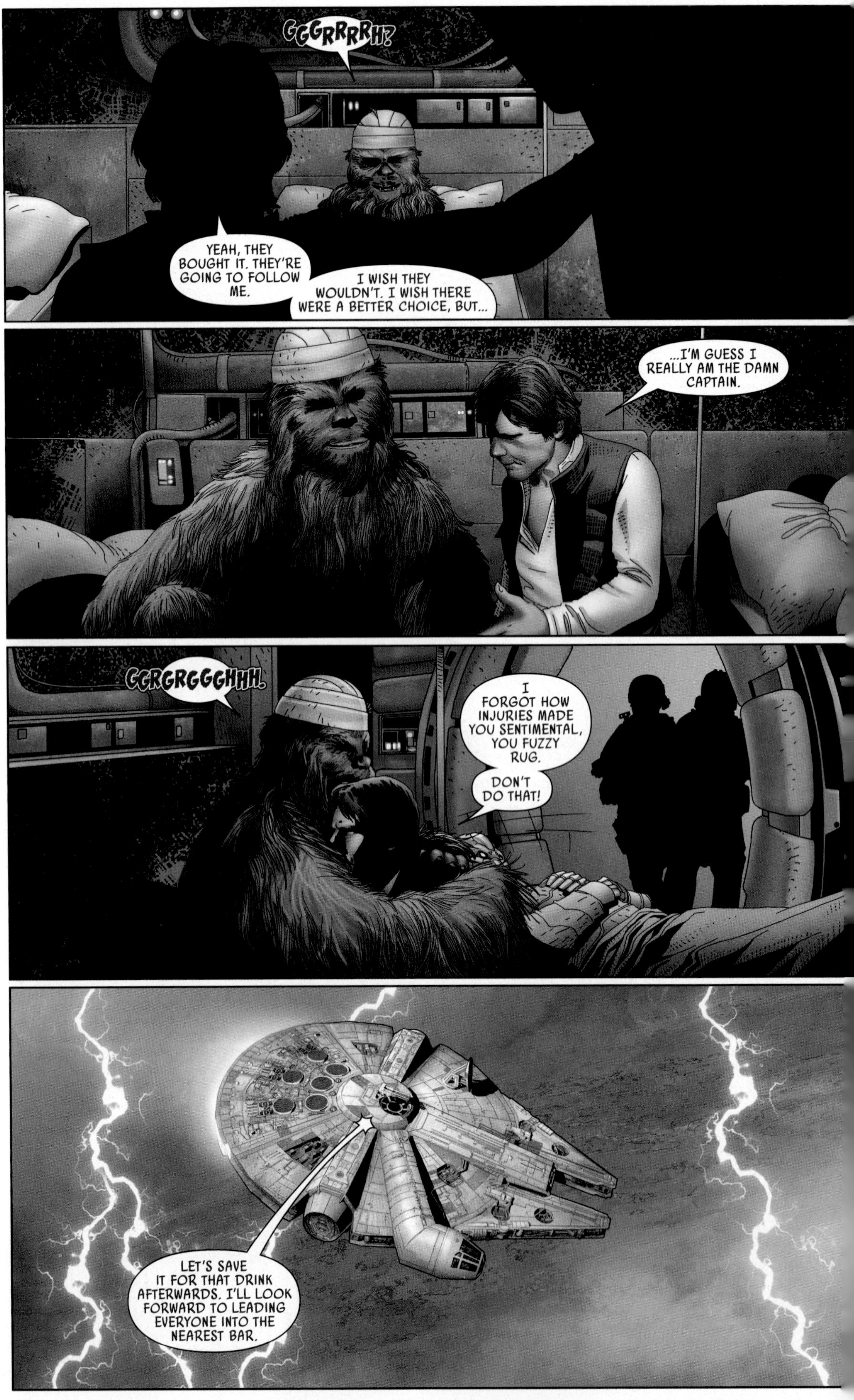
GGGRRRRH?
YEAH, THEY BOUGHT IT. THEY'RE GOING TO FOLLOW ME.
I WISH THEY WOULDN'T. I WISH THERE WERE A BETTER CHOICE, BUT...
...I'M GUESS I REALLY AM THE DAMN CAPTAIN.
GGRGRGGGHHH.
I FORGOT HOW INJURIES MADE YOU SENTIMENTAL, YOU FUZZY RUG.
DON'T DO THAT!
LET'S SAVE IT FOR THAT DRINK AFTERWARDS. I'LL LOOK FORWARD TO LEADING EVERYONE INTO THE NEAREST BAR.

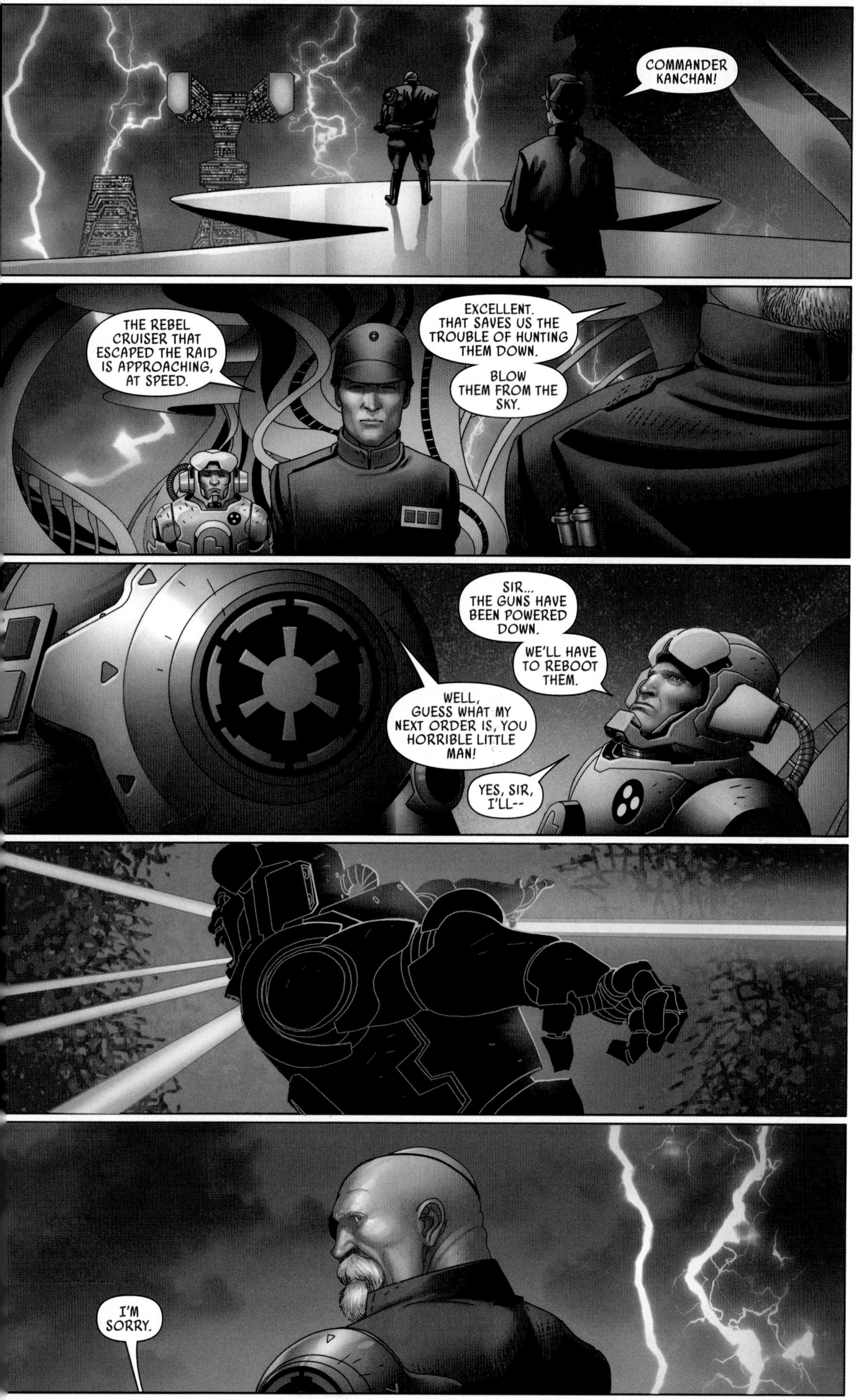
COMMANDER KANCHAN!
THE REBEL CRUISER THAT ESCAPED THE RAID IS APPROACHING, AT SPEED.
EXCELLENT. THAT SAVES US THE TROUBLE OF HUNTING THEM DOWN.
BLOW THEM FROM THE SKY.
SIR... THE GUNS HAVE BEEN POWERED DOWN.
WE'LL HAVE TO REBOOT THEM.
WELL, GUESS WHAT MY NEXT ORDER IS, YOU HORRIBLE LITTLE MAN!
YES, SIR, I'LL--
I'M SORRY.

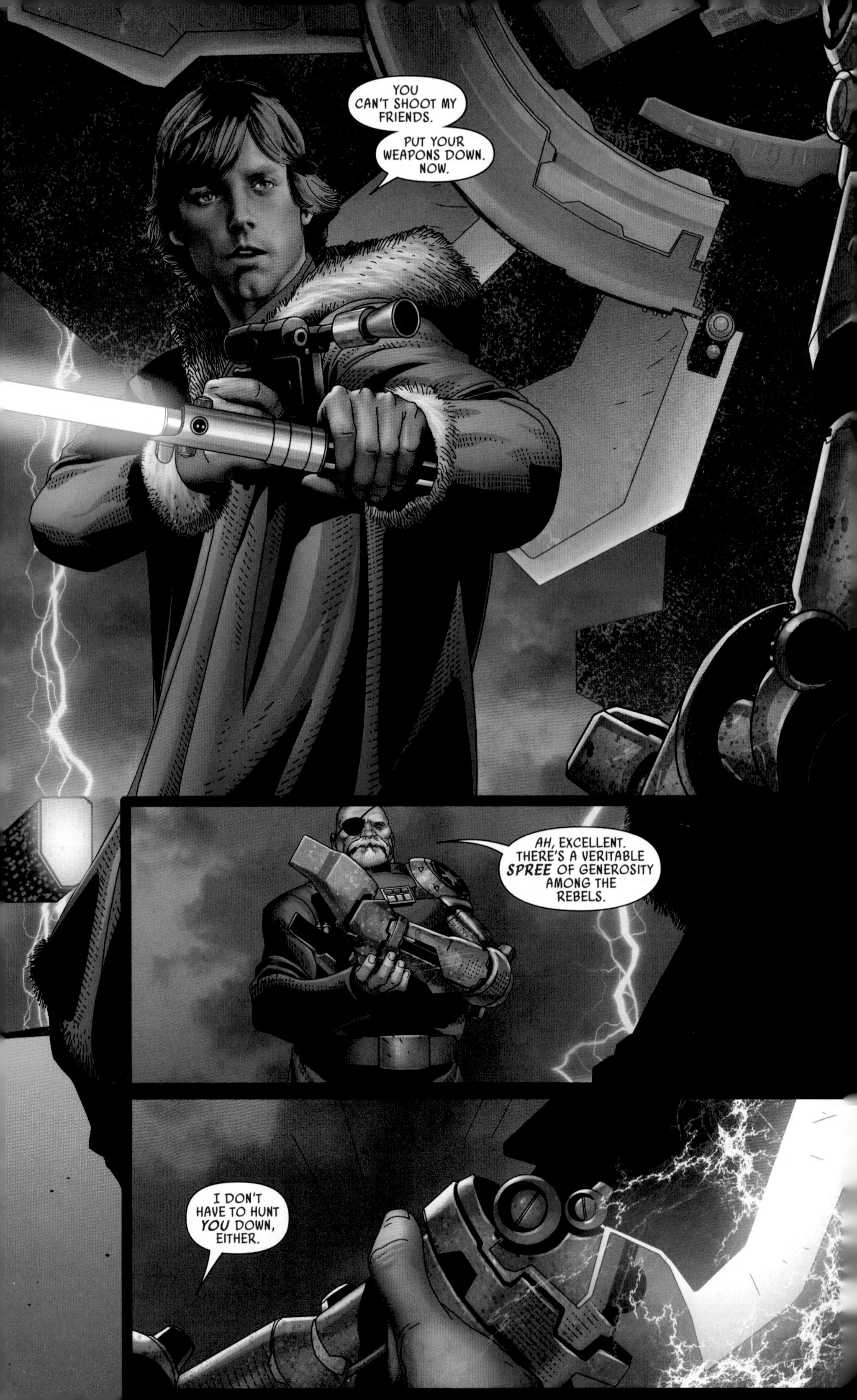
YOU CAN'T SHOOT MY FRIENDS.
PUT YOUR WEAPONS DOWN. NOW.
AH, EXCELLENT. THERE'S A VERITABLE SPREE OF GENEROSITY AMONG THE REBELS.
I DON'T HAVE TO HUNT YOU DOWN, EITHER.

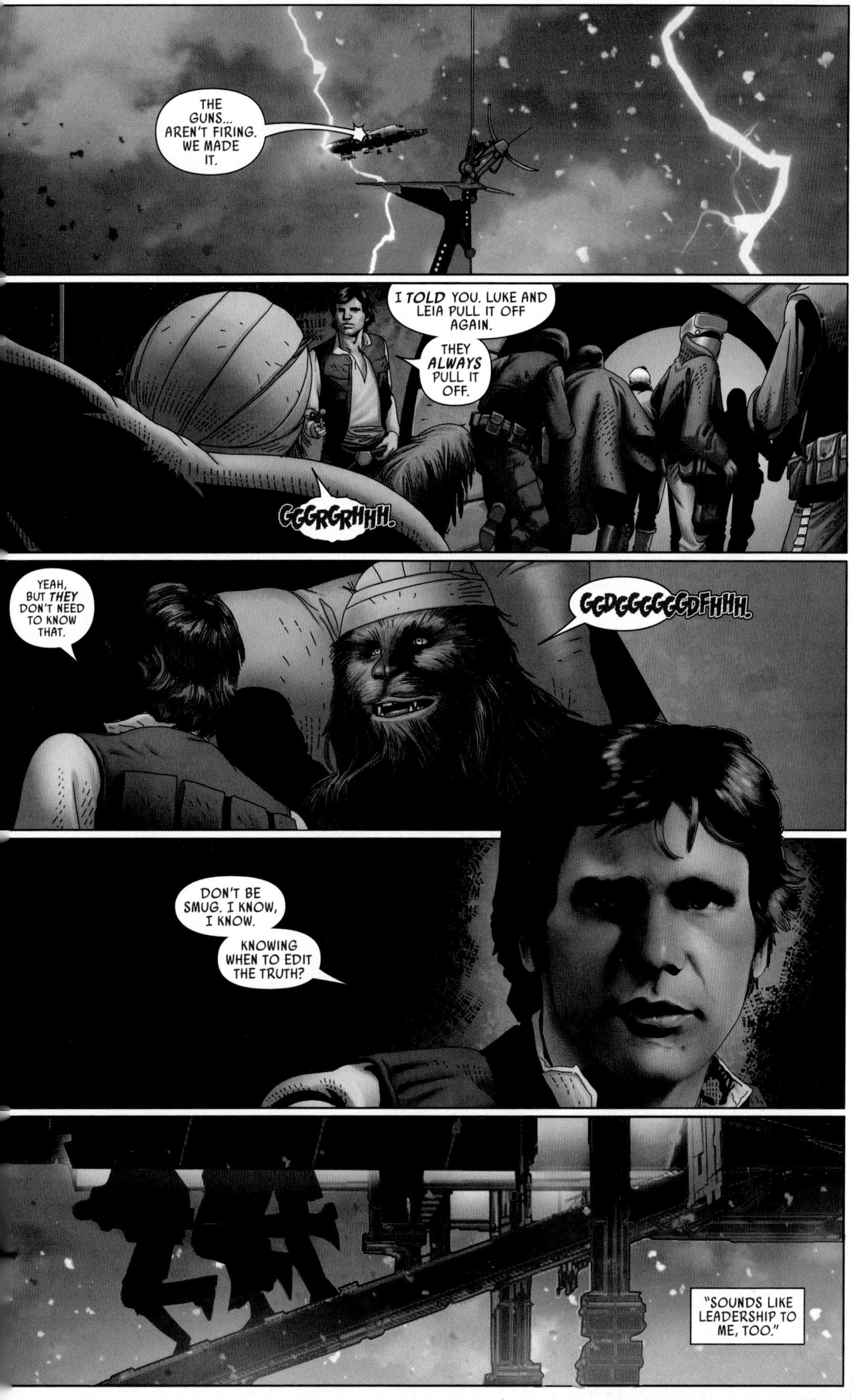
THE GUNS... AREN'T FIRING. WE MADE IT.
I TOLD YOU. LUKE AND LEIA PULL IT OFF AGAIN.
THEY ALWAYS PULL IT OFF.
GGGRGRHHH.
YEAH, BUT THEY DON'T NEED TO KNOW THAT.
GGDGGGGGGDFHHH.
DON'T BE SMUG. I KNOW, I KNOW.
KNOWING WHEN TO EDIT THE TRUTH?
"SOUNDS LIKE LEADERSHIP TO ME, TOO."

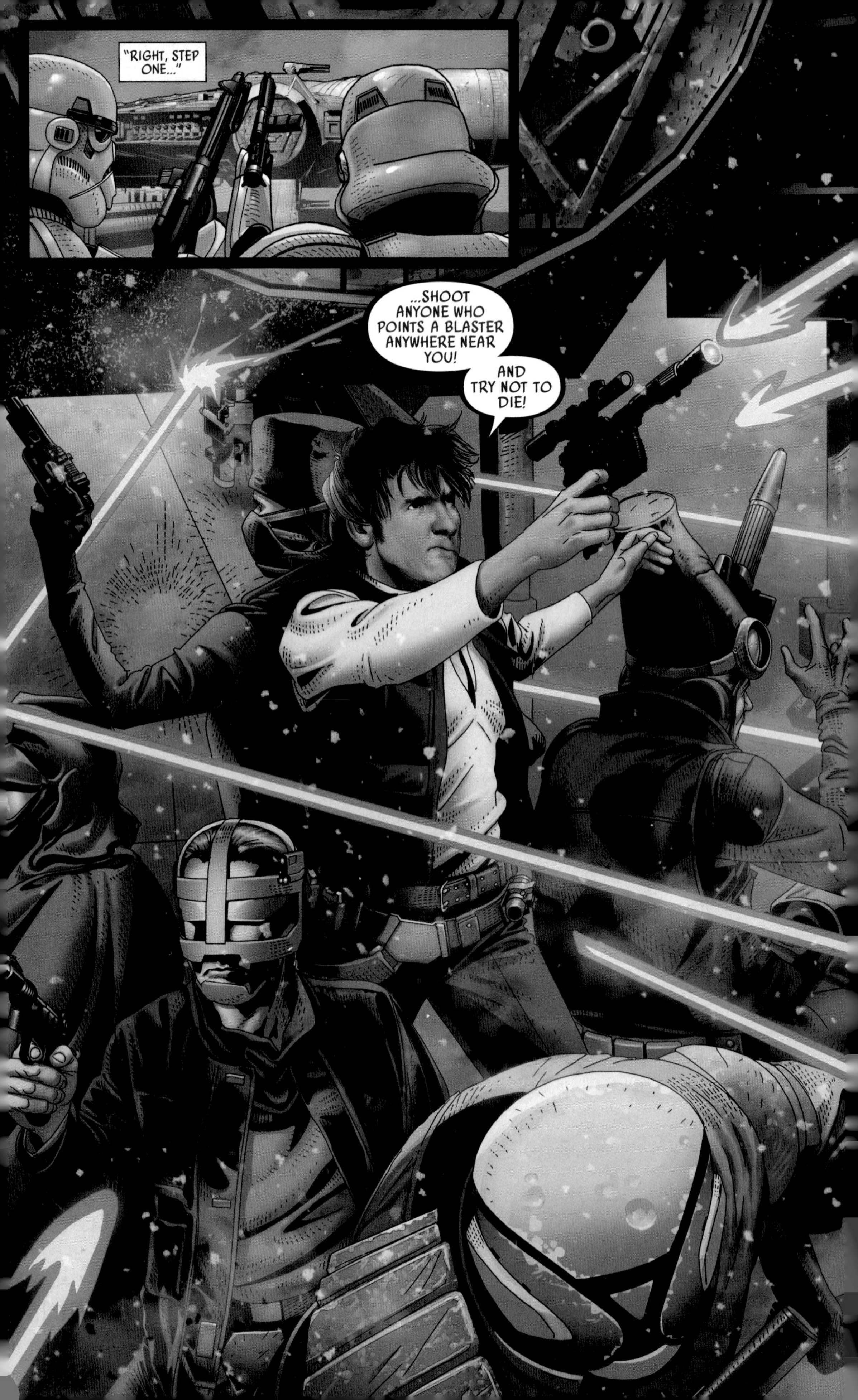
"RIGHT, STEP ONE..."
...SHOOT ANYONE WHO POINTS A BLASTER ANYWHERE NEAR YOU!
AND TRY NOT TO DIE!

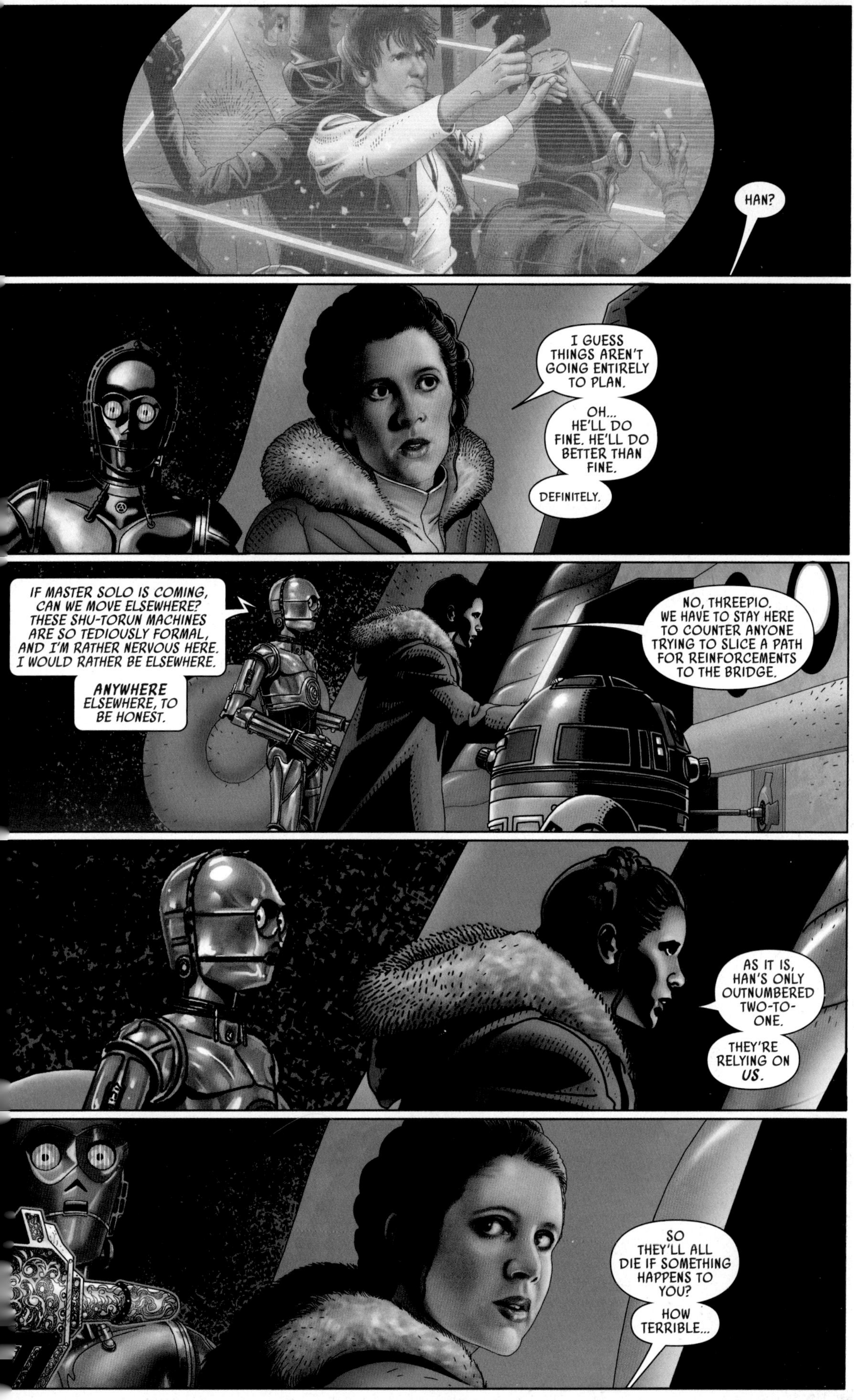
HAN?
I GUESS THINGS AREN'T GOING ENTIRELY TO PLAN.
OH... HE'LL DO FINE. HE'LL DO BETTER THAN FINE.
DEFINITELY.
IF MASTER SOLO IS COMING, CAN WE MOVE ELSEWHERE? THESE SHU-TORUN MACHINES ARE SO TEDIOUSLY FORMAL, AND I'M RATHER NERVOUS HERE. I WOULD RATHER BE ELSEWHERE.
ANYWHERE ELSEWHERE, TO BE HONEST.
NO, THREEPIO. WE HAVE TO STAY HERE TO COUNTER ANYONE TRYING TO SLICE A PATH FOR REINFORCEMENTS TO THE BRIDGE.
AS IT IS, HAN'S ONLY OUTNUMBERED TWO-TO-ONE.
THEY'RE RELYING ON US.
SO THEY'LL ALL DIE IF SOMETHING HAPPENS TO YOU?
HOW TERRIBLE...

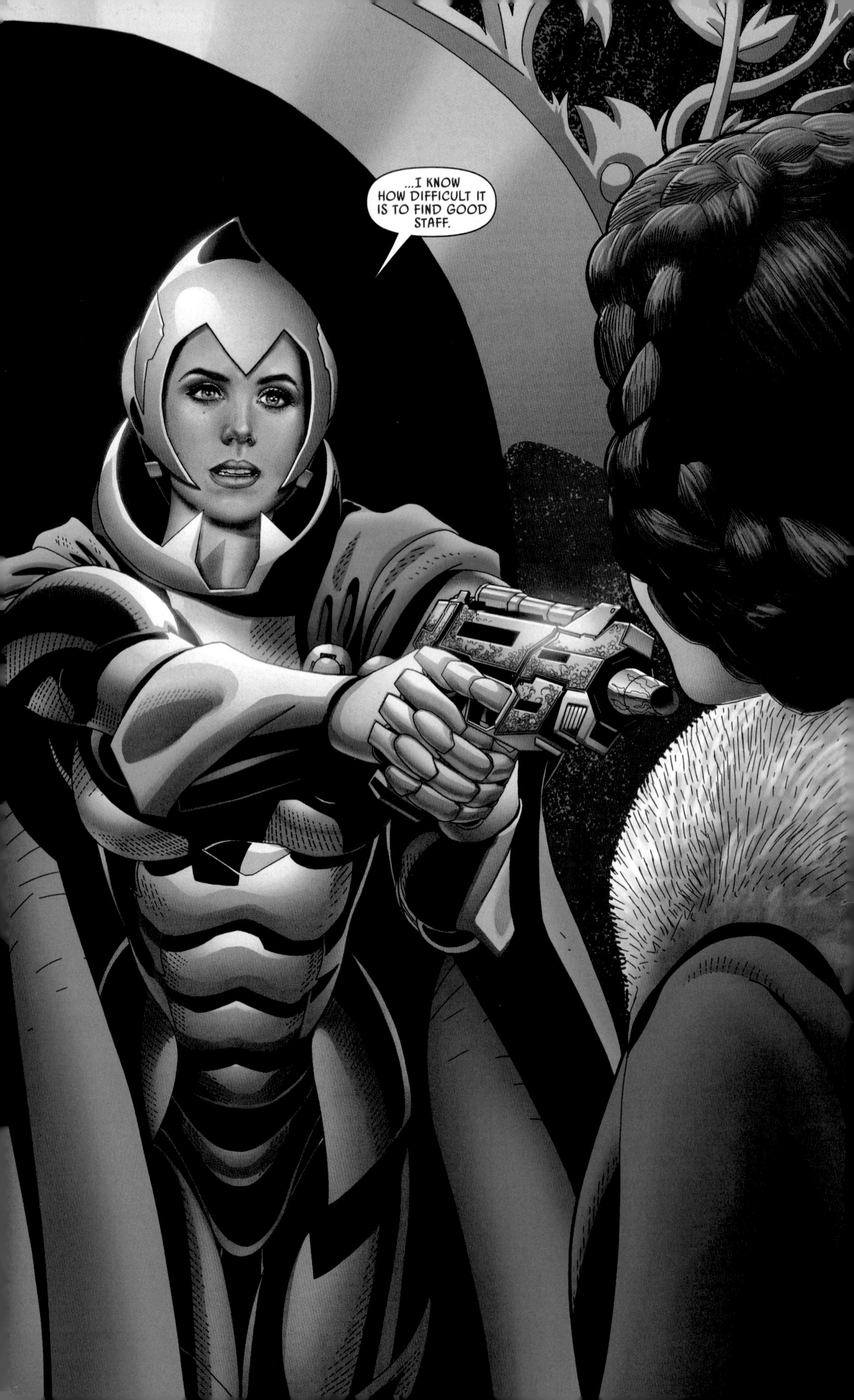
...I KNOW HOW DIFFICULT IT IS TO FIND GOOD STAFF.

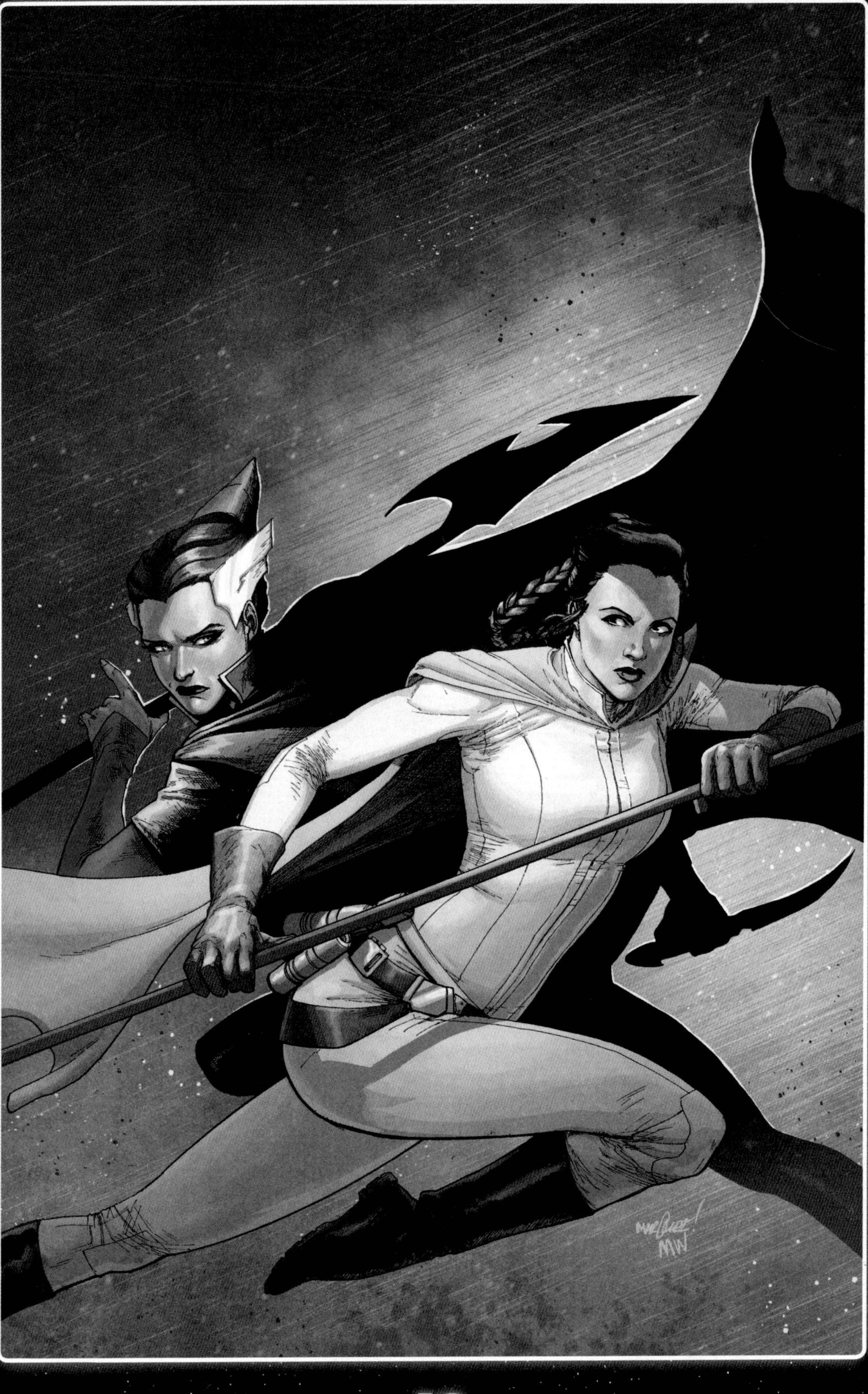

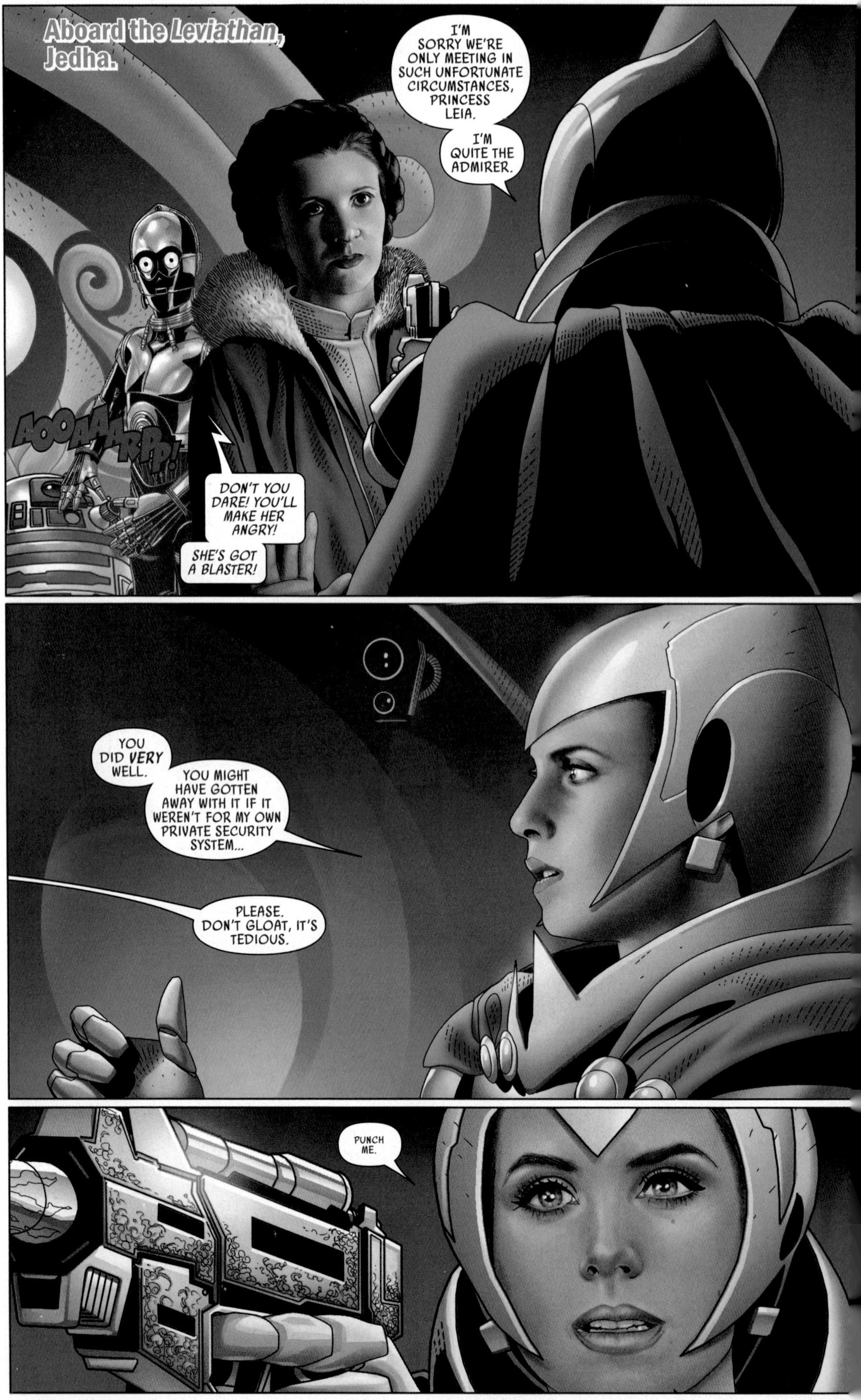

Aboard the *Leviathan*, Jedha.
I'M SORRY WE'RE ONLY MEETING IN SUCH UNFORTUNATE CIRCUMSTANCES, PRINCESS LEIA.
I'M QUITE THE ADMIRER.
AOOAAARPP!
DON'T YOU DARE! YOU'LL MAKE HER ANGRY!
SHE'S GOT A BLASTER!
YOU DID VERY WELL.
YOU MIGHT HAVE GOTTEN AWAY WITH IT IF IT WEREN'T FOR MY OWN PRIVATE SECURITY SYSTEM...
PLEASE. DON'T GLOAT, IT'S TEDIOUS.
PUNCH ME.

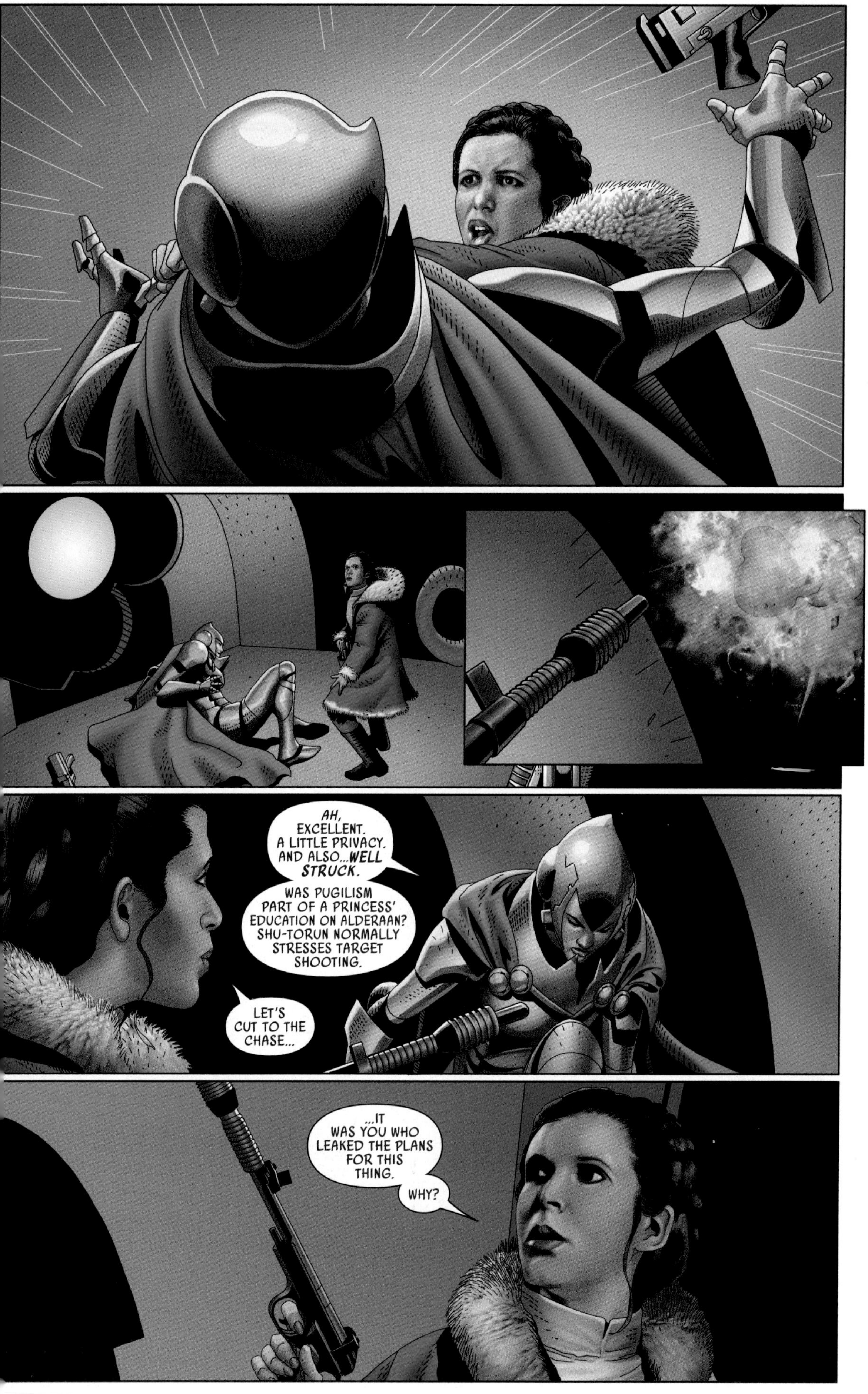

AH, EXCELLENT. A LITTLE PRIVACY. AND ALSO...WELL STRUCK.
WAS PUGILISM PART OF A PRINCESS' EDUCATION ON ALDERAAN? SHU-TORUN NORMALLY STRESSES TARGET SHOOTING.
LET'S CUT TO THE CHASE...
...IT WAS YOU WHO LEAKED THE PLANS FOR THIS THING.
WHY?

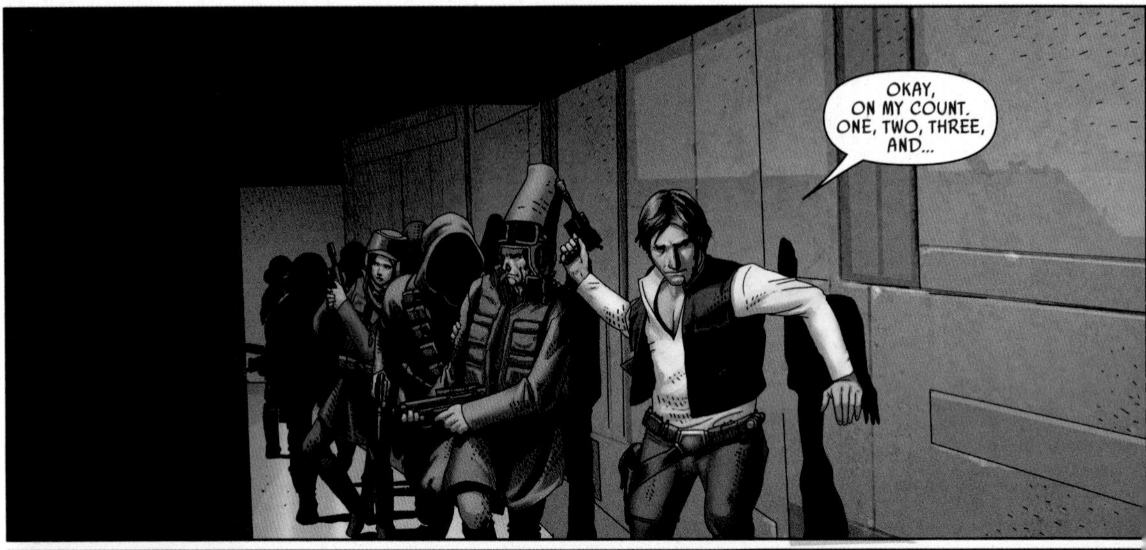
OKAY, ON MY COUNT. ONE, TWO, THREE, AND...

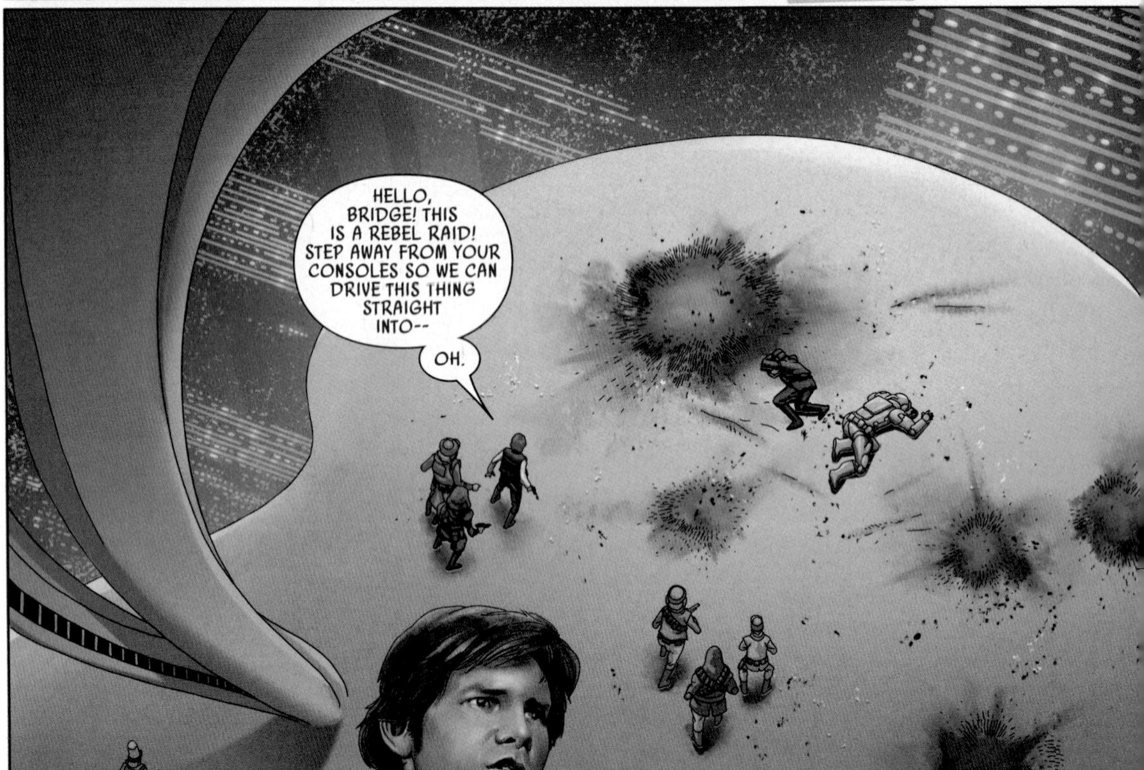
HELLO, BRIDGE! THIS IS A REBEL RAID! STEP AWAY FROM YOUR CONSOLES SO WE CAN DRIVE THIS THING STRAIGHT INTO--
OH.

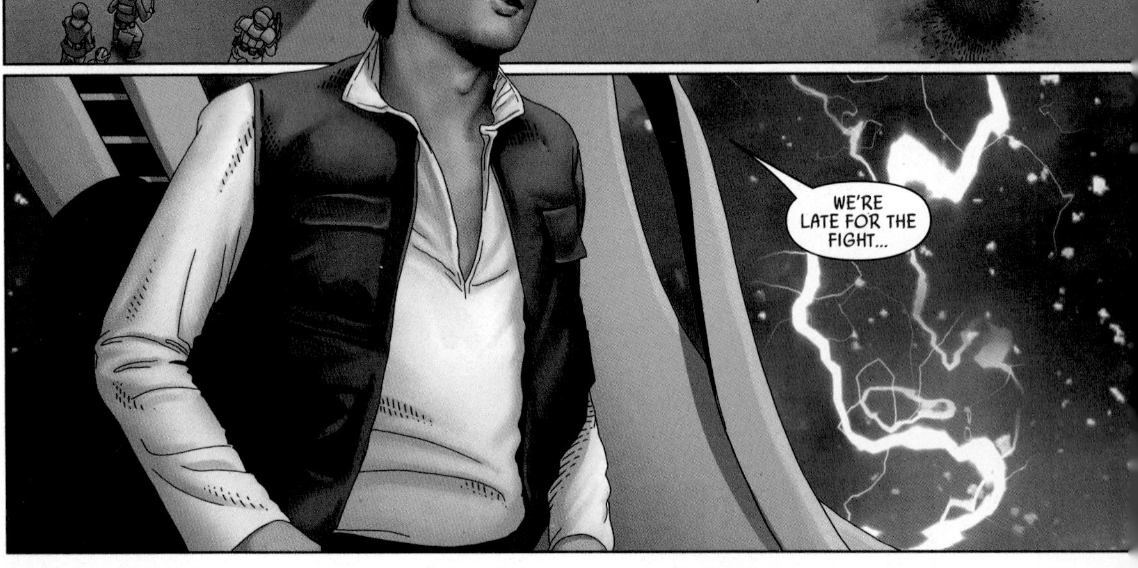
WE'RE LATE FOR THE FIGHT...

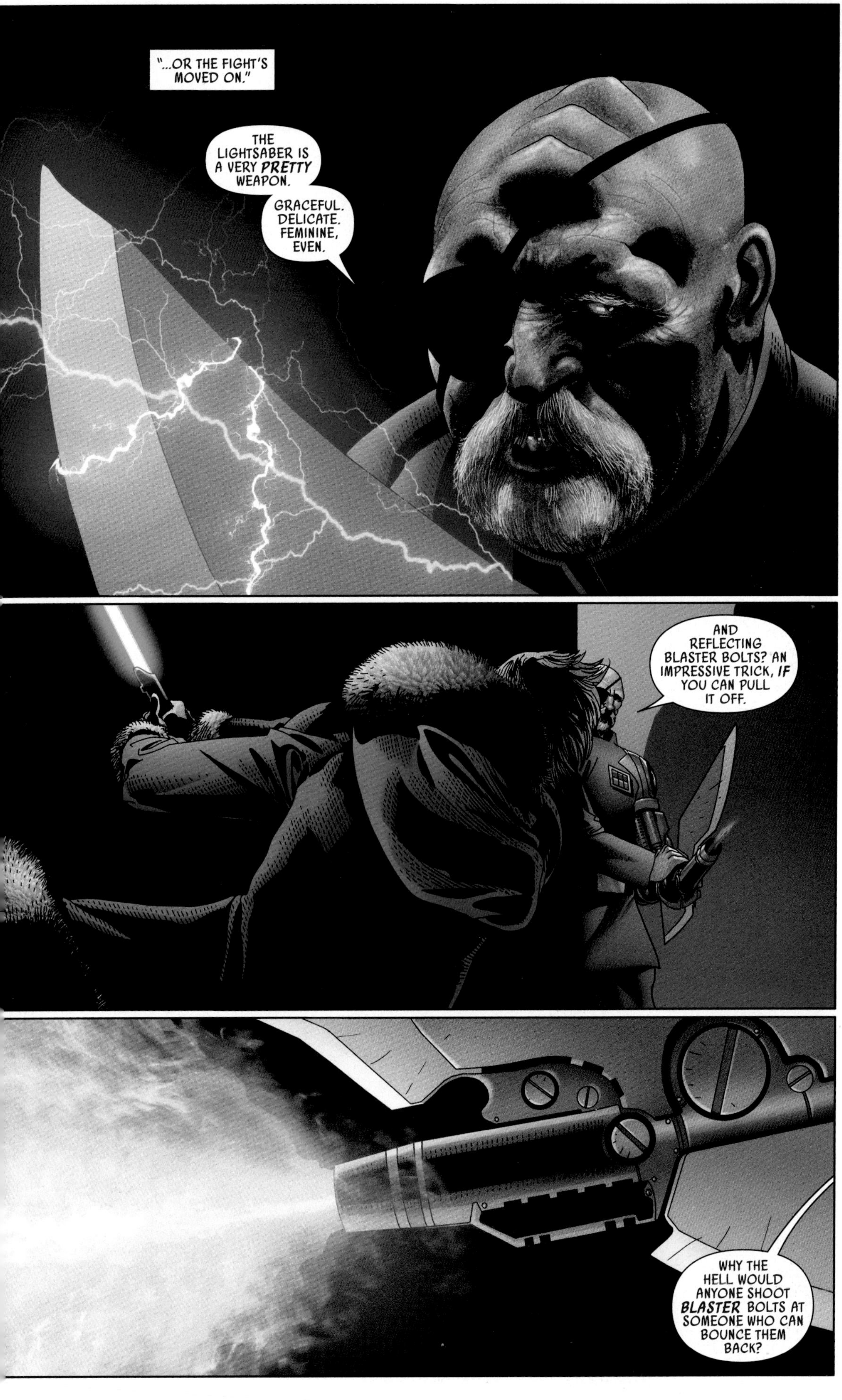
"...OR THE FIGHT'S MOVED ON."
THE LIGHTSABER IS A VERY PRETTY WEAPON.
GRACEFUL. DELICATE. FEMININE, EVEN.
AND REFLECTING BLASTER BOLTS? AN IMPRESSIVE TRICK, IF YOU CAN PULL IT OFF.
WHY THE HELL WOULD ANYONE SHOOT BLASTER BOLTS AT SOMEONE WHO CAN BOUNCE THEM BACK?

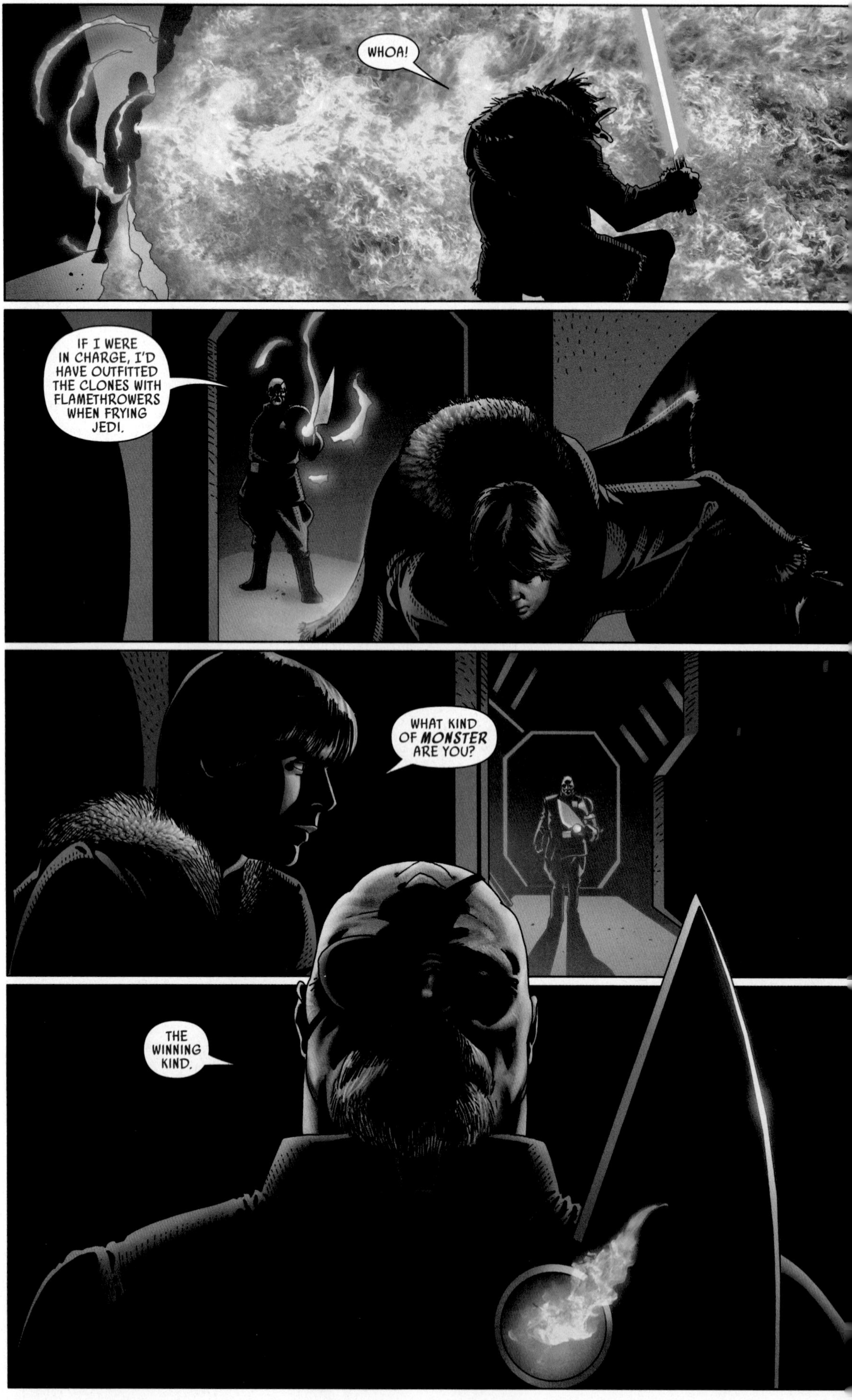
WHOA!
IF I WERE IN CHARGE, I'D HAVE OUTFITTED THE CLONES WITH FLAMETHROWERS WHEN FRYING JEDI.
WHAT KIND OF MONSTER ARE YOU?
THE WINNING KIND.

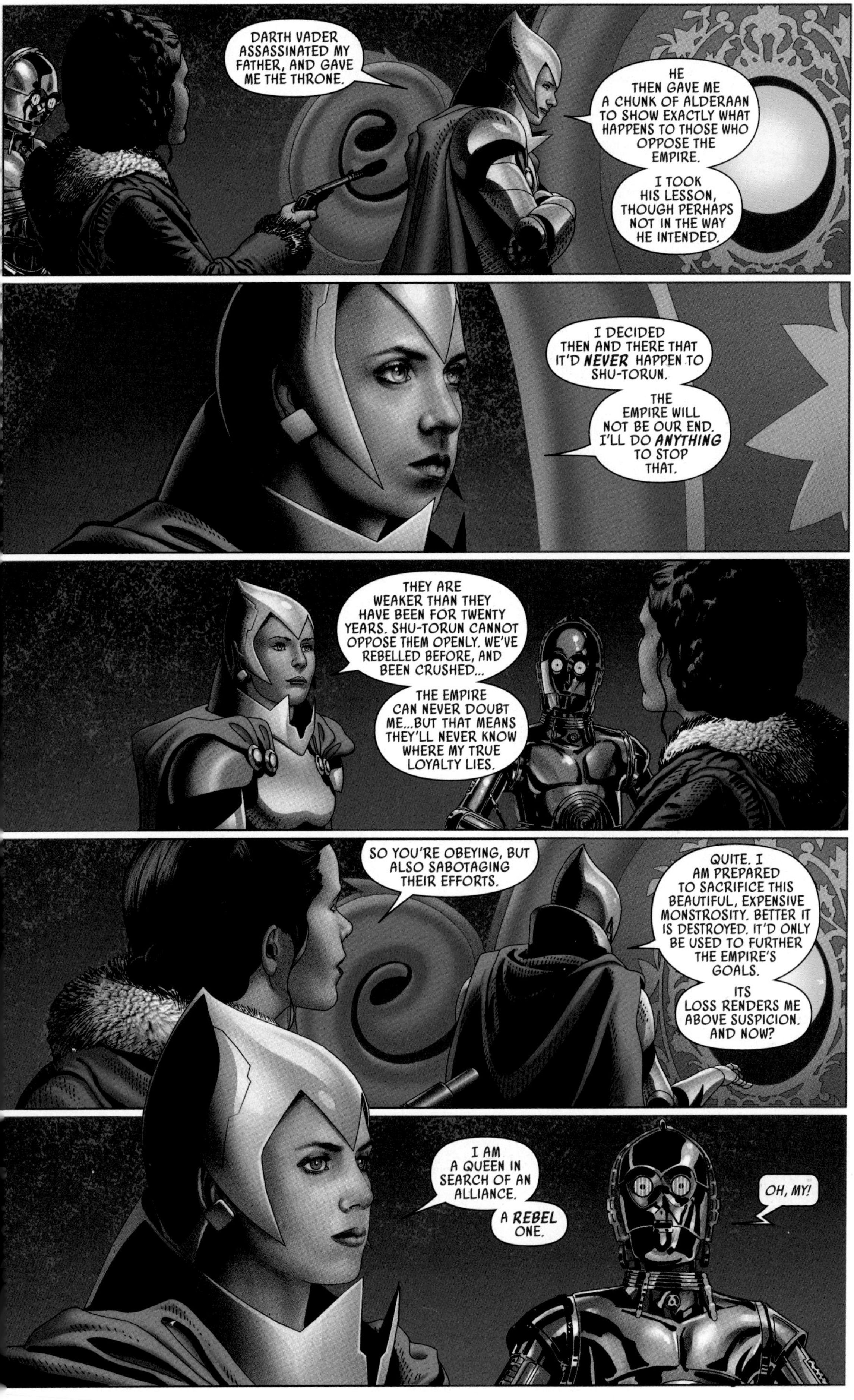
DARTH VADER ASSASSINATED MY FATHER, AND GAVE ME THE THRONE.
HE THEN GAVE ME A CHUNK OF ALDERAAN TO SHOW EXACTLY WHAT HAPPENS TO THOSE WHO OPPOSE THE EMPIRE.
I TOOK HIS LESSON, THOUGH PERHAPS NOT IN THE WAY HE INTENDED.
I DECIDED THEN AND THERE THAT IT'D NEVER HAPPEN TO SHU-TORUN.
THE EMPIRE WILL NOT BE OUR END. I'LL DO ANYTHING TO STOP THAT.
THEY ARE WEAKER THAN THEY HAVE BEEN FOR TWENTY YEARS. SHU-TORUN CANNOT OPPOSE THEM OPENLY. WE'VE REBELLED BEFORE, AND BEEN CRUSHED...
THE EMPIRE CAN NEVER DOUBT ME...BUT THAT MEANS THEY'LL NEVER KNOW WHERE MY TRUE LOYALTY LIES.
SO YOU'RE OBEYING, BUT ALSO SABOTAGING THEIR EFFORTS.
QUITE. I AM PREPARED TO SACRIFICE THIS BEAUTIFUL, EXPENSIVE MONSTROSITY. BETTER IT IS DESTROYED. IT'D ONLY BE USED TO FURTHER THE EMPIRE'S GOALS.
ITS LOSS RENDERS ME ABOVE SUSPICION. AND NOW?
I AM A QUEEN IN SEARCH OF AN ALLIANCE.
A REBEL ONE.
OH, MY!

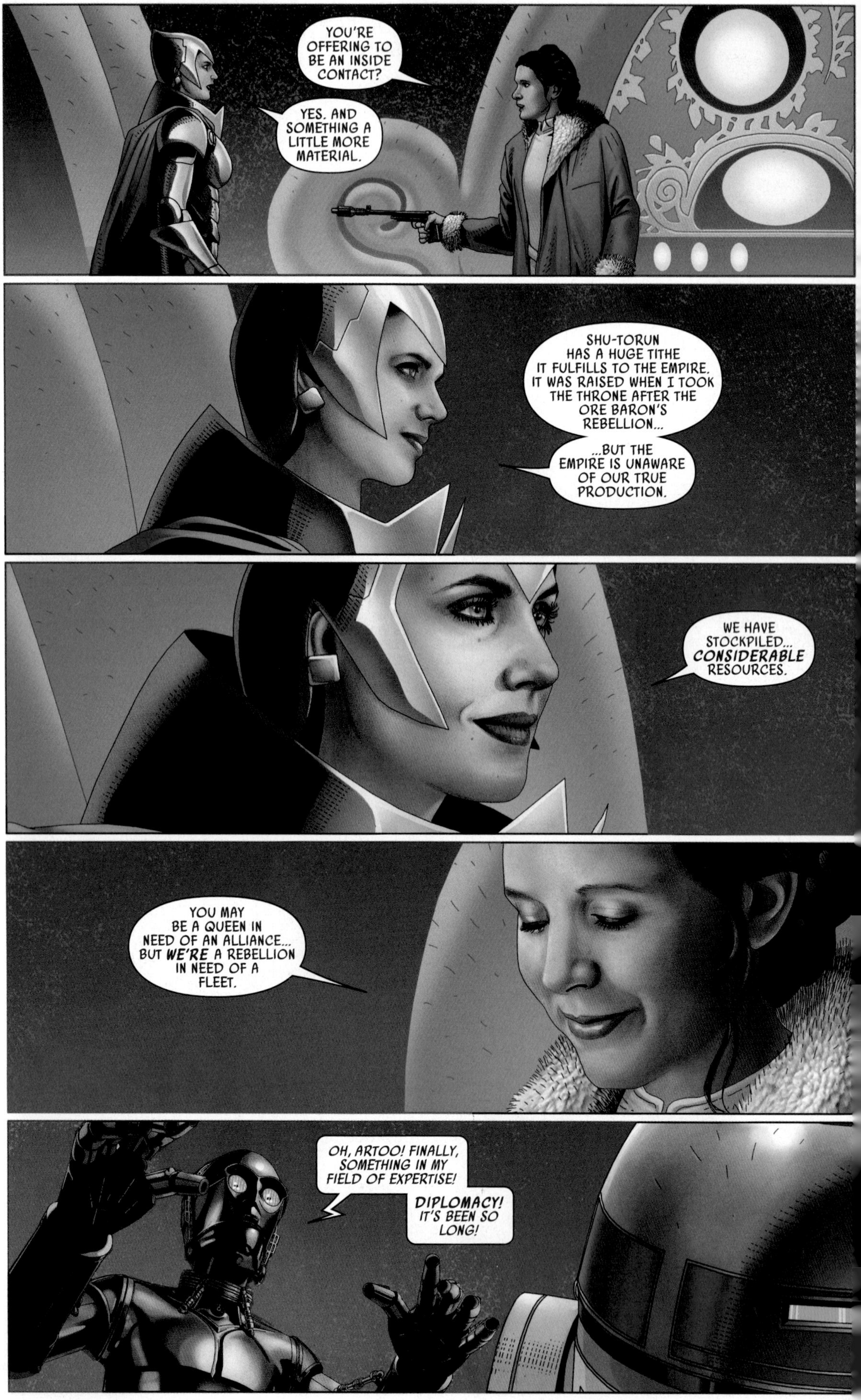
YOU'RE OFFERING TO BE AN INSIDE CONTACT?
YES. AND SOMETHING A LITTLE MORE MATERIAL.
SHU-TORUN HAS A HUGE TITHE IT FULFILLS TO THE EMPIRE. IT WAS RAISED WHEN I TOOK THE THRONE AFTER THE ORE BARON'S REBELLION...
...BUT THE EMPIRE IS UNAWARE OF OUR TRUE PRODUCTION.
WE HAVE STOCKPILED... CONSIDERABLE RESOURCES.
YOU MAY BE A QUEEN IN NEED OF AN ALLIANCE... BUT WE'RE A REBELLION IN NEED OF A FLEET.
OH, ARTOO! FINALLY, SOMETHING IN MY FIELD OF EXPERTISE!
DIPLOMACY! IT'S BEEN SO LONG!

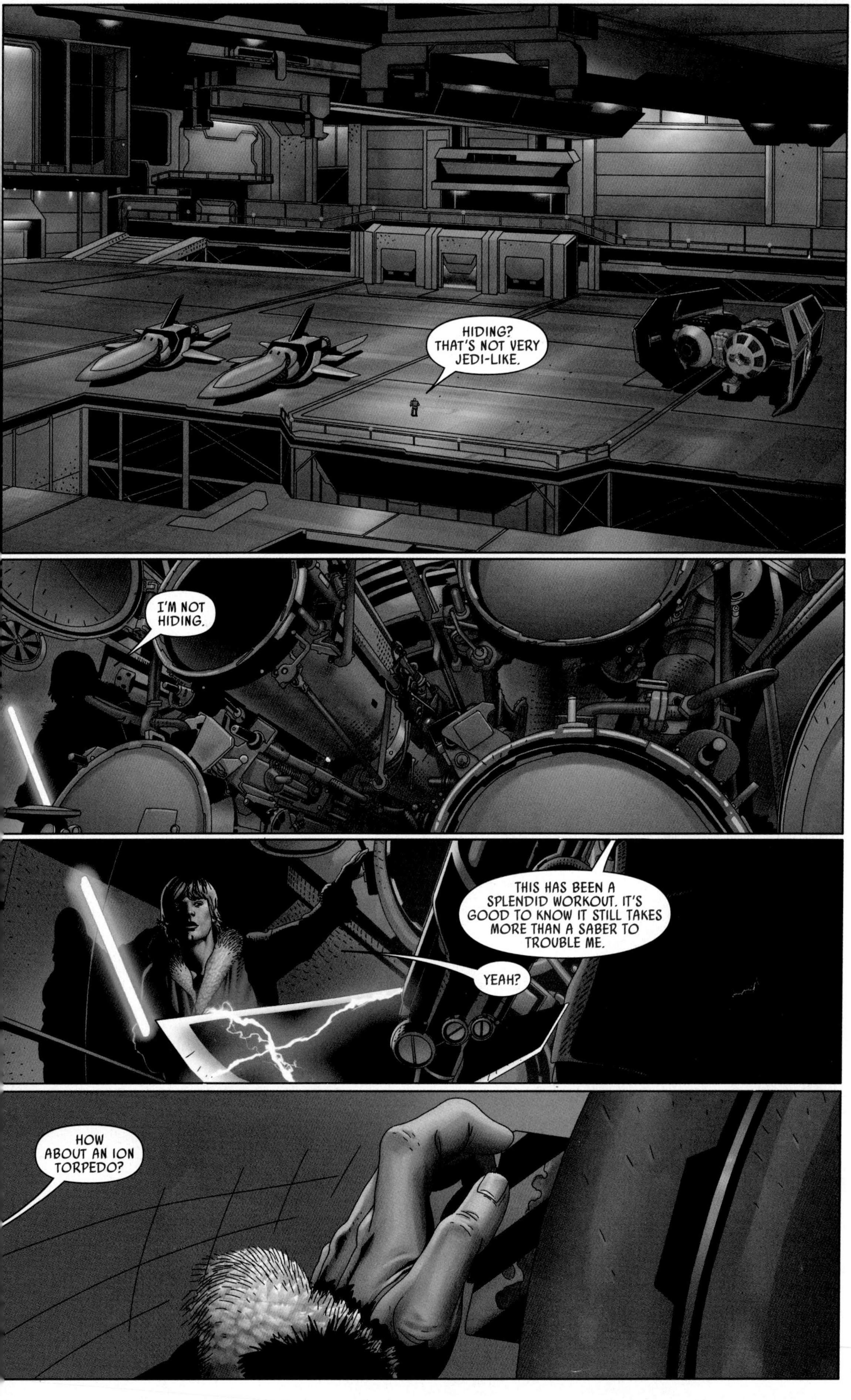
HIDING? THAT'S NOT VERY JEDI-LIKE.
I'M NOT HIDING.
THIS HAS BEEN A SPLENDID WORKOUT. IT'S GOOD TO KNOW IT STILL TAKES MORE THAN A SABER TO TROUBLE ME.
YEAH?
HOW ABOUT AN ION TORPEDO?

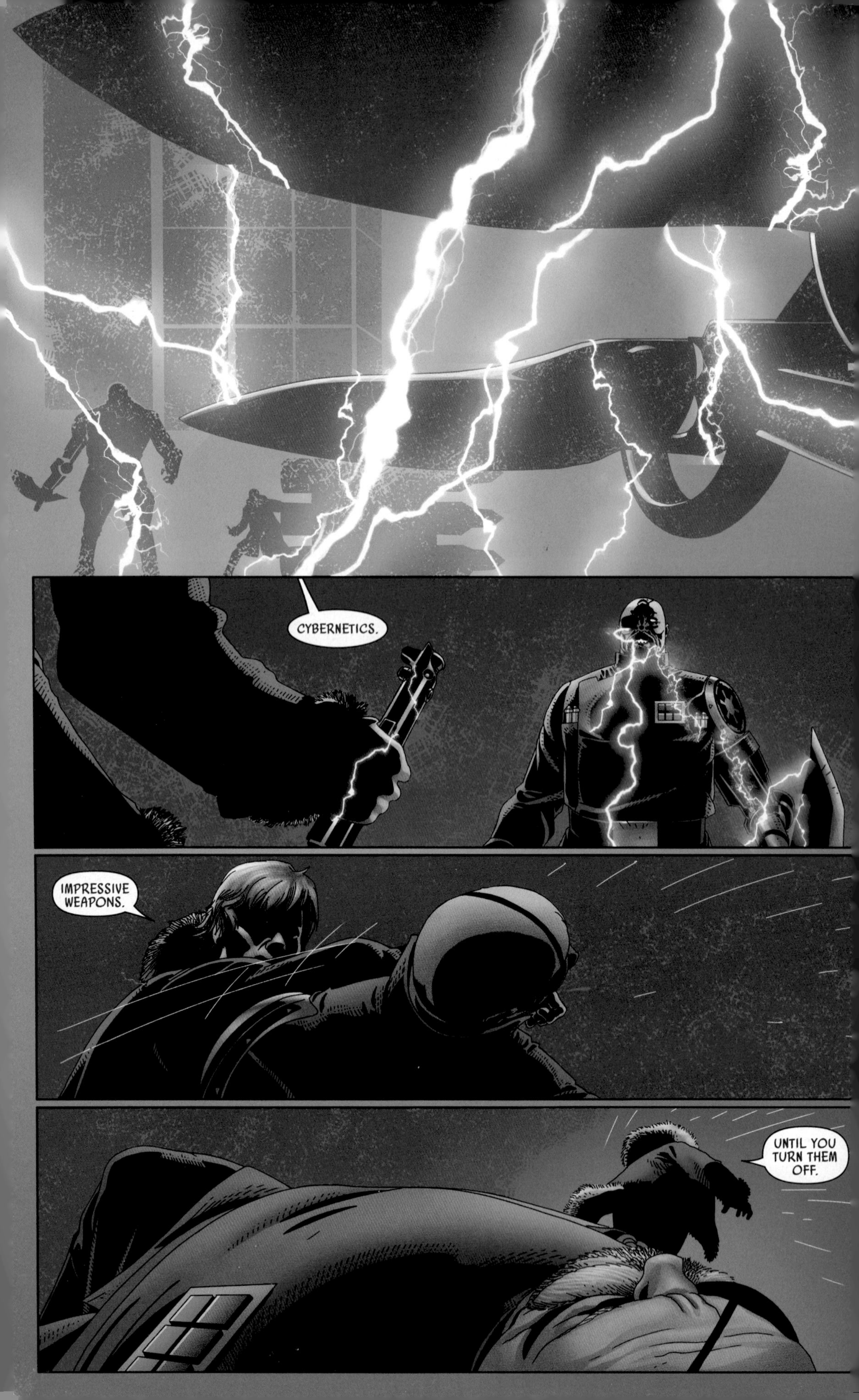
CYBERNETICS.
IMPRESSIVE WEAPONS.
UNTIL YOU TURN THEM OFF.

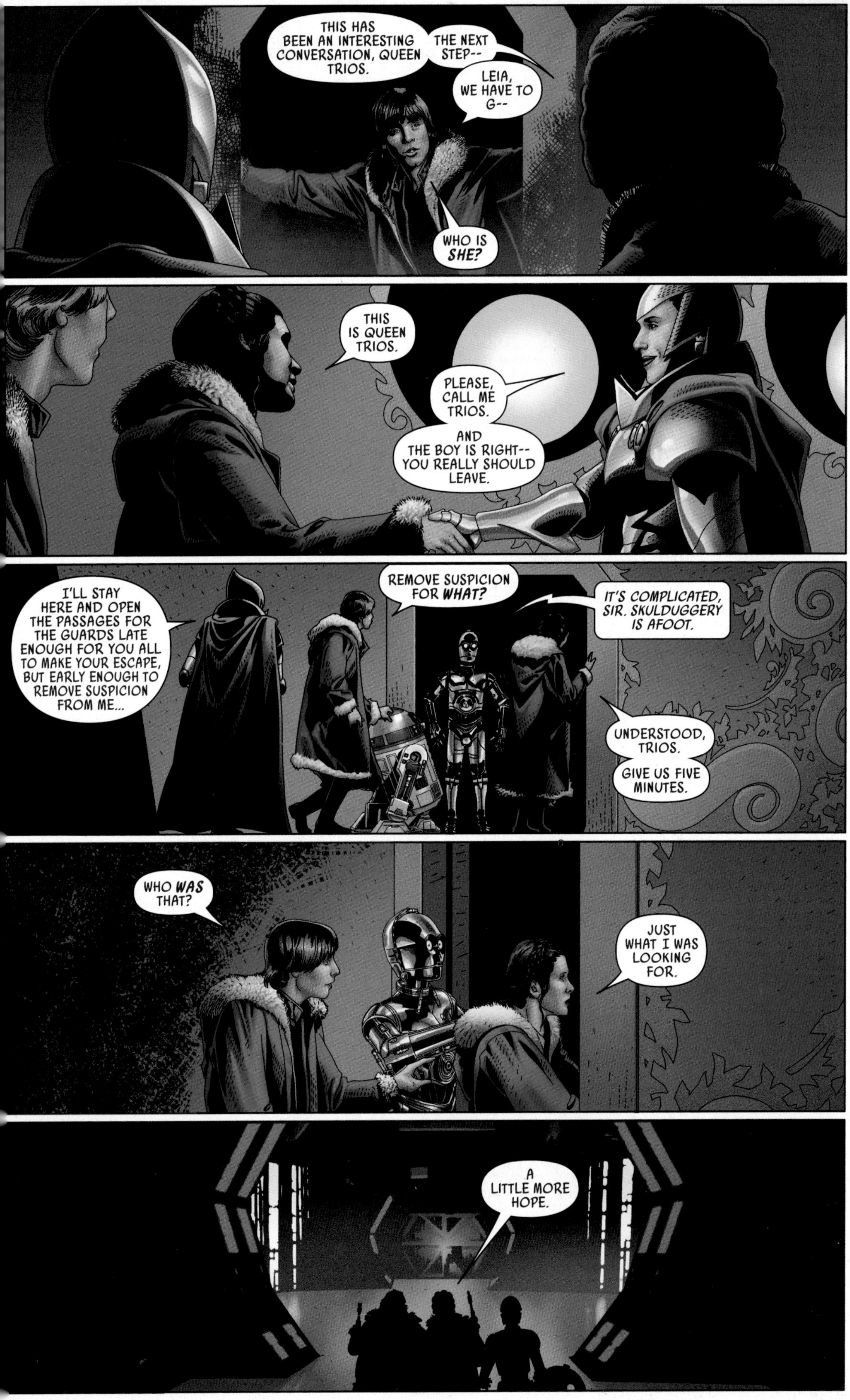
THIS HAS BEEN AN INTERESTING CONVERSATION, QUEEN TRIOS.
THE NEXT STEP--
LEIA, WE HAVE TO G--
WHO IS SHE?
THIS IS QUEEN TRIOS.
PLEASE, CALL ME TRIOS.
AND THE BOY IS RIGHT-- YOU REALLY SHOULD LEAVE.
I'LL STAY HERE AND OPEN THE PASSAGES FOR THE GUARDS LATE ENOUGH FOR YOU ALL TO MAKE YOUR ESCAPE, BUT EARLY ENOUGH TO REMOVE SUSPICION FROM ME...
REMOVE SUSPICION FOR WHAT?
IT'S COMPLICATED, SIR. SKULDUGGERY IS AFOOT.
UNDERSTOOD, TRIOS.
GIVE US FIVE MINUTES.
WHO WAS THAT?
JUST WHAT I WAS LOOKING FOR.
A LITTLE MORE HOPE.

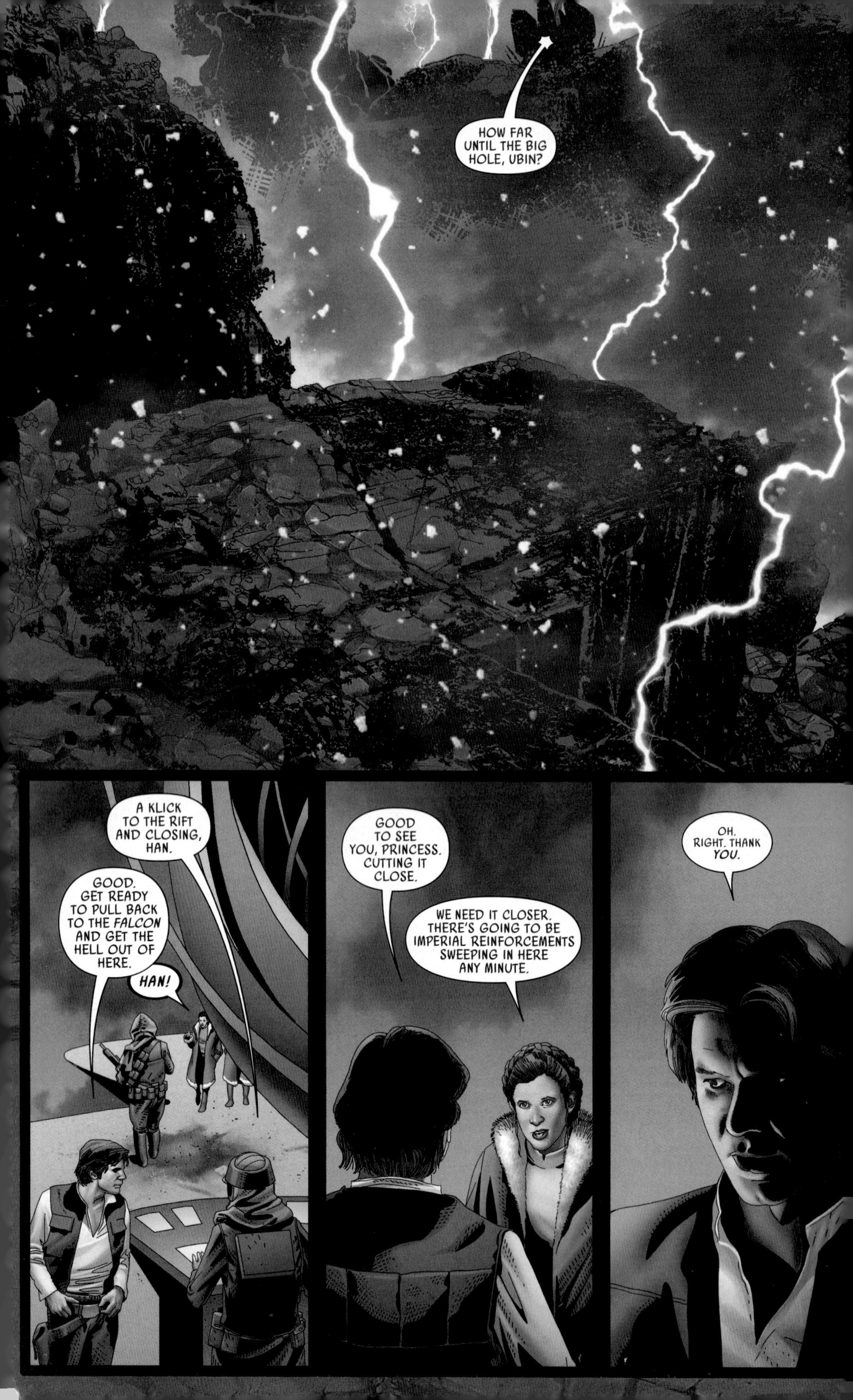
HOW FAR UNTIL THE BIG HOLE, UBIN?
A KLICK TO THE RIFT AND CLOSING, HAN.
GOOD. GET READY TO PULL BACK TO THE *FALCON* AND GET THE HELL OUT OF HERE.
HAN!
GOOD TO SEE YOU, PRINCESS. CUTTING IT CLOSE.
WE NEED IT CLOSER. THERE'S GOING TO BE IMPERIAL REINFORCEMENTS SWEEPING IN HERE ANY MINUTE.
OH. RIGHT. THANK *YOU*.

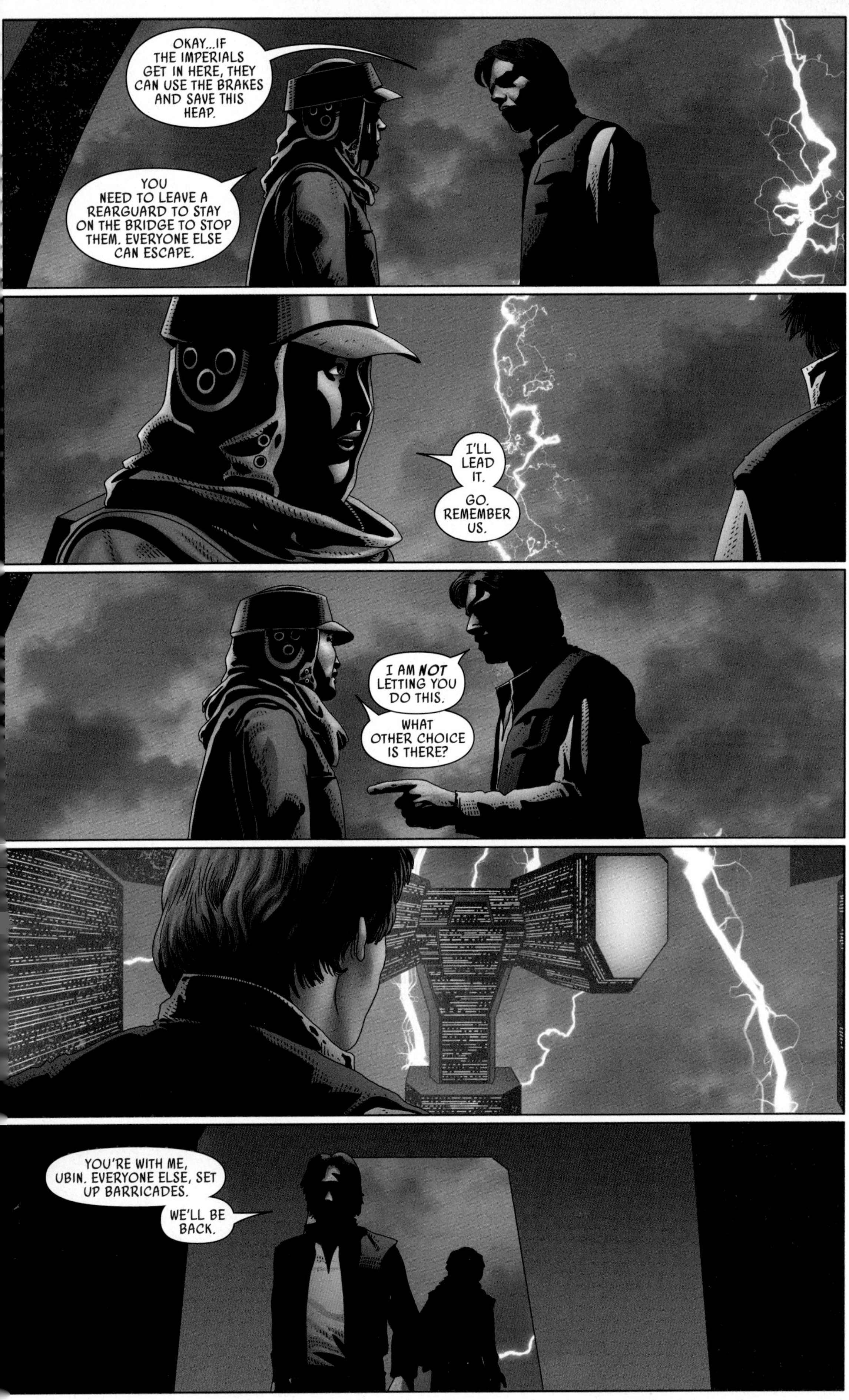

OKAY...IF THE IMPERIALS GET IN HERE, THEY CAN USE THE BRAKES AND SAVE THIS HEAP.
YOU NEED TO LEAVE A REARGUARD TO STAY ON THE BRIDGE TO STOP THEM. EVERYONE ELSE CAN ESCAPE.
I'LL LEAD IT.
GO. REMEMBER US.
I AM ***NOT*** LETTING YOU DO THIS.
WHAT OTHER CHOICE IS THERE?
YOU'RE WITH ME, UBIN. EVERYONE ELSE, SET UP BARRICADES.
WE'LL BE BACK.

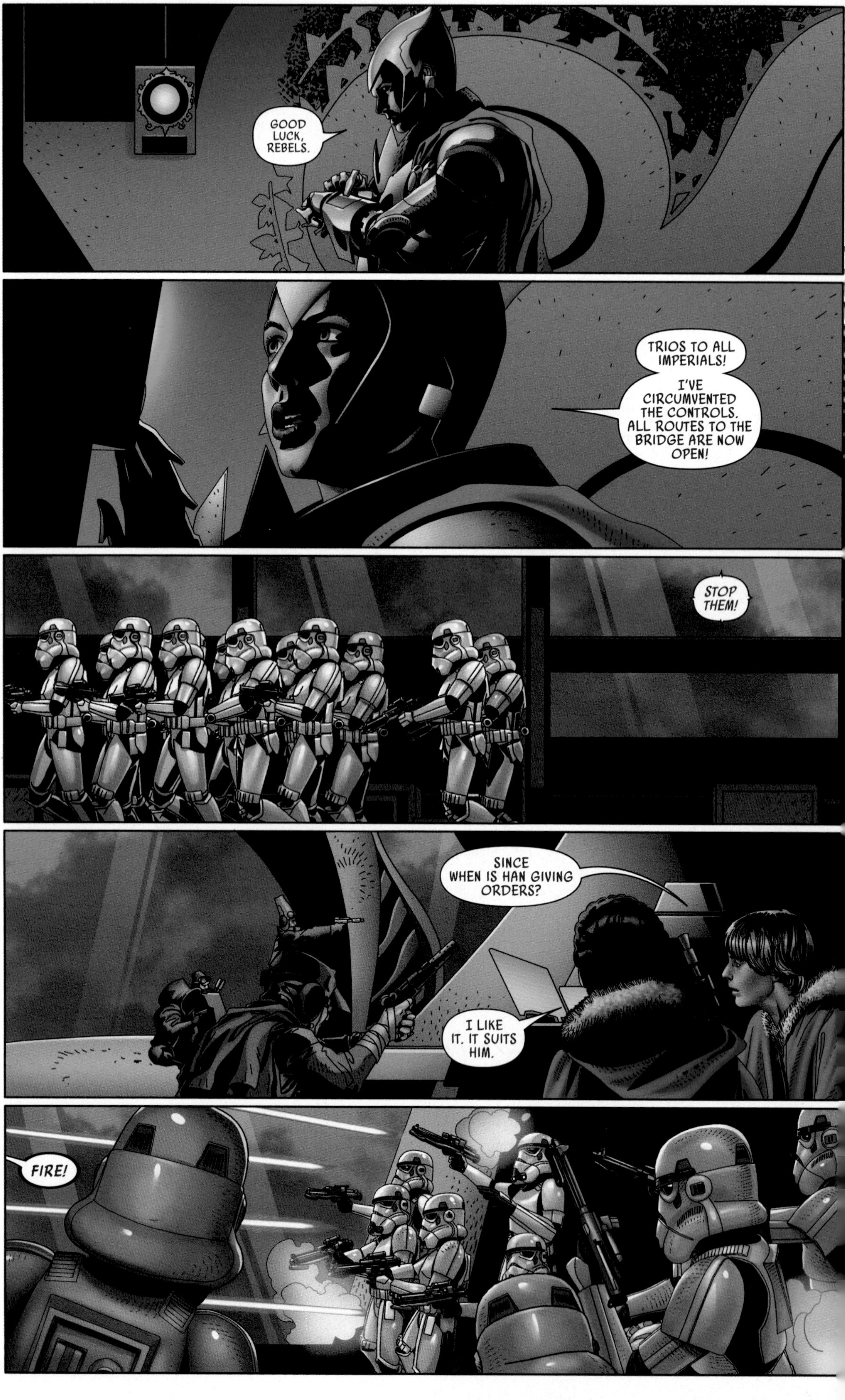
GOOD LUCK, REBELS.
TRIOS TO ALL IMPERIALS!
I'VE CIRCUMVENTED THE CONTROLS. ALL ROUTES TO THE BRIDGE ARE NOW OPEN!
STOP THEM!
SINCE WHEN IS HAN GIVING ORDERS?
I LIKE IT. IT SUITS HIM.
FIRE!

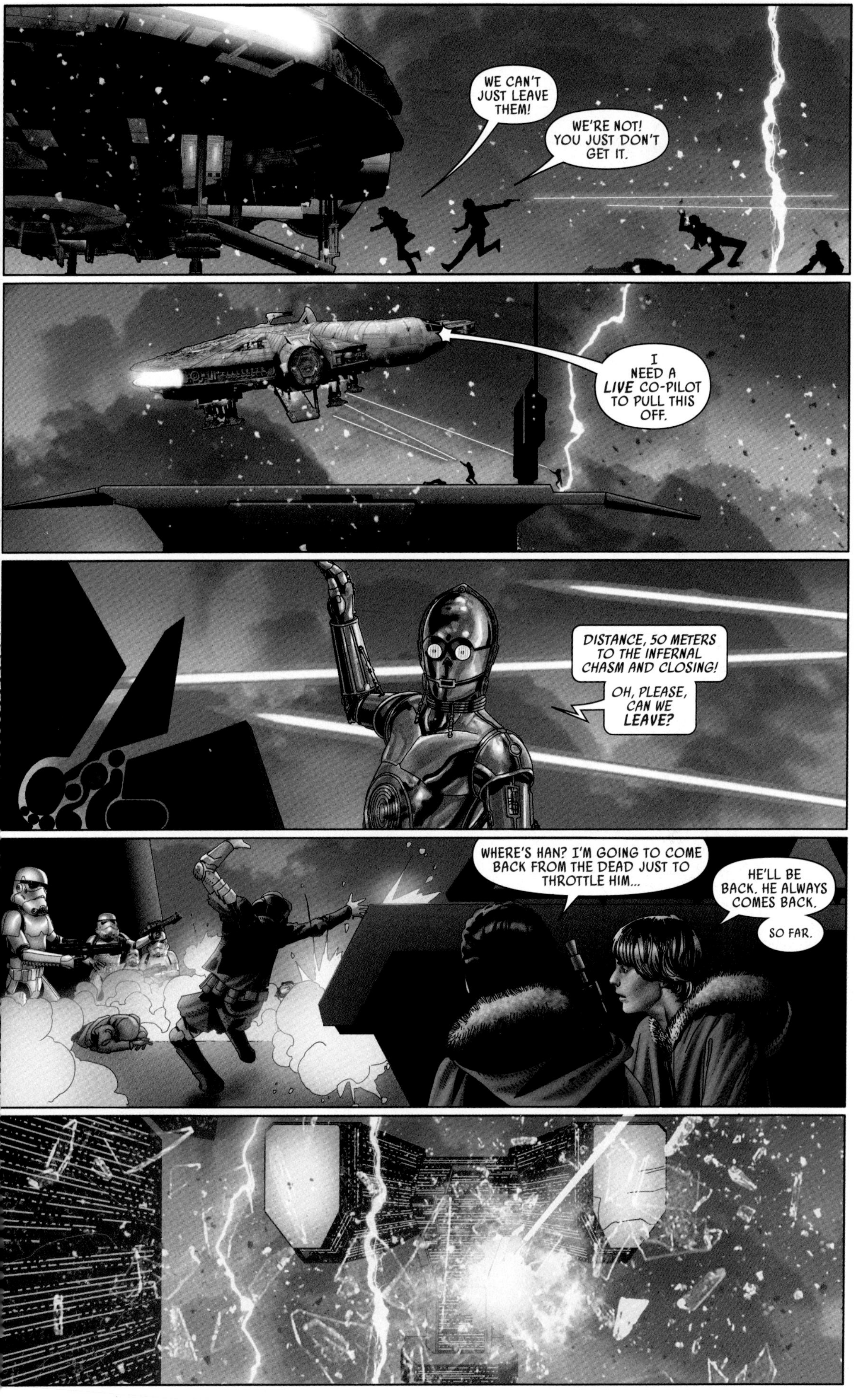
WE CAN'T JUST LEAVE THEM!
WE'RE NOT! YOU JUST DON'T GET IT.
I NEED A LIVE CO-PILOT TO PULL THIS OFF.
DISTANCE, 50 METERS TO THE INFERNAL CHASM AND CLOSING!
OH, PLEASE, CAN WE LEAVE?
WHERE'S HAN? I'M GOING TO COME BACK FROM THE DEAD JUST TO THROTTLE HIM...
HE'LL BE BACK. HE ALWAYS COMES BACK.
SO FAR.

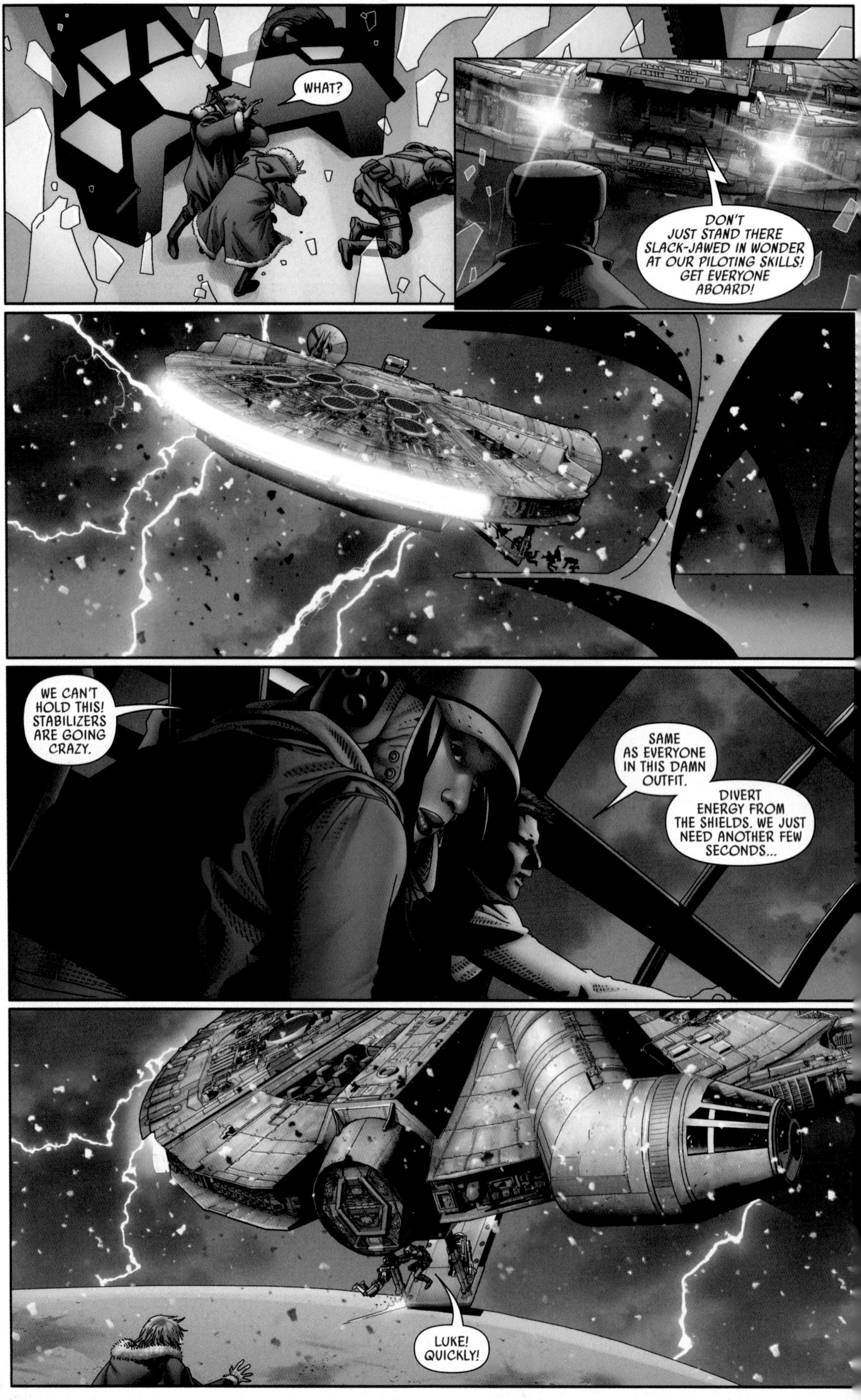
WHAT?
DON'T JUST STAND THERE SLACK-JAWED IN WONDER AT OUR PILOTING SKILLS! GET EVERYONE ABOARD!
WE CAN'T HOLD THIS! STABILIZERS ARE GOING CRAZY.
SAME AS EVERYONE IN THIS DAMN OUTFIT.
DIVERT ENERGY FROM THE SHIELDS. WE JUST NEED ANOTHER FEW SECONDS...
LUKE! QUICKLY!

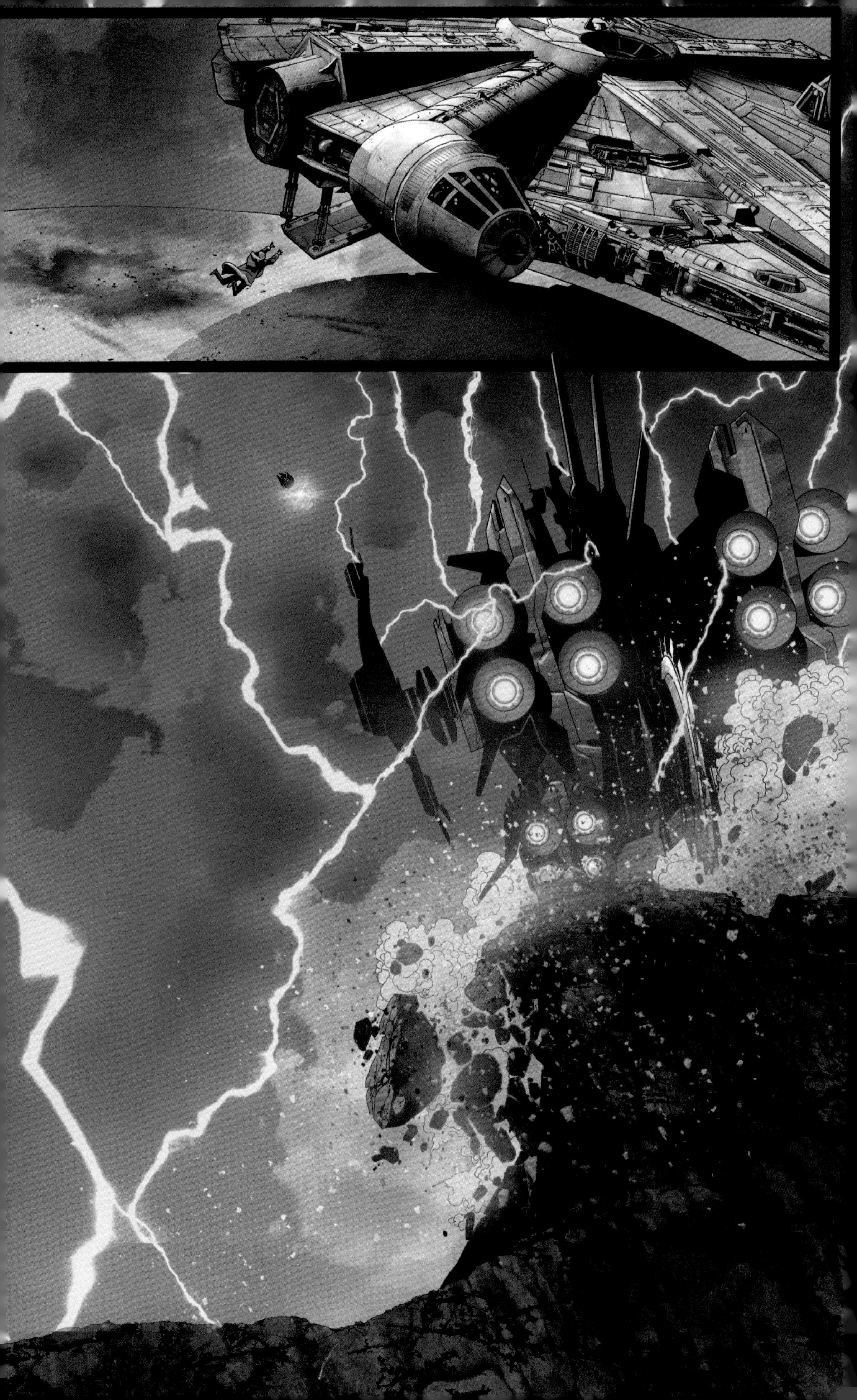

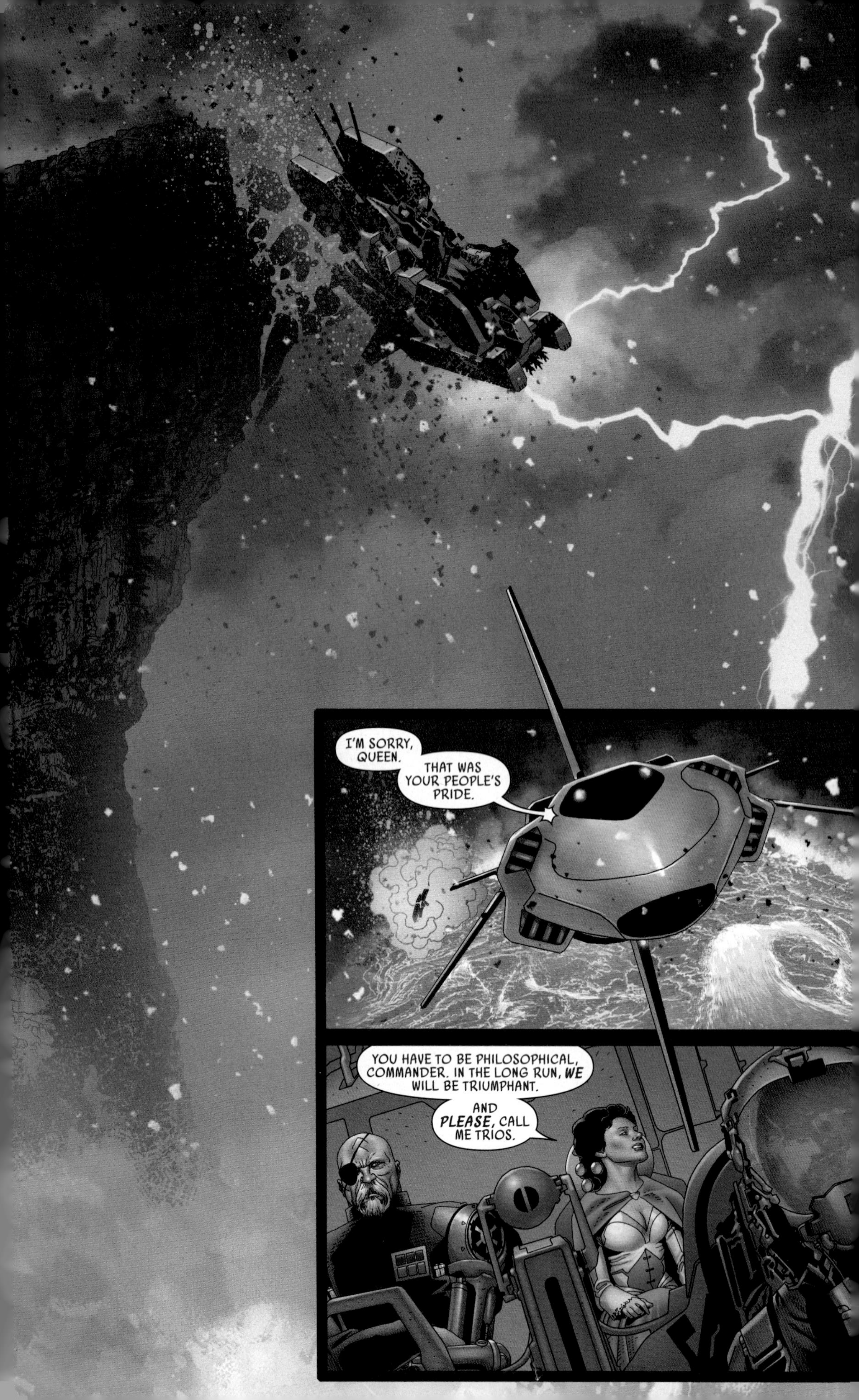
I'M SORRY, QUEEN.
THAT WAS YOUR PEOPLE'S PRIDE.
YOU HAVE TO BE PHILOSOPHICAL, COMMANDER. IN THE LONG RUN, *WE* WILL BE TRIUMPHANT.
AND *PLEASE*, CALL ME TRIOS.

ᱯᱠᱢᱢ ᱡᱛᱷᱛᱪᱠᱨᱛ�. ᱯᱠᱨ ᱪᱢᱛᱛᱨᱨ ᱧᱨᱡᱢᱪᱷ...

...ᱧᱨᱶ ᱯᱠᱪ ᱪᱧᱪᱣᱠᱶ ᱧᱠᱥᱥ ᱧᱠᱴ ᱣᱠᱶᱥᱶᱧ ᱧᱨᱥᱧ ᱯᱪᱨ ᱧᱪᱩᱶᱯ ᱨᱯᱛᱷᱪᱪ.

I'LL RECOVER. THE PLANET WON'T...

...BUT THE EMPIRE WILL NOT PROFIT FROM HER DEATH THROES.

ᱧᱪᱪᱶᱶ ᱪᱩᱧᱛᱶ ᱯᱪᱪ ᱧᱪᱨᱪᱪ ᱩᱨ ᱛᱪᱪᱧᱧ ᱪᱶᱛᱪᱧ !ᱛᱪᱪ ᱪᱪᱴᱣᱪ ᱯᱪᱪᱨ ᱧᱪᱴᱧ ᱪᱶᱸ.

ᱯᱪᱪ ᱛᱪᱪᱪᱧ ᱣᱪᱶᱶ ᱧᱪᱴ ᱛᱪᱪᱪ ᱧᱪᱪᱨ ᱧᱪᱪᱶ ᱛᱪᱪᱧ ᱛᱪᱪᱪᱨ ᱛᱪᱪᱪ.

WE'LL GUARD THE ASHES OF JEDHA UNTIL IT'S GONE, THEN MOVE ON.

THE DREAM WILL NOT DIE, EVEN WHEN JEDHA DOES.

WE'RE DIFFERENT, BUT WE CAN WORK TOGETHER, BENTHIC.

THAT'S WHAT "ALLIANCE" MEANS.

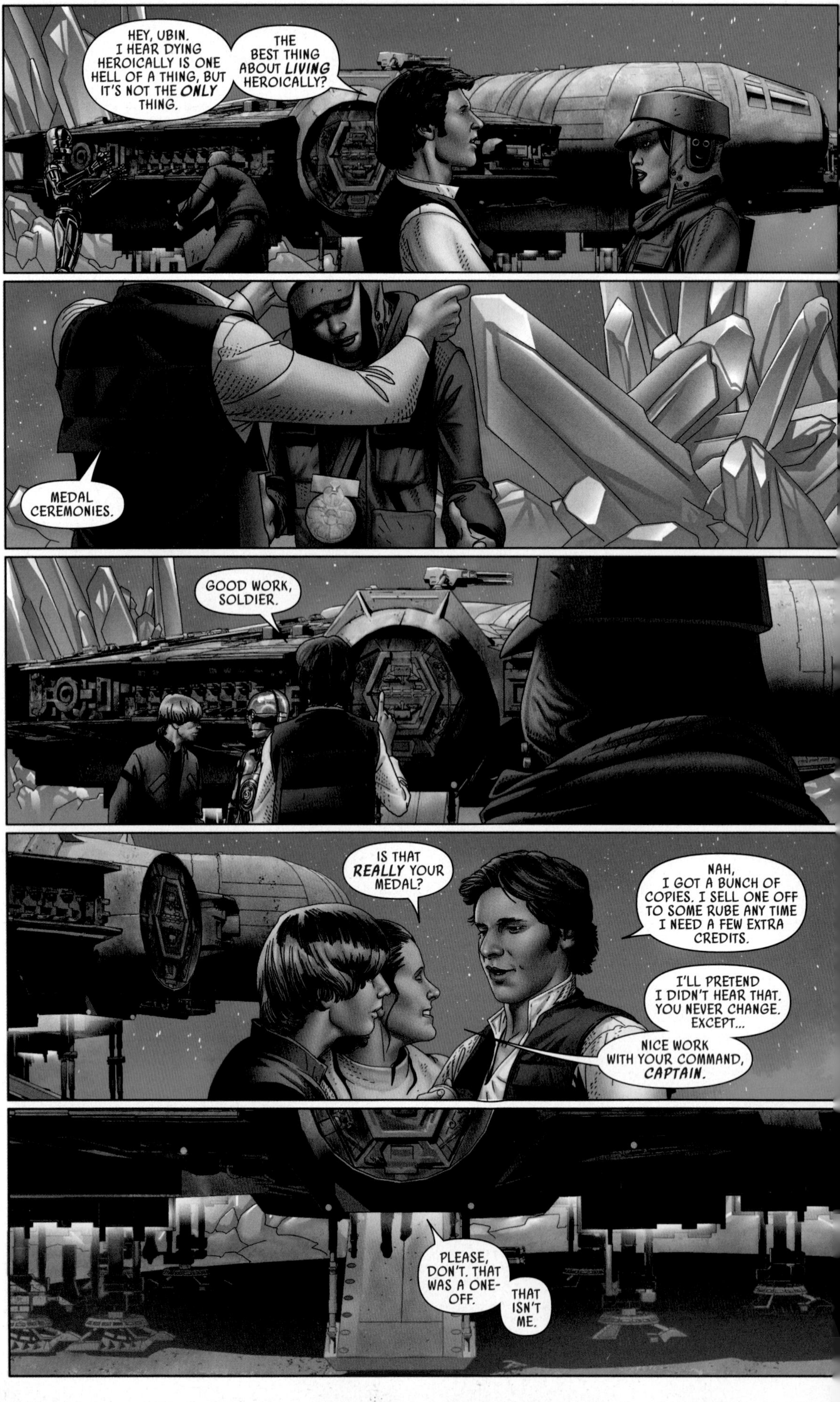
HEY, UBIN. I HEAR DYING HEROICALLY IS ONE HELL OF A THING, BUT IT'S NOT THE ONLY THING.
THE BEST THING ABOUT LIVING HEROICALLY?
MEDAL CEREMONIES.
GOOD WORK, SOLDIER.
IS THAT REALLY YOUR MEDAL?
NAH, I GOT A BUNCH OF COPIES. I SELL ONE OFF TO SOME RUBE ANY TIME I NEED A FEW EXTRA CREDITS.
I'LL PRETEND I DIDN'T HEAR THAT. YOU NEVER CHANGE. EXCEPT...
NICE WORK WITH YOUR COMMAND, CAPTAIN.
PLEASE, DON'T. THAT WAS A ONE-OFF.
THAT ISN'T ME.

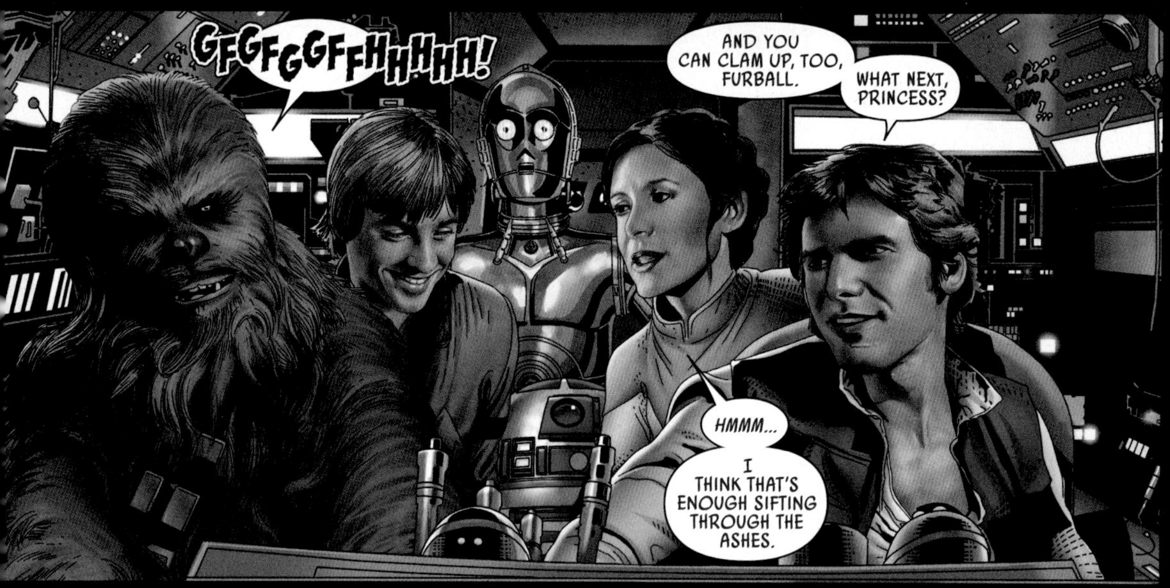
GFGFGGFFHHHHH!
AND YOU CAN CLAM UP, TOO, FURBALL.
WHAT NEXT, PRINCESS?
HMMM...
I THINK THAT'S ENOUGH SIFTING THROUGH THE ASHES.

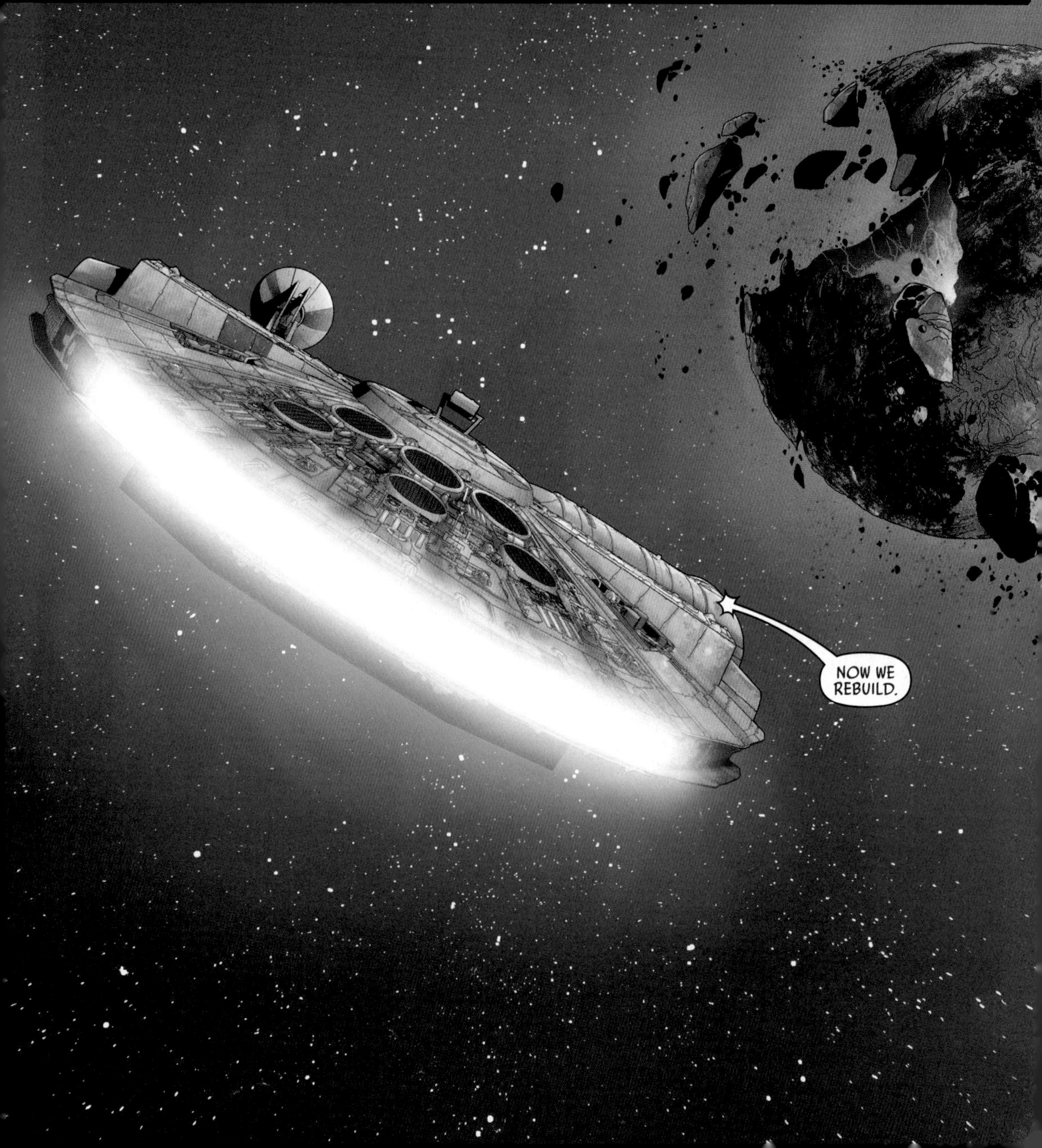
NOW WE REBUILD.

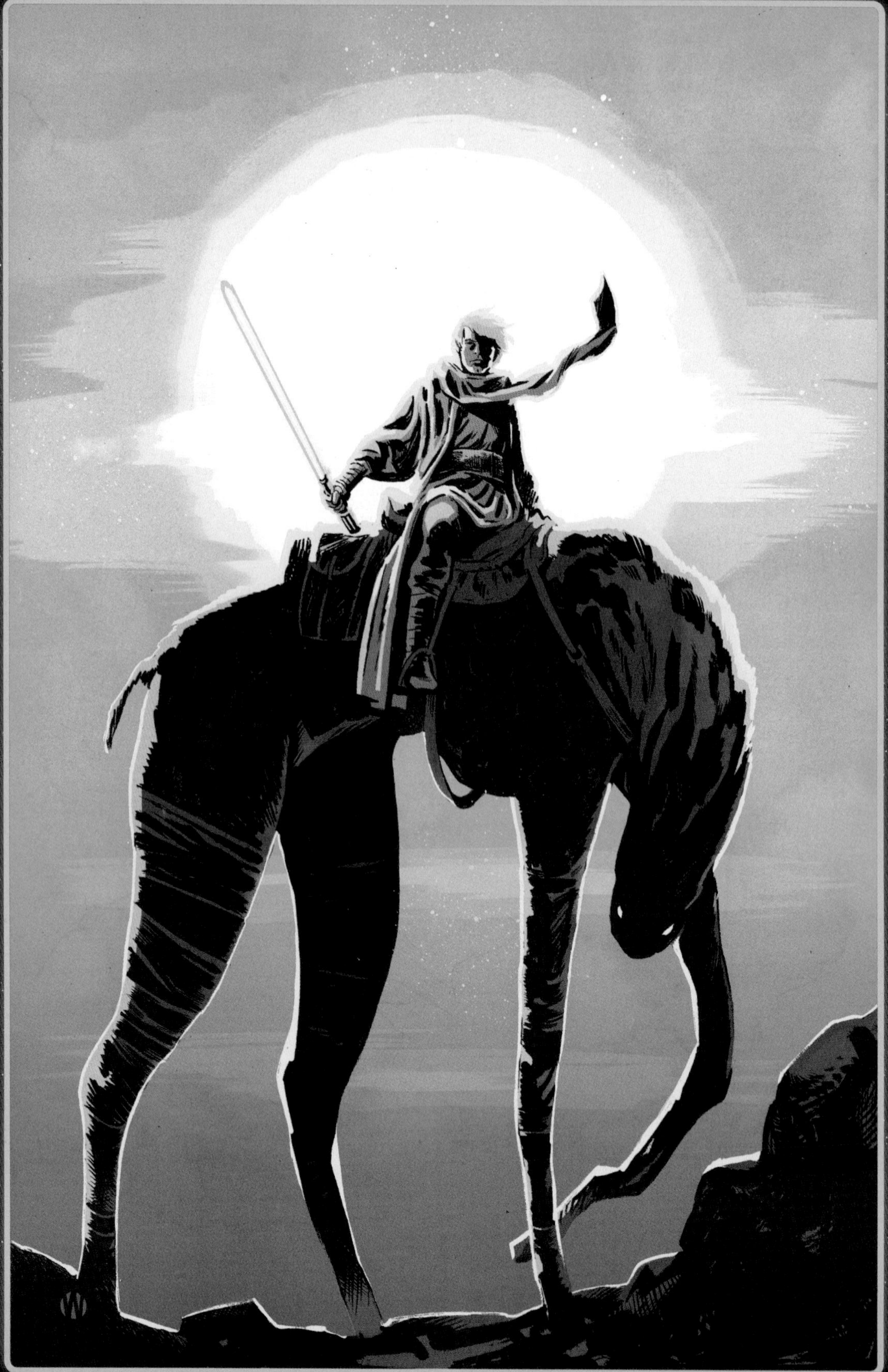

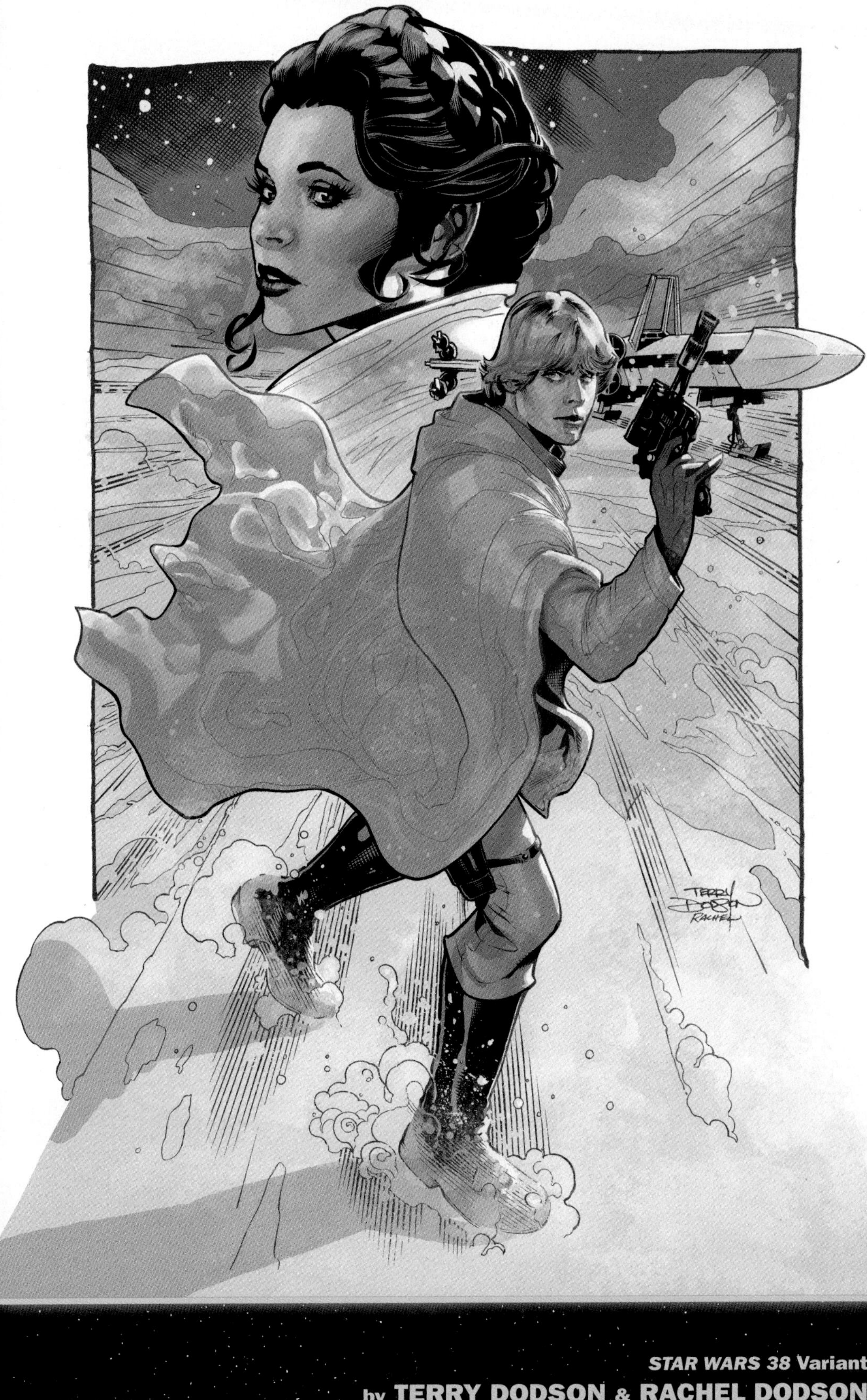
TERRY DODSON
RACHEL

***STAR WARS* 38 Variant**

by TERRY DODSON & RACHEL DODSON

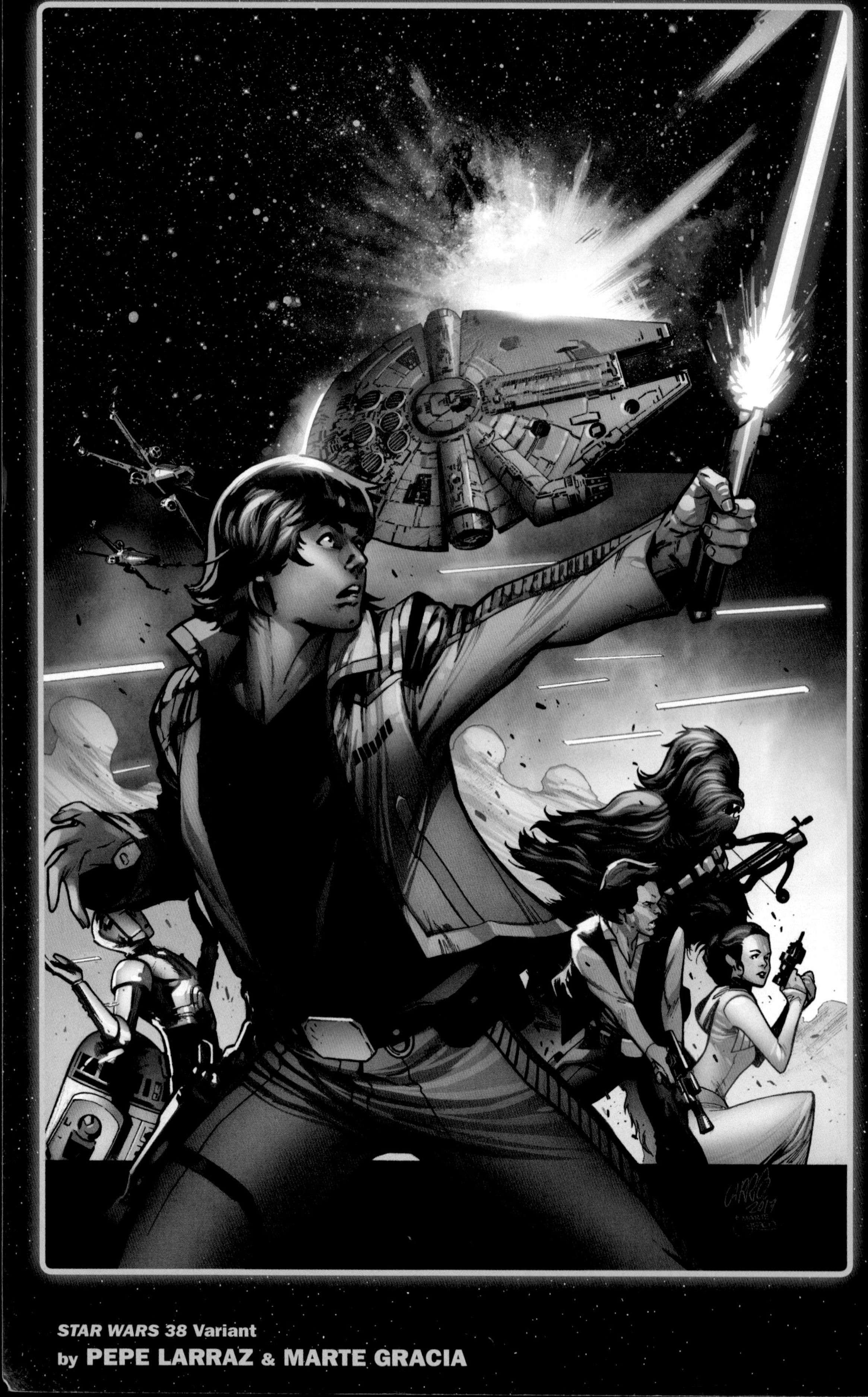

STAR WARS 38 Variant
by **PEPE LARRAZ & MARTE GRACIA**

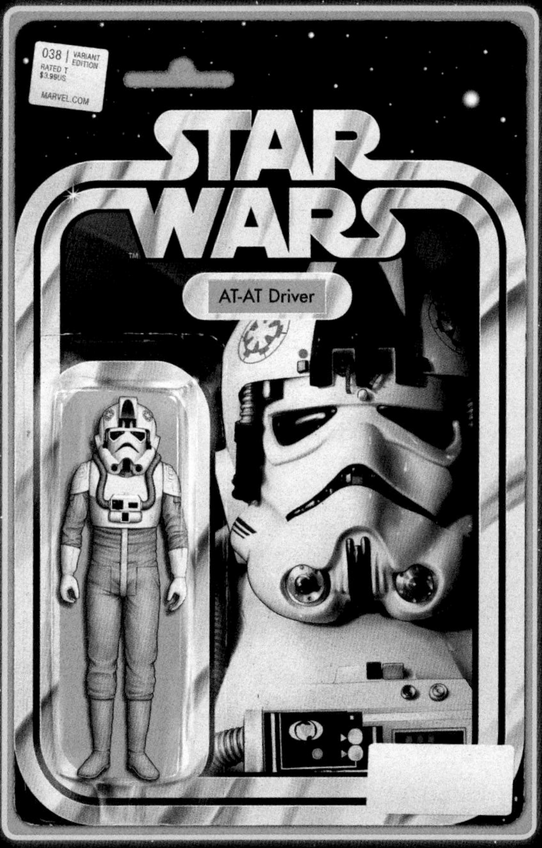
038 VARIANT EDITION
RATED T $3.99US
MARVEL.COM
STAR WARS
AT-AT Driver

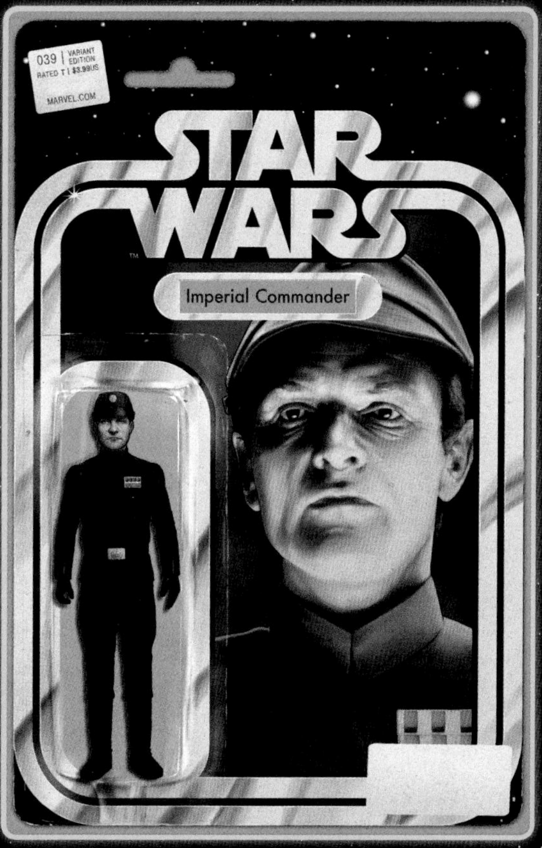
039 VARIANT EDITION
RATED T $3.99US
MARVEL.COM
STAR WARS
Imperial Commander

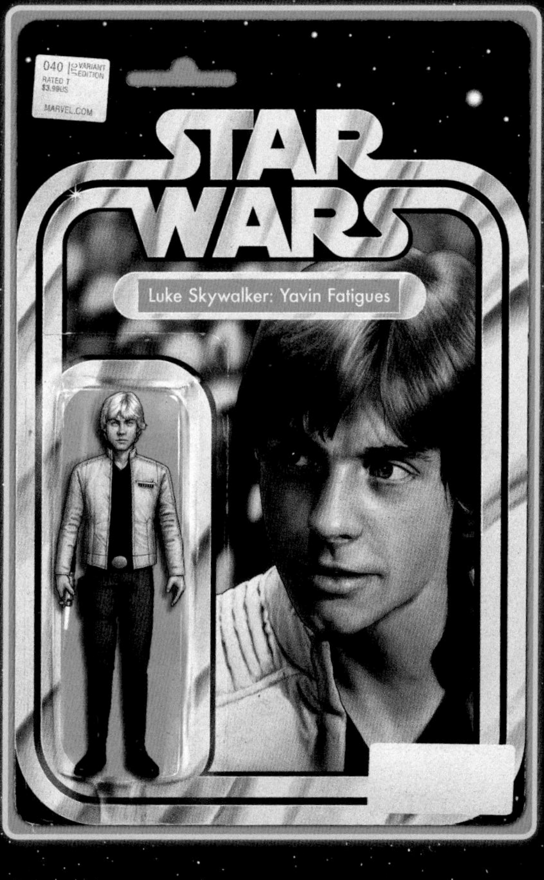
040 VARIANT EDITION
RATED T $3.99US
MARVEL.COM
STAR WARS
Luke Skywalker: Yavin Fatigues

***STAR WARS* 38-40 Action Figure Variants**
by JOHN TYLER CHRISTOPHER

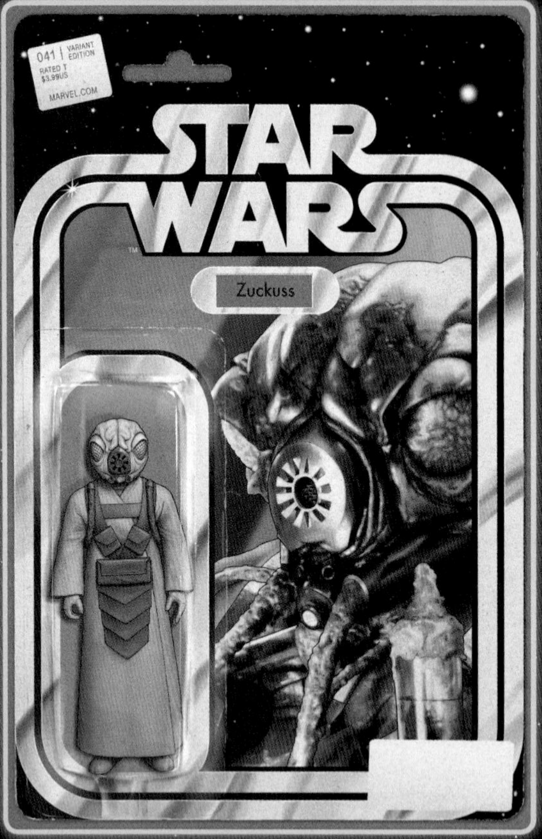
041 VARIANT EDITION
RATED T
$3.99US
MARVEL.COM
STAR WARS
Zuckuss

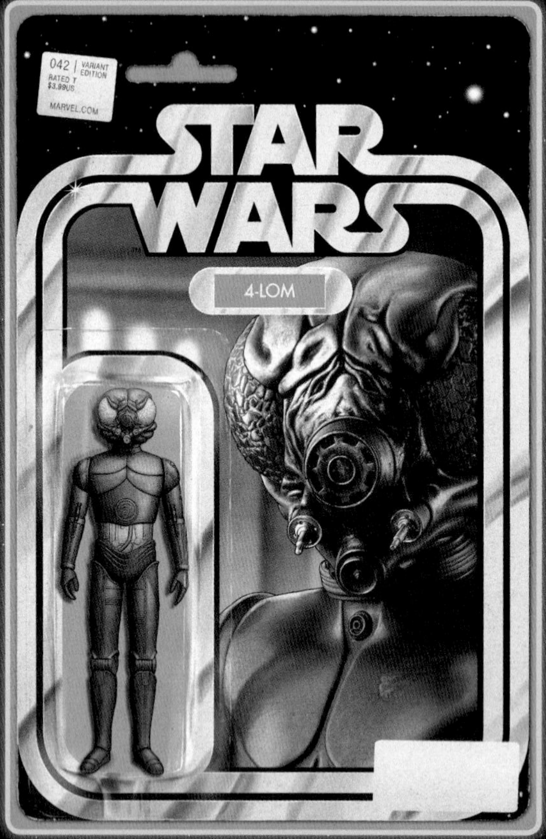
042 VARIANT EDITION
RATED T
$3.99US
MARVEL.COM
STAR WARS
4-LOM

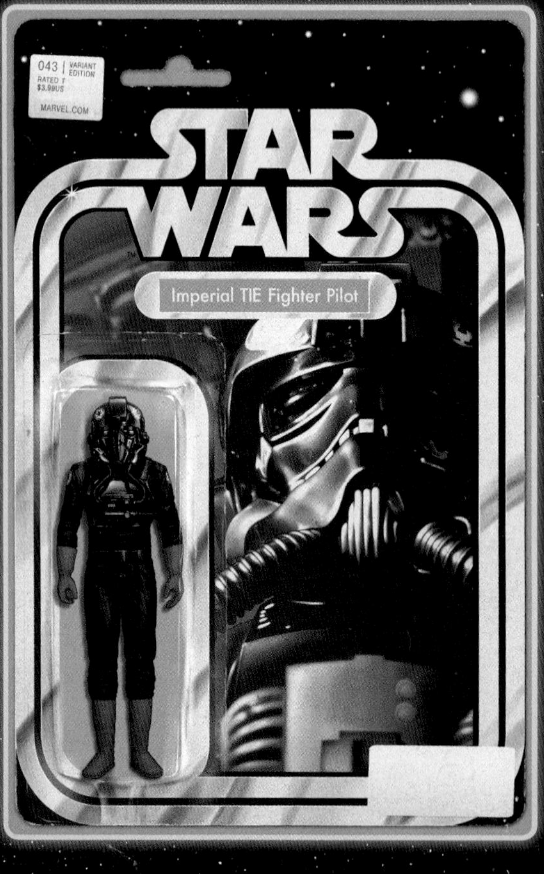
043 VARIANT EDITION
RATED T
$3.99US
MARVEL.COM
STAR WARS
Imperial TIE Fighter Pilot

***STAR WARS* 41-43 Action Figure Variants**

by JOHN TYLER CHRISTOPHER

WHAT IS A PRINCESS WITHOUT A WORLD?

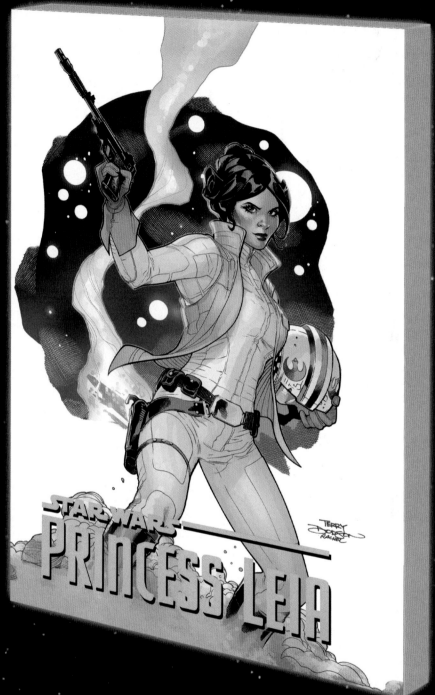

STAR WARS: PRINCESS LEIA TPB

978-0-7851-9317-3

ON SALE NOW!

THE DARK LORD OF THE SITH'S FIRST DEADLY MISSION

**STAR WARS: DARTH VADER: DARK LORD OF THE SITH
VOL. 1: IMPERIAL MACHINE TPB
978-1302907440**

ON SALE NOVEMBER 2017
WHEREVER BOOKS ARE SOLD

TO FIND A COMIC SHOP NEAR YOU, VISIT COMICSHOPLOCATOR.COM

BETRAYED BY HIS MASTER AND CRAVING VENGEANCE, MAUL STRIKES BACK!

STAR WARS: DARTH MAUL - SON OF DATHOMIR
978-1302908461

ON SALE NOVEMBER 2017
WHEREVER BOOKS ARE SOLD

TO FIND A COMIC SHOP NEAR YOU, VISIT COMICSHOPLOCATOR.COM

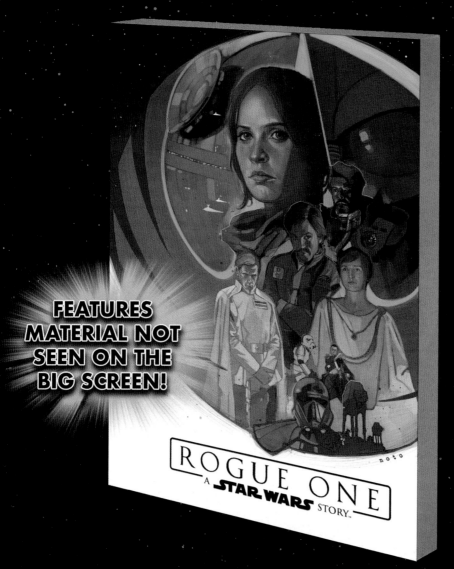